ENVIRONM... SC...

Roger Johnson
and Peter Morrell

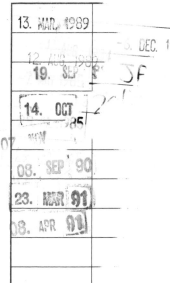

THE LONDON BOROUGH

Blackie

ENVIRONMENTAL
SCIENCE

ISBN 0 216 91151 6

First published 1982

Published by Blackie and Son Limited
Bishopbriggs, Glasgow G64 2NZ
Furnival House, 14–18 High Holborn, London, WC1V 6BX

Printed in Great Britain by
Thomson Litho Ltd, East Kilbride, Scotland

Contents

Acknowledgments

The authors and publishers are grateful to the following organizations for permission to reproduce copyright material.

National Coal Board: Figs 1.2, 2.6, 2.8, 2.9, 2.10, 2,11, 7.7. United Kingdom Atomic Energy Authority: Figs 1.7, 1.10, 1.13, 2.28, 2.29 (also British Nuclear Fuels Ltd), 6.39. Central Electricity Generating Board: Figs 1.14, 2.26. North of Scotland Hydro-Electric Board: Figs 1.18, 1.19. Lucas Energy Systems Ltd: Fig. 1.23. TI (Group Services) Ltd: Fig. 1.24. High Commissioner for New Zealand: Fig. 1.25. British Petroleum Company Ltd: Fig. 2.1. The Royal Society for the Protection of Birds: Figs 2.4, 3.3, 5.13. Aerofilms Ltd: Figs 2.12, 3.13, 6.14, 7.4, 7.5. Building Research Establishment: Figs 2.13, 6.7, 6.8. Severn Trent Water Authority: Figs 2.5, 4.14, 4.22, 7.10. National Society for Clean Air: Figs 2.15, 2.16, 2.17, 2.22, 2,23. British Farmer and Stockbreeder Ltd: Fig. 3.1. Agricultural Press Ltd: Fig 5.10, (Farmers Weekly) and Fig. 5.21 (Fish Farmer). Northwood Publications Ltd (Big Farm Management): Figs 3.2, 5.8, 5.14, 5.17, 6.1, 7.3. ICI Ltd Fig. 5.11 (Agricultural Division) and Figs 3.8, 5.15, (Plant Protection Division). Director, Institute of Geological Sciences (NERC): Figs 3.11, 6.15, 6.16, 6.23, 6.24 (NERC Copyright reserved). Forestry Commission: Figs 3.12, 6.6. Camera Press Ltd: Figs 3.15, 6.20, 6.21. Natural History Photographic Agency: Fig. 4.1. National Water Council: Figs 4.3, 4.10, 4.12, 4.18, 4.19, 4.20. Ministry of Agriculture: Figs 4.6, 5.7, (Crown copyright). Houseman (Burnham) Ltd (Permutit Domestic Division): Figs 4.7, 4.8. The Jersey New Waterworks Company Ltd: Fig. 4.23. Centre for World Development Education: Figs 5.1, 5.6. Danish Food Centre: Fig. 5.2. Institute of Oceanographic Sciences: Fig. 5.3. The Outspan Organization: Fig. 5.4. World Health Organization: Fig. 5.5. Unilever Ltd: Figs 5.22, 5.23, 5.24. HJ Heinz Co Ltd: Fig. 5.25. Findus Ltd: Fig. 5.26. Courtaulds Ltd: Figs 6.2, 6.4. Wira: Fig. 6.3. Ronald Sheridan: Fig. 6.5. Timber Research and Development Association: Fig. 6.9. British Tar Industry Association: Fig. 6.10. Cement and Concrete Association: Figs 6.30, 7.1. British Steel Corporation: Fig. 6.35. The Coca Cola Export Corporation: Fig. 6.36. RTZ Ltd: Figs 6.37, 6.38. Tom Weir: Fig. 7.11. Peter Wakely: Figs 7.12, 7.13. Nature Conservancy Council: Figs 7.15, 7.16. National Trust: Fig. 7.17. British Broadcasting Corporation: Fig. 7.14. Grower Publications Ltd (Grower Books): Fig. 5.16. D Gulland: Fig. 5.19. Gordon Lyall: Fig. 6.29. D. Gulland, Staffordshire College of Agriculture: Fig. 5.18. M. S. Phillips: Fig. 7.6. Fig 7.9. The Controller of Her Majesty's Stationery Office: Tables 4.3, 4.4 and 4.6.

The cover photograph of a rock drilling bit was supplied by the Hughes Tool Company Ltd.

Preface

Environmental science has been introduced into school curricula for a variety of reasons. Invariably, however, the demand for the subject has stemmed from an increasing public awareness of environmental issues. This awareness has produced a requirement that individuals be educated in environmental matters. The aim of this book is to assist in the development of this area of education. It is hoped that the book will impart a body of environmental knowledge and, in turn, help to develop an awareness of environmental problems. Finally, it is hoped that each individual, in studying the material in the book, will develop a personal concern for the environment.

For convenience, the book has been presented in eight chapters. However, it must be appreciated that the purpose of environmental science is to allow for an inter-disciplinary approach to, and an all-encompassing view of, environmental issues. To ensure that these aims are met within the book within any one chapter several references may be found to material in other chapters. Alternatively, in some cases material presented in one chapter may well be presented again in summary form in another chapter. This technique may present difficulties to some readers but it is felt that this is the most satisfactory way of ensuring that the reader appreciates the extent to which all environmental issues are inter-related.

Energy and Energy Sources 1

ENERGY

The term **energy** is one that is in common use and everybody has some idea of its meaning. For instance, we know that energy is used up if we run a race and we know that energy is necessary to make a car work. However, if you try to tell somebody precisely what energy 'is', it becomes very difficult.

Energy is defined scientifically as 'the capacity for doing work'. In order to do work, energy is used; and if energy is used, then work is done. The term **work** also needs to be defined, and we can do so by stating that 'work is done when a force moves its point of application'. This wording has been carefully chosen by scientists, but at first sight appears to be difficult to understand. In general terms, a force can be thought of as a mass pressing down on some part of the Earth. Whenever the mass is moved, it moves its 'point of application' (the area over which the mass presses down), and so work is done. Work is done, then, every time a mass is moved, and in order to move the mass, energy is used.

It is also often convenient to think of work being done when an energy change occurs. When an electric light is turned on, energy is used and so work is done. It is not easy to see that a force is moved (though, of course, electrons are being moved through the conductor), but it is quite easy to see that a change of energy is taking place, i.e. electricity to light and heat.

Energy is usually measured in units called **joules**. One joule is the amount of energy necessary to move a force of one **newton** a distance of one metre— energy (in joules)=force (in newtons)×distance (in metres). A newton is the force necessary to give a mass of one kilogram an acceleration of one metre per second per second. In the case of our mass pressing down on the Earth, the force with which it presses down can be found by multiplying the mass (measured in kilograms) by the acceleration due to gravity (9·81 metres per

Fig. 1.1 *Work is done when a force moves its point of application!*

second per second); e.g. a mass of 2kg presses downwards with a force of $2 \times 9.81 = 19.62$ newtons. Using this example, the work done (energy used) in raising this mass 4 metres off the ground $= (2 \times 9.81) \times 4 = 78.48$ joules.

A second unit of energy is the **calorie**. This unit, though it is not an SI unit, still appears in many textbooks, particularly books concerned with food sciences. A calorie is defined as 'the energy required to raise the temperature of one gram of water by one degree centigrade'; e.g. if 1g of water is raised in temperature by 1°C then 1 calorie of energy has been used. Similarly, if 20g (20cm³) of water are raised by 4°C, then 80 calories of energy have been used. Calories may be converted into joules by multiplying by 4.18 (there are 4.18 joules in 1 calorie). A kilojoule and a kilocalorie are 1000 joules and 1000 calories respectively.

Finally, it is necessary to consider **power**. Power is a measure of the rate at which work is done or energy used and is measured in joules per second. A rate of work of 1 joule per second is known as a **watt**. A kilowatt is 1000 watts or 1000 joules per second.

A unit of energy that has not yet been mentioned, but which is frequently used, is the **kilowatt-hour**. This is the amount of energy used when 1000 watts (joules per second) are used for 1 hour. (This equals 3.6×10^6 joules.) This value also corresponds to 1 **unit** of electricity—the unit used when calculating the electricity used in a house.

Energy can take many forms. The forms of energy of most concern to environmental scientists are:

1   electrical energy
2   thermal (heat) energy
3   nuclear energy
4   chemical energy (the energy present in the bonds between atoms and molecules in an element or a compound)
5   kinetic energy (energy something has because of its movement)
6   potential energy (energy something has because of its position)
7   light energy
8   sound energy.

Many readers will perhaps also be aware of the increasing use of the term **solar energy**. This is a convenient way of talking about the heat and light energy that comes from the Sun.

There are two properties of energy that are of such importance that they have been stated in what are referred to as the **laws of thermodynamics**. The first of these laws says that energy cannot be created nor destroyed but may be converted from one form to another. The second law is rather more complex, but includes the idea that whenever energy conversions take place, some of the energy is *always* converted into heat energy. It also says that when energy conversions take place, there is less useful energy left than there was at the start.

The practical importance of these two laws can be seen if you think of how an electric lamp works. Firstly, in order for the lamp to give off light, electrical energy must be supplied and this is generally converted from the chemical energy in fossil fuels, via a generating station. In terms of the first law of thermodynamics we can see that although the coal (and also the chemical energy) has disappeared, it has not been destroyed but has been changed into light energy. In terms of the second law, although the purpose of a lamp is to give light, heat is automatically produced as well, though it is of no real value. Also, if the amount of light energy produced is measured (the useful energy), it would be found to be less than the electrical energy required to produce the light, and the amount of electrical energy is only about one-third of the chemical energy originally present in the fossil fuel.

Fig. 1.2 A fossil leaf found in a coal measure

ENERGY SOURCES

Until recently the most important sources of energy for man have been the **fossil fuels**—coal, oil and gas.

Coal

Coal is the term used to describe a number of substances which have been formed from the fossilized remains of plant material (see Fig 1.2). The plants important in coal formation were mainly of the **Pteridophyte** family. Present day members of this family include ferns, horsetails and clubmosses, but the plants that formed coal were much larger than the ferns of today. Many of the important species were the size of trees and thrived in the rather swampy, humid environments of the **Carboniferous period** about 300 million years ago.

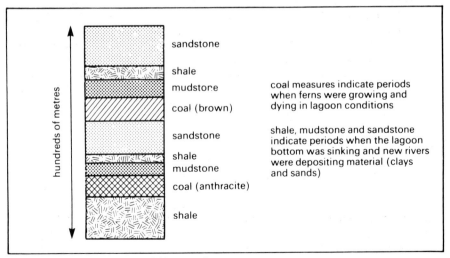

Fig. 1.3   Core of rock extracted from a coal measure

The series of events that led to coal formation was as follows. The plants that eventually formed coal grew in and around the edges of swamps and when they died they fell into the water. As the water was lacking in oxygen, the plants only partly decomposed, and as more plants died and fell into the water, so the depth of partly-decayed plant material increased. Naturally, as the depth of decaying plant material increased, so the water became shallower, so more plants were able to grow in the shallows. This plant material would also eventually die so that the decaying vegetation would gradually become many metres deep and the water would become less and less deep. Occasionally, perhaps partly because of the mass of plant material lying on the Earth's crust, or as a result of geological activity, the area of ground sank and became flooded again. Plants would then begin to grow round the water's edge again, and death and decay would follow so that a cycle of events took place (see Fig. 1.3).

Gradually, as the partly-decayed plant material became buried deeper in the Earth's crust, so its form changed. A combination of pressure and heat in the Earth's crust, working over long periods of time, caused both physical and chemical changes. The amount of change depended upon the extent to which each of the factors mentioned above operated. The degree to which the material changed can be seen in the **coal series.** This series is made up of the materials peat, lignite (brown coals), bitumous coals (black coals), and anthracite. Peat has been buried for the least time and at the least depth, while anthracite has been buried for the longest time and at the greatest depth.

Oil and Gas

There is less certainty about the way in which oil and gas have been formed but they are thought mainly to have been formed from the remains of **marine plankton** (this plankton is made up of the microscopic plants and animals that are found in the surface layers of the world's oceans). It is thought that these organisms died and fell to the bottom of the seas where they accumulated in very large numbers. Over long periods of time, the dead organisms became covered by the clay, silt and sand that is carried into the sea by rivers. This process then repeated itself many times over until the pressure that was exerted by the vast depth of deposited material changed the fluids of the organisms into oil and gas (see Fig. 1.4). The major oil deposits in the world were formed during the last 200 million years.

Because oil (also referred to as crude oil or crude petroleum) and gas are able to move through **permeable** rock strata, they are often found at great distances from the site of formation. Both oil and gas will move until they meet rock strata that is **impermeable.** Such areas then form oil or gas traps. Some examples of the way in which oil and gas can be trapped are shown in Fig. 1.5 and Fig. 1.6.

Fig. 1.4 Oil and gas are formed from the remains of dead plankton

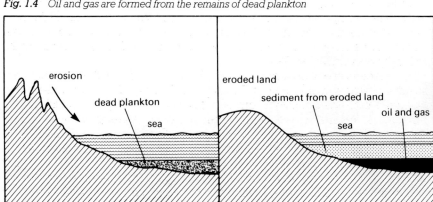

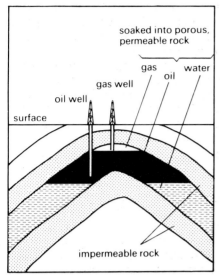

Fig. 1.5 *An anticlinal oil trap*

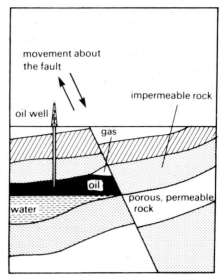

Fig. 1.6 *A fault trap*

The energy present as chemical energy in the fossil fuels can be released as heat (and light) energy by breaking the high-energy bonds holding together the molecules present in the fuels. At the same time, other molecules are allowed to form which require less energy to hold them together. The spare energy appears as heat and light. Some energy is required to start the reaction, but once started the reaction is **exothermic**; that is, it releases its own heat and some of this heat is used to continue the reaction. A typical example would be the burning (**oxidation**) of natural gas (methane).

$$CH_4 + 2O_2 \longrightarrow CO_2 + 2H_2O + heat$$

methane + oxygen → carbon dioxide + water + heat

The energy required to hold the molecules of methane and oxygen together is more than that required to hold together the carbon dioxide molecule and the water molecules.

Nuclear Fuels

Since the early 1940s it has been realized that certain atoms of uranium (^{235}U) are capable of releasing vast quantities of energy by a process known as **nuclear fission**. The energy released as a result of this process was first used in the atom bombs that were dropped on Hiroshima and Nagasaki in 1945. The enormous quantities of energy released caused so much destruction that it hastened the end of the Second World War.

The peaceful use of this form of energy began in 1956 with the construction of the first nuclear power station, at Windscale in Cumbria. Since this time nuclear power has increased considerably as can be seen from Fig. 1.7 and Fig. 1.8.

In outline, the energy released by uranium-235 is released when an atom of this material splits (fissions) into two smaller parts. (This may occur naturally or be made to do so when certain conditions are present.) The energy that is required to hold all the atomic particles together in the large uranium atom is much more than the energy required to hold the atomic particles together in each of the two atoms formed when the uranium atom splits. The excess, or spare, energy is released mainly as heat.

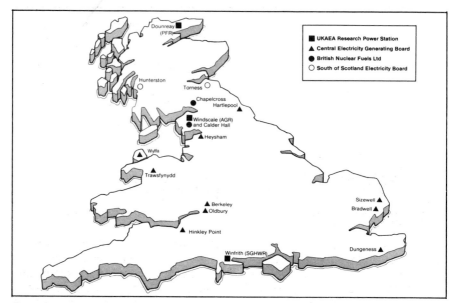

Fig. 1.7 *UK nuclear installations*

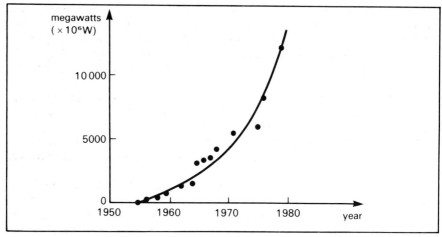

Fig. 1.8 *Growth of UK nuclear electricity output*

In a nuclear reactor the energy released when uranium undergoes fission is controlled. To understand how the reactor operates, some basic understanding of the structure of atoms is necessary. In general, the atom can be thought of as being made up of three types of particle—**neutrons, protons** and **electrons.** The protons and neutrons are grouped towards the centre of the atom, while electrons move in paths, or orbits, round this central part. The proton and the electron each carry an electrical charge of exactly the same size. However, because the proton is positively charged and the electron is negatively charged (and there are equal numbers of protons and electrons), the atom as a whole is electrically neutral. The neutron carries no charge at all.

The number of particles present in an atom is noted in shortened form and this is explained in the following examples. The symbol $^{12}_{6}C$ refers to a carbon atom having six protons, indicated by the lower number (or **atomic number**). It also has a total of twelve protons plus neutrons, indicated by the upper number (or **mass number**). An atom of $^{12}_{6}C$ is shown in Fig. 1.9. Because the mass number

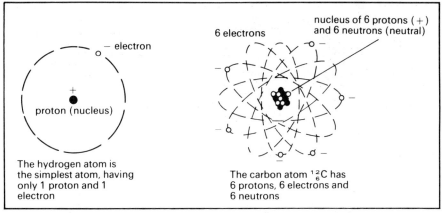

Fig. 1.9 *Atomic Structure*

is twelve, and the atomic number shows that there are six protons, there must also be six neutrons. Also, because in any atom there is the same number of electrons as protons, these two numbers tell us a great deal about the structure of an atom. In a similar way, $^{16}_{8}O$ indicates an atom of oxygen containing eight protons, eight neutrons and eight electrons. Finally, it is quite possible for different atoms of the same substance (**element**) to have different numbers of neutrons. For instance, the $^{12}_{6}C$ atom referred to earlier may also exist as $^{14}_{6}C$—a carbon atom, having six protons, six electrons and eight neutrons. Atoms of the same element with differing numbers of neutrons are known as **isotopes**. As atoms become larger and thus have a greater number of atomic particles in them, so it becomes more likely that the number of neutrons is greater than the number of protons.

The uranium that we have mentioned as being of value in providing nuclear fuel is $^{235}_{92}U$, often referred to simply as 'U–235'. Unfortunately, most uranium that occurs naturally is ^{238}U and only a small fraction of the uranium is ^{235}U. (In fact 99·3% of natural uranium is ^{238}U.) To make fuel for reactors, the amount of ^{235}U often needs to be increased. The uranium is then referred to as **enriched uranium**.

When the uranium fuel (in the form of **fuel rods**—See Fig. 1.10) is placed in the reactor, some of the ^{235}U will undergo fission spontaneously. When this occurs, an atom of ^{235}U changes into two different atoms of smaller size. Also, some of the spare neutrons in the large uranium atom (which are not needed by the two smaller atoms that are formed) are released. There is also a very large quantity of thermal (heat) energy released. For every kilogram of ^{235}U that undergoes fission, as much energy is released as is contained in about 10 000 kilograms (10 tonnes) of fossil fuel.

If the neutrons that are released when the ^{235}U fissions are travelling at the right speed, a neutron might be captured by another atom of ^{235}U. This will make the ^{235}U atom undergo fission and the process described above repeats itself (see Fig. 1.11). If the series of reactions is to continue, then a **critical mass** of ^{235}U must be present, and in this case a **chain reaction** is set up. (A critical mass is said to exist if there is sufficient ^{235}U present for a chain reaction to take place.)

In order to control the large quantities of energy that might be released in a nuclear reactor, every reactor contains two particularly important parts— **moderators** and **control rods.** Moderators (often made of blocks of graphite) are necessary to reduce the speed of neutrons so that they are the correct speed to be caught by, and cause fission of, ^{235}U. Control rods (often made of boron) are placed in the reactor to capture some of the spare neutrons. If this were not

Fig. 1.10 *Fuel rods in the core of a fast-breeder reactor*

Fig. 1.11 *A* ^{235}U *atom captures a neutron and undergoes fission*

neutron

^{235}U nucleus

nucleus splits
(fissions)

two smaller elements
are formed called
fission products

free neutrons +
heat energy

done, then too many neutrons would cause too many ^{235}U atoms to undergo fission at the same time. The energy would be released so quickly, and in such large quantities, that the reactor would break down and could release large quantities of radioactive material into the environment.

Normally the heat produced during fission is carried away from the reactor by water or a gas such as carbon dioxide, and this passes to a **heat exchanger**. The heat is used to change water into steam which is then used to produce electricity by turning turbines and generators (see Fig. 1.12). Reactors using this method are commonly known as **burner** or **thermal reactors**.

A second type of nuclear reactor is called a **fast-breeder reactor**. In these reactors, the starting fuel is a compact mixture of uranium oxide and plutonium surrounded by a blanket of ^{238}U. The chain reaction begins as in the thermal reactor, but in this instance moderators are not used to reduce the speed of the neutrons that are released as fission occurs. These fast neutrons are captured by the atoms of ^{238}U, which are converted to ^{239}U. Several changes then take place in the ^{239}U which ends in it becoming plutonium-239 (^{239}Pu). This

Fig. 1.12 *Plan of an air or water-cooled thermal nuclear reactor*

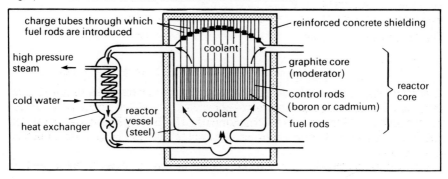

charge tubes through which
fuel rods are introduced

reinforced concrete shielding

high pressure
steam

coolant

graphite core
(moderator)

cold water

control rods
(boron or cadmium)

reactor
core

heat exchanger

reactor
vessel
(steel)

coolant

fuel rods

Fig. 1.13 *Fast-breeder reactor at Dounreay, Caithness*

plutonium is **fissile,** that is, it undergoes fission in much the same way as ^{235}U does.

The term 'breeder' is used because the reactor 'breeds' its own fuel. More plutonium may be produced than is required in the reactor to keep the chain reaction going and so has to be removed. This plutonium can be treated in a way that makes it useful as a fuel in other fast-breeder reactors.

Though there are many possible disadvantages of this system (it is discussed in Chapter 2), the greatest advantage is that relatively useless ^{238}U is converted into useful plutonium-239. This can be used as a fuel in future reactors, and as we have seen, ^{238}U is far more common than ^{235}U.

The Non-Renewable Nature of Fuels

All of the energy sources that have been discussed so far are **finite** and **non-renewable**. This means that there is a fixed quantity of each of the sources. None of them is being formed at this moment or, if they are being formed, it will take so long for them to form that it is not possible that they will be of any use to man in the foreseeable future.

This feature of these energy sources has of course been known for a long time, but the full consequences of this knowledge have only been fully realized in recent years. We are now becoming very concerned because we realize that these resources will not last us for very much longer. We can estimate just how long these resources will last by finding out how much of each fuel is present in the Earth and the rate at which we are using it. An example of the means by which such an estimate is obtained is given below.

Estimated reserves of North Sea gas (1976)$= 1443 \times 10^9 \, m^3$
Production values (1976) per year $= 3941 \times 10^7 \, m^3$

Predicted depletion date $= \dfrac{1443 \times 10^9}{3941 \times 10^7}$

$= $ approximately 37 years.

A similar calculation can be used to estimate the depletion date of UK coal reserves. It is estimated that there are approximately 98×10^9 tonnes left and we are using 125×10^6 tonnes each year. Similarly, North Sea oil reserves are about 2300×10^6 tonnes. In 1980 we were using about 80×10^6 tonnes per year, but this is increasing.

Often the estimated depletion dates that are given cause a great deal of argument. This is for two main reasons. Firstly, it is very difficult to calculate how much of a fuel is likely to be available to us in the future. Secondly, it is not easy to decide how fast the fuel will be used up in the future. Some of the difficulties that are met will be obvious if you think for a while. For a start, you will probably realize that it is very difficult to measure exactly how much fuel there is in any one area when it might be several hundreds of metres below the Earth's surface. It is even more difficult to be certain that all the fuel present in the Earth's crust has been discovered. Also, if it is felt that there is more to be discovered, it is obviously difficult to estimate how much of such a fuel there might be. Some of these problems can be seen by looking at values estimated for North Sea oil reserves and production.

North Sea oil reserves are estimated at between 1.9×10^9 tonnes and 4.1×10^9 tonnes. These differences arise because the value chosen depends upon whether you use those reserves which, to date, are *proven* to be present, or whether you accept certain estimates about what *might* become available in the future. The amount that is likely to be produced each year is equally difficult to estimate. Production values for 1976 were about 15×10^6 tonnes, and at that time this value was expected to increase to 80×10^6 tonnes by 1980. This expectation has, in fact, been fulfilled.

Another problem is that as fuels become in short supply, the cost of fuel will increase. Because of this, it should be possible to afford to extract fuels which at the moment are too expensive, i.e. at today's prices it would cost more to extract them than would be obtained by selling them. For instance, oil is known to occur in combination with shale (oil shale) and sand (tar sands) in deposits several times larger than the traditional oil sources. Until the 1970s the cost of extracting oil from these sources was too high, but by the mid 1970s the extraction of oil from tar sands was becoming **economically viable** from the richest deposits in Canada. (This means that the oil could be sold for more money than was needed to obtain it.)

Some oil shale deposits are known to occur in the UK and have been commercially mined in Scotland. Though some low grade reserves (those containing small amounts of useful material) still exist in Scotland, it is unlikely that they will become economic to work. However, it is hoped that oil shales present in the quite extensive kimmeridge clays of south and east England may well hold suitable concentrations. The environmental problems of using these energy sources, however, will be enormous. This is particularly true of oil shales because of the very large quantities of waste materials that will be produced in extracting the oil from the shale. Many of the wastes may also be toxic (poisonous).

New ways of extracting fuels might also be found that will enable us to obtain fuels that we cannot use at the moment—perhaps because they are buried too deeply in the Earth's crust, or perhaps because they are under the deepest parts of the oceans.

Table 1.1 *World depletion dates for the main energy sources.*

Energy source	Depletion date (years from now)
crude oil	25–35
natural gas	25–35
coal	700–1 400
uranium–235	20–25
uranium–238	$\times 10^3$–10^{4*}

*If used in fast breeder reactors

Despite all of these difficulties it is necessary that we should at least attempt to predict when our fuels are likely to run out so that we can decide when it will be necessary to find some alternative means of producing the energy we need. Many experts agree that depletion dates are likely to be approximately as shown in Table 1.1. (The larger value for coal assumes that coal will continue to be used at the present rate and that our estimation of the amount of coal yet to be discovered is not too high. If coal is used to replace oil, then obviously it will become depleted much more quickly.)

Electricity

Because electrical energy is so important in industrialized societies, it is important to know how electricity is produced. In fact, the Central Electricity Generating Board (CEGB) uses about 67% of the coal produced in Britain and supplies industry with the largest proportion of its energy requirements. Very nearly every house in the country is supplied with electricity. Enormous amounts of money are spent in producing this electrical energy. In fact , one large fossil fuel powered generating station may cost hundreds of millions of pounds; a nuclear power station will cost over one thousand million pounds.

The first stage in the production of electricity is the conversion of the chemical energy in coal, oil or gas into heat energy. (In a nuclear-fuelled power station, the energy binding the atomic particles together in the nucleus of uranium is converted into heat.) This heat is used to change water into steam. The steam is taken through pipes to a **turbine** and causes the turbine shaft to turn at high speed (the energy is now present as kinetic energy). The shaft of the turbine is connected to an electromagnet (the **rotor**) in the **generator**. This magnet is situated inside a large coil of wire (the **stator**). As the magnet rotates it produces a current in the coil. These machines are so vast that it can take many hours to reach peak power output, and because of the laws of energy conversion and heat transfer only 25–30% of the energy in the fuel is converted into electrical energy. A 500 megawatt turbo-generator is shown in Fig. 1.14.

A large generating station may generate electricity at about 25 000 volts. However, to distribute this electricity efficiently over long distances the voltage may be increased to 132 000, 275 000 or 400 000 volts. The voltage used depends upon distance and current to be distributed (the **load**). When the electricity reaches the area in which it is to be used, the voltage is reduced again. If it is to be used in heavy industry it will be reduced to 33 000 volts, for light industry to 11 000 volts and for domestic supply to 240 volts.

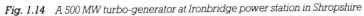

Fig. 1.14 *A 500 MW turbo-generator at Ironbridge power station in Shropshire*

The electricity is increased or decreased in voltage by using **transformers**. The transformer works on a very simple principle. This is explained in Fig. 1.15:

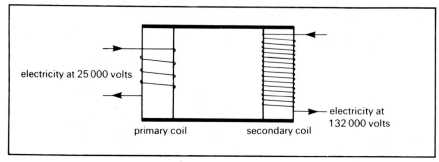

Fig. 1.15 *Simplified diagram of a transformer*

An **alternating current** (a.c.) passes through the coil of wire shown on the left-hand side of the diagram (the **primary coil**). The term 'alternating' means that the electricity passes through the coil first in one direction and then in the other. As the current changes direction so it causes a current to be produced in the coil on the right (the **secondary coil**). By having more turns of wire in the coil on the right than on the left, the voltage can be increased (stepped up). If the incoming current passes through a coil having more turns than the 'outgoing coil', then the voltage is reduced (stepped down).

The electricity may be transmitted by either underground or overhead cables. Overhead cables have to be supported well above the ground on electricity pylons which are rather unsightly but which are much cheaper than underground cables.

ALTERNATIVE AND RENEWABLE ENERGY SOURCES

Because our traditional energy sources are in danger of running out within the next few decades, an increasing amount of research and development is being directed at alternative energy sources. Many of these alternative sources are also **renewable**. This means they rely on natural flows of energy or cycles of matter that have been present on Earth practically since its formation and will be present until its final destruction. We can, therefore, be confident that if we are able to use these energy sources they will never run out.

Wind

The wind on our planet is the result of large-scale air movements that result from the Sun's heat energy warming up different parts of the planet faster than others. As the air above the surface of the Earth warms up, it becomes less dense and begins to rise. As it does so, an area of low pressure is formed and cool air (which is more dense) moves in to equalize the pressure. As the warm air moves upwards, so its gets cooler and more dense and tends to fall again. In the upper atmosphere, air tends to move from the equator to the poles and in the lower atmosphere it tends to move from poles to equator. However, because of the spin of the Earth and the distribution of sea and continents, the air follows a rather more complex pattern.

The energy contained in these air movements has been used in many ways throughout man's history. The most obvious example is in driving windmills that have in turn driven stone wheels to grind corn for flour or pump water from drainage ditches (East Anglia and Holland). What is new about windmills in the context of alternative energy sources is the idea that they can be used to produce electricity, in which case they are called **aerogenerators.** Fig. 1.16 shows various types of wind-energy devices.

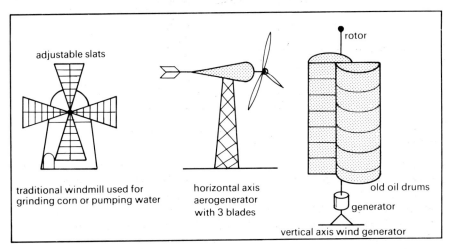

Fig. 1.16 Wind energy devices

Many calculations have been done on how much electrical energy could be generated from windmills of conventional design and the answer depends, of course, on the size of the windmill and the speed of the wind. Given that a mean wind speed in the most exposed sites in the UK is about 7 metres per second and that a windmill is constructed with 2 blades, each 50 metres in diameter, it is expected that about 1000 kilowatts (1 megawatt) of electricity might be generated. (A moderately large fossil fuel powered generating station might generate 500 megawatts.) Windmills of this size *can* be constructed! In 1974, a windmill in Ohio having blades of about 40 metres in diameter generated 100 kilowatts of electricity, and a windmill capable of generating 1250 kilowatts was constructed in Vermont in the 1940s.

The United Kingdom is placed in a favourable position to use wind energy because it is situated in one of the windiest areas of the world. However, many people might object to large numbers of windmills being built in the countryside, particularly as the most favourable (windy) sites tend to be in areas of great natural beauty. The present generating capacity in the UK (1978) is over 65 000 megawatts. If all our electricity were generated by windmills each generating 1 megawatt, then obviously we would need 65 000 of them! One possible way of overcoming these objections is to build the windmills in shallow waters off the coast—and in this case many could be built on the North Sea oil rigs when the oil finally runs out.

Another rather more practical problem is that windmills will only generate electricity when the wind blows—and this is inconsistent. This problem is partly compensated for by the fact that the wind blows most consistently at times of highest energy demand—during the winter.

In 1981 work was in hand to construct an aerogenerator in the Orkneys to produce electricity for the inhabitants. The Orkney islands are not connected to the national grid on the mainland because of the difficulties of transmitting electricity to them.

The occupants of farms and other isolated dwellings are becoming increasingly interested in producing their own electricity from aerogenerators.

Energy from Water

Energy from water can be obtained in several ways. The most successful of the possible techniques has been used for many years in most parts of the world. This involves using the kinetic energy obtained by water in falling large distances to drive turbines and generators to produce electricity. Generating stations that utilize this technique are referred to as **hydro-electric** stations (see Fig. 1.17).

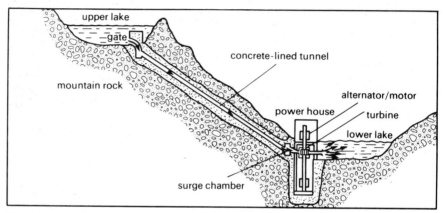

Fig. 1.17   How hydro-electric power is generated

Hydro-electric power

The amount of energy that can be generated in this way depends upon the volume (or mass) of water falling and the distance through which it falls. For this reason, most hydro-electric stations are situated in mountainous regions.

At present in the UK over 1500 megawatts of electricity are generated by hydro-electric power (HEP)—a little over 2% of the total. There are several environmental objections to increasing the amount of electricity generated in this way. Objections that are raised are levelled at the need to create large concrete dams. Many people consider these to be out of place in the wild countryside of Wales, North-West England and Scotland, where most of these stations are necessarily built. Also, flooding land reduces the natural habitat of a wide range of plants and animals. The flooded area is normally agricultural land

Fig. 1.18   Lednock dam, Tayside Region. The surrounding land is used for hill-sheep farming

Fig. 1.19   *The machine hall of Cruachan power station*

(though generally of poor quality, suitable only for extensive grazing of sheep or hardy cattle), and any loss of this land in the UK must be considered carefully. Finally, it is occasionally necessary to flood the valleys in which people live and these people must subsequently lose their homes.

The greatest restriction to a large extension of hydro-electric power in the UK however, is the lack of suitable sites. Not only is it necessary to find a site where water falls as far a distance as possible but also to find a site where, if possible, rainfall maintains sufficient water in the reservoir to replace that which generates the electricity. This problem is met at Cruachan in Scotland. The hydro-electric power station here works in conjunction with conventional power stations. At times of peak electricity demand, both the conventional and the hydro-electric stations produce electricity for distribution through the national grid. The water that flows from the upper reservoir and through the turbines is impounded (captured) in a lower reservoir. At times of low demand, the electricity generated by the conventional station is used to pump the water back into the upper reservoir. This system is often referred to as a **pumped storage scheme**. This is particularly interesting at Cruachan since the generators are built inside a mountain and are about 400m below ground. The machine hall is shown in Fig. 1.19. Fig. 1.20 shows the arrangement of shafts and tunnels under the ground.

In 1980 the Government sponsored research into the idea of using the small streams in Wales to produce electricity by hydro power. It was felt that several hundred sites could be made available so that each could provide upwards of 25kW of electrical energy. This would be sufficient electricity to power a farm or a hamlet and would be a start towards the day when fossil fuels run out.

Fig. 1.20   *Cruachan is a pumped-storage scheme*

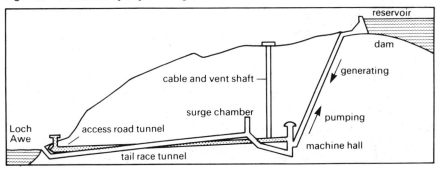

On a world scale, most of the suitable sites for hydro-electric stations that remain are in underdeveloped countries. The sites are difficult to reach and often great distances from civilization. To use such sites would be very expensive and, because many of these countries are politically unstable, there is no guarantee that the country that installs the necessary equipment would be allowed to benefit from it.

Tidal power

The second technique for extracting energy from water is, in principle, very similar to conventional hydro-electricity and is called **tidal power**. The major difference is that instead of using a low discharge (small volume) of water falling through a large distance, a large discharge is used, passing through a small distance. The sites where these criteria are likely to be met are river estuaries. One such site that has been exploited to produce electricity is La Rance estuary in France where the installation can generate 62 megawatts of electricity.

One of the most suitable sites in the world for constructing such a system is the Severn Estuary which some experts calculate would be capable of producing between 10% and 20% of our present electricity requirements.

Tidal movements (and thus the energy in them) are produced by the force of gravity that the Moon exerts on the Earth. As the Moon orbits the Earth it drags round a 'bulge' in the oceans which creates a high tide. However, due to the spin of the Earth, another 'balancing bulge' forms on the side of the Earth away from the Moon. This creates another high tide. Because the Moon passes any point on the Earth once in every twenty-four hours, there are two high tides— one as the Moon passes the point, and a second as the 'balancing bulge' passes the point. As the rise and fall of the tides causes water to move in and out of estuaries, the water can be made to pass through turbines situated in a barrage across the estuary, which can then turn generators to produce electricity. A cross-section of a tidal barrage is shown in Fig. 1.21.

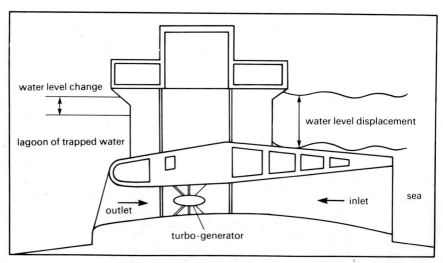

Fig. 1.21 *Cross-section of a tidal barrage. Rising water is allowed to pass through the inlet sluice as the tide comes in. The water is then trapped in a lagoon and is allowed to leave through turbo-generators when electricity is required*

One practical problem of the system is that the tides are not regular (the Moon does not pass over the same point at exactly the same time on successive days) and thus the times when electricity can be generated will vary. This can be overcome by storing the water after a high tide behind the barrage and allowing it to pass out through the turbines when the electricity is required.

It is possible to arrange the barrage so that a high level of water can be maintained in the lagoon of trapped water for shipping and perhaps for recreation. A lock system can be designed to allow ships to pass in and out when water levels are low.

Some possible environmental problems (other than the visual impact) include: the effect on wildlife that inhabits the estuary and the changing rate of deposition of silt. Some forms of wildlife are specially adapted to living in conditions where for part of the time they are covered in water and part of the time no water is present; they are also able to withstand the changing salt content of the water as sea and fresh water mix in different amounts. If the natural change of tides is interfered with then perhaps these animals will die (some people argue, however, that the suggested changes will allow more animals to live in the area, so overall it will be beneficial). A tidal barrage will also change the rate at which silt and other materials (including materials in solution and suspension that animals and plants use as food) are carried from the rivers into the sea. This may also have a harmful effect on wildlife. It is unlikely that migrating fish would be affected very much because it is thought that the fish will be able to swim through the blades of the turbines that are built into the barrages. Alternatively fish ladders can be constructed.

Wave power

A final means of obtaining electricity from water is to use the energy present in waves which are generated by high winds far out at sea. Most of the energy in a wave is in an up and down direction, and a number of devices have been designed to convert this energy into electrical energy. Two of these devices are shown in Fig. 1.22. The UK is in an advantageous position to use this

Fig. 1.22 Wave power devices

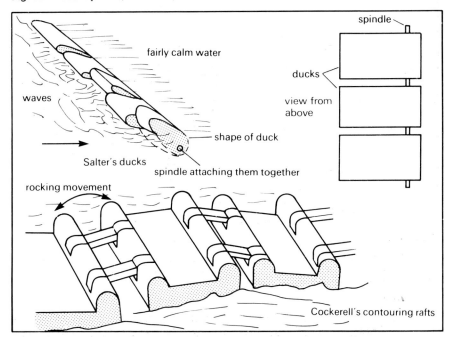

technology because large waves are frequently generated off our coasts (waves off the north-west coast of Scotland might produce 15 kW of electricity per metre of their length). It has been suggested that a power station made of suitable devices measuring in total about 80 kilometres long and 7–8 metres high, might generate 1% of our present electrical energy requirements. One important advantage of this system is that the waves (and thus the electricity generated) are greatest during winter, when we have our highest energy demand.

The latest suggestion to harness wave power is to diffract the waves through a series of slits so that they focus on to one point. The combined effects of the waves would enable the water level to be raised many feet above normal. A reservoir situated at this point could be used to store the water and release it to produce conventional hydro-electric power.

Even wave power has possible environmental disadvantages, because if energy is removed from waves there will be less energy available in them to transport material up and down coastlines. This might affect fish breeding areas.

Energy from the Sun

The energy that reaches the Earth from the Sun is called **solar energy,** and is a combination of heat and light energy. Under the right conditions, both forms of energy can be used.

Fig. 1.23 *A solar cell array*

Solar cells

The light energy can be utilized by using solar cells. These are made from special materials which produce an electric current when light energy falls on them (see Fig. 1.23). The light falling on the solar cell causes electrons to be released and so an electric current can be generated. Selenium (a metal), cadmium disulphide (a compound of the metal cadmium) and amorphous silicon are examples of materials used in solar cells.

Solar cells are faced with two main problems. Firstly, the materials that generate the electric current are very expensive and a large panel is required to produce a useful current. Secondly, electricity is only generated when the sun shines! A possible means of overcoming this last problem is by using the solar cells to charge storage batteries. The batteries could be charged when the sun is strong and more electricity is produced than is needed. The batteries could then produce electricity whenever it is required.

Despite these problems, this means of using solar energy is utilized by France along the Marseilles autoroute (motorway), where an emergency telephone system operates along its entire length and is powered by solar cells which charge storage batteries.

The heat energy present in sunlight can be utilized in two different ways—by **solar furnaces** and **solar panels.**

Solar furnaces

This system operates by using mirrors to reflect the Sun's heat energy onto a focal point. This heat can be used to change water to steam and so drive a turbo-generator. The first electricity generating station of any notable size that works on this principle was constructed in Italy in 1981 and can generate 1 MW of electricity.

Solar panels

This system is currently generating a lot of interest among home owners in the UK because it is one of the few renewable energy forms that can be used by individuals. The panels are made of two parts, a black material which absorbs the solar energy, and a glass cover which allows solar energy to pass in but reduces the amount able to pass out. Water is allowed to trickle over the black backing, or pass through pipes which lie on the surface of the backing. In doing so, the water becomes warmer (see Fig. 1.24).

In general, this system is used to heat domestic water by allowing the water that has passed through the solar panel to pass through a copper coil immersed in a lagged tank. The water from the panel passes its heat to the water in the tank and then passes back to the panel for further warming.

The greatest practical problem is again that the system only operates when the sun is shining and tends, at the moment, to be very expensive. It costs a lot of money to set up a panel and a relatively small quantity of heat is obtained. Naturally, the final temperature reached by the water in the lagged tank will depend upon the size of the panel and the quantity of energy present in the sunlight.

Fig. 1.24 One form of solar panel. The copper piping absorbs heat from the sun and warms the water circulating in the pipes

Fig. 1.25 A geyser erupting

Geothermal Energy

Present in the Earth's crust are certain areas where the heat that is normally deep within the Earth's crust and in the **mantle** (the part beneath the crust) comes relatively close to the surface. Often, groundwater moves downwards until it reaches the areas of high temperature and becomes hot. On occasions, this hot water is apparent on the surface as **geysers**.

Areas of high temperature which are sufficiently large and near enough to the Earth's surface to be used commercially are found in New Zealand, Italy, Iceland and some parts of the USA. The first commercially used energy from this type of source was in Italy early in this century, and the Italians now generate 4 megawatts of electricity from 16 generating stations using geothermal energy. An even greater output is now achieved in the USA.

The United Kingdom is poorly situated to utilize this energy source and so far it has achieved little attention in this country. Nevertheless, several areas of 'hot rock' have been found close enough to the surface to be of use, if we can develop the technology required to inject water down to this area so that it would be heated prior to returning to the surface with its 'captured' energy. One

Fig. 1.26 Extracting heat from hot rock areas in the Earth's crust

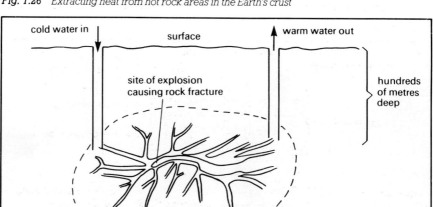

possibility is to detonate an explosive charge that will fracture the hot rock. Water could then be pumped through the fractures as illustrated in Fig. 1.26.

Assuming a suitable source of geothermal energy exists, there are two practical difficulties that emerge. The first of these is that the hot water or steam has to be conveyed via pipelines to the site where it is to be used (e.g. the turbo-generators) before it loses too much of its heat. The second problem is even more difficult to solve. Eventually, either the hot water is removed faster than groundwater supplies can replace it, or, if the groundwater can replace it, it has the effect of cooling the area to the point where it is no longer of any value. To overcome this problem it is hoped to develop a technique whereby waste water from generating stations (which still contains heat) might be re-injected into the area so that the cooling effect will not be so great.

The environmental effects are two-fold. The extensive network of pipes is generally considered to look unpleasant and the areas tend to smell very strongly of the sulphur which is often associated with these geothermal areas.

Biological Energy Sources

Sources of biological energy have been used by man for centuries and they still play a major role in some areas. Excluding the fossil fuels, which are of course biological in origin, it is possible to use wood, peat and dried animal excreta.

More recently, an increasingly important source of energy is the sludge that is left in sewage treatment works after the purified effluent is released into water systems (see Chapter 4). The sludge is placed into containers or **digestors** at about 37°C and kept under **anaerobic** conditions (anaerobic means without oxygen). Under these conditions anaerobic bacteria break down the sludge (which to the bacteria is a food source) and release (among other things) methane gas (see Fig. 1.27). The amount and proportion of methane released depends upon many factors, including the time for which the digestor is allowed to operate, but eventually the gases can be purified and the methane burnt. (Methane is the gas referred to as North Sea gas or natural gas.) The importance of this energy source is probably fairly limited, but a number of modern sewage works produce methane from sludge and are able to use the energy present in it for space heating and for generating electricity for lighting, vehicles and pumps.

A number of instances have been quoted of individuals making their own digestors which run on animal excreta, and at least one person has modified a car to run off the methane produce from poultry manure. Another form of biological fuel that is creating a lot of interest is alcohol. In South America, large

Fig. 1.27 A methane digestor

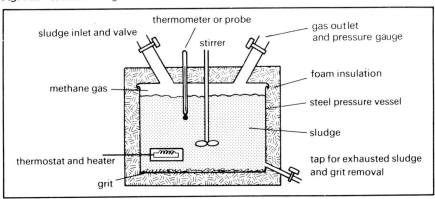

areas of land are planted with sugar cane and the sugar that is obtained from the crop can be converted into alcohol. This alcohol can be mixed with petrol and the mixture used to fuel cars. In Brazil, petrol contains up to 20% alcohol. It has been suggested that we grow sugar beet in the UK for the same purpose, but we have very little land available for such a scheme.

Nuclear Fusion

A final source of energy that holds out great hope for the future is that of **nuclear fusion**. The principle is to combine two atoms of very small mass into one of greater mass. This reaction has been made to occur in the 'H'-bomb, but in this instance the reaction is uncontrolled.

The most suitable material to use is likely to be **deuterium**—an atom of hydrogen having a neutron rather than none at all as is the case in normal hydrogen. There is a very large quantity of deuterium available in sea water. One possible reaction would be:

$$^{2}_{1}H \quad + \quad ^{2}_{1}H \quad \longrightarrow \quad ^{3}_{2}He \quad + \quad n \quad + \quad energy$$

deuterium + deuterium → helium + one neutron + energy

In such a reaction one gram of $^{2}_{1}H$ undergoing fusion would release $7{\cdot}7 \times 10^{10}$ joules of energy, so weight-for-weight the fusion reaction would produce two and a half million times as much energy as burning coal.

At the present time, however, controlled fusion reactions have not been maintained for more than a fraction of a second. The major practical problem is of maintaining the reactants under suitable conditions at a temperature of about $10^{8}\,°C$.

ACTIVITIES

Recognizing forms of energy

This series of experiments is concerned with the law of conservation of energy (or the first law of thermodynamics). This law states that energy can neither be created nor destroyed but may be converted from one form to another.

1 Set up the experiment in Fig. 1.28. You should be able to recognize electrical energy, kinetic energy and potential energy. Copy the diagram into your book and write:
a) a letter A where electrical energy is converted to kinetic energy;
b) a letter B where kinetic energy is converted to potential energy.

Fig. 1.28

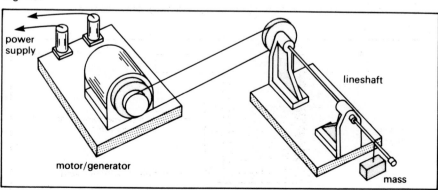

2 Set up the experiment in Fig. 1.29 using a two-way switch. Allow the motor to drive the flywheel and then move the switch to allow the flywheel to light the lamp. You should be able to recognize electrical energy, kinetic energy, heat and light energy.

Fig. 1.29

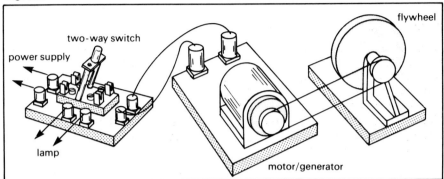

Copy the diagram in your book and write:
a) a letter *A* where electrical energy is converted to kinetic energy;
b) a letter *B* where kinetic energy is converted to electrical energy;
c) a letter *C* where electrical energy is converted to heat and light energy.

3 Set up the experiment in Fig. 1.30. Copy this diagram into your book and state what form of energy is being produced and what form of energy it is converted from.

Fig. 1.30

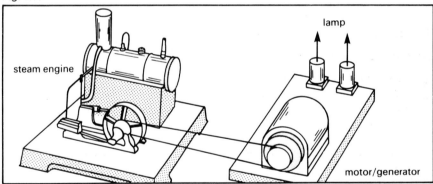

4 Set up the experiment in Fig. 1.31. Copy the diagram into your book and write:
a) an *A* where chemical energy is converted to electrical energy;

Fig. 1.31

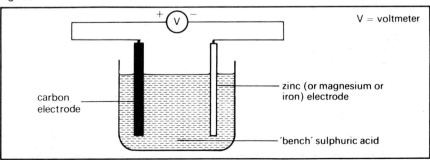

b) a *B* where kinetic energy appears;

Measuring energy

It is important in this series of experiments that you become familiar with units of energy and how energy is measured. It is also important that you should appreciate the second law of thermodynamics. This law states that whenever one form of energy is converted to another form, some useful energy is 'lost'. (In most cases the energy that is 'lost' appears as heat and could be measured if you had sufficiently accurate equipment.)

5   This experiment shows you how to measure the maximum amount of energy produced in experiment 4. Set up the experiment in Fig. 1.32.
Using the formula $E=VIt$ calculate the maximum amount of energy produced. Hint: you will have to take your values in the time *before* the current produced begins to fall below its maximum value.

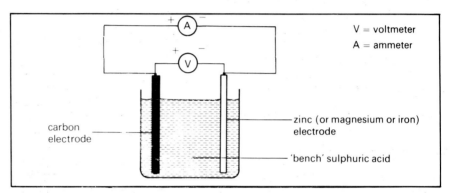

Fig. 1.32

6   Experiment to measure the amount of heat given out when a fuel burns. For this you will need a spirit lamp, ethanol, boiling tube, thermometer plus an accurate balance.
Note: be careful not to place your ethanol anywhere close to a naked flame because it is *highly* inflammable.
a) Carefully pour some ethanol into the spirit lamp until it is about half full, insert the wick and place the cap on the spirit lamp.
b) Weigh the spirit lamp (plus cap). Leave the cap over the wick.
c) Pour a measured volume of water into your boiling tube (remember 1 cm³ of water weighs 1 gram). Measure the water temperature.
d) Remove the cap from over the wick of your spirit lamp and light the wick.
e) Immediately place your boiling tube containing water over the spirit lamp so that the heat produced will heat the water. Carefully place the thermometer in the water.
f)   After a suitable time has passed (say five minutes) take the temperature of the water and put out the flame by placing the cap over it.
g) After your spirit lamp has cooled, weigh it again (with its cap on).
By subtracting this weight from the weight of the spirit lamp plus its original amount of ethanol, you can calculate how much ethanol has been burnt.
Calculate the temperature increase of the water. The amount of heat energy released (in calories) can be calculated from the following equation.

$$\text{Energy} = \text{mass of water} \times \text{temperature increase}$$

(One calorie is the amount of heat necessary to raise 1g of water by 1°C.)
To calculate the energy in 1g of ethanol this value must be divided by the mass of ethanol burned. Therefore,

$$\text{energy in 1g of ethanol} = \frac{\text{mass of water} \times \text{temperature increase}}{\text{mass of ethanol burned}}$$

To convert this value (measured in calories) into joules it should be multiplied by 4·18.

Questions

1   Calculate the potential energy in each of the following:
a) a mass of 2kg raised 2m off the floor;
b) a mass of 4kg raised 6m off the floor;
c) a mass of 500g raised 4m above the ground;
d) a mass of 400g raised 50cm above the ground.
2   Suppose a water engineer constructs a dam in a valley so that water leaving the dam falls 120m to the valley floor and flows through a turbo-generator.
a) How much potential energy is present in each litre of water (1 litre$=1\times10^3$ cm^3 and 1 cm^3 has a mass of 1g)?
b) Assume that all of this potential energy is converted into kinetic energy as the water falls, how much energy would there be in 1 million litres of water?
c) If the turbo-generator is 80% efficient, how much electrical energy would be available from the 1 million litres of water?
d) Suppose 1 million litres of water falls every 6 seconds. How much power could be obtained from the water?
3   A person makes a wind-powered machine to raise water for an irrigation system. The machine raises 4kg of water at a time in a container weighing 1kg. The water is raised a distance of 2·5m. If 2500 loads of water are raised in 24 hours, how much wind energy is tapped during this time? (Assume the machine is 50% efficient.)
4   A machine to produce energy works by moving up and down on sea waves. In a preliminary investigation, 100 of these machines were placed 1m apart on a sea with waves 0·75m high. Each machine is raised with a force of 12N. How much wave energy was extracted in total from the 100 machines?
5   Use your electricity bills for the last twelve months to calculate how much electrical energy your family uses.
Give an answer in kilowatt-hours ('units' of electricity) and in joules.
6   a) Find out how much power (joules per second or watts) each electrical item in your house uses.
b) Estimate how many hours in a week each electrical item is used for.
c) Estimate how many joules each item uses in a week.
d) Place the items in order of those using most electricity down to those using least.
e) For the two items which use most electricity, make some practicable suggestions as to how you could reduce the amount of energy each one uses.
7   In a pumped storage scheme, suggest during which periods of the day it is most likely that water is being pumped into the upper reservoir. Give a reason for your answer.

2 Energy and the Environment

THE ENVIRONMENTAL EFFECTS OF EXTRACTING FOSSIL FUELS

Oil and Gas

As described in Chapter 1, oil and gas are often found several hundreds of metres below the surface of the Earth's crust, and to reach the oil a hole has to be drilled.

The cutting end of the drill (the **bit**) is fastened to a rotating hollow steel pipe. As the bit cuts away the rock, a fluid (**drilling mud**) is pumped down through the hollow pipe to keep the bit cool and to wash out the rock fragments as they are cut away. The fluid (mostly clay suspended in water) also helps to seal the sides of the rock as the bit cuts through it. This mud comes up to the surface and is analysed every hour or so to determine the chemical composition of the rock and to see if any hydrocarbons are present. As the hole increases in depth, a steel sleeve is inserted into the hole and cemented in place to give support to the walls of the hole.

Generally, as the bit makes contact with the **reservoir rock** (rock containing oil and gas), the oil and gas flow to the surface because of the pressure they are under. A series of valves at the top of the drill hole make sure that the flow is under control. Eventually, the pressure forcing the oil out of the reservoir becomes less and so the oil has to be pumped out. Very often secondary recovery techniques are then used. Water or a gas is forced down into the reservoir rock through another drill hole, to force yet more oil out. In many instances some of the oil underground is burned. This releases heat that makes the remaining oil less viscous (more runny). In this way more oil can be pumped out.

The main danger to the environment at this stage is a **blow-out.** This is what happens if the valves at the top of the drill hole are unable to control the flow of oil due to the pressure exerted on them. If this should occur, then hundreds of cubic metres of oil would flow out into the sea (in the case of an off-shore rig) or onto the land. This happened in the North Sea on the Ekofisk rig in 1977. If gases are associated with the oil, then a spark could very easily ignite the gas and oil.

The oil that flows up the drill hole might be loaded onto an oil tanker or piped ashore to an onshore refinery (where the crude petroleum is split into groups of oil products in a **fractionating column** such as that shown in Fig. 2.3). Accidents occurring during the transfer of oil to the tanker, or a fracture of the oil pipeline, will of course result in oil being released into the sea.

It is also important to realize that the UK is still an oil-importing country and any accident involving oil tankers off the coast of the UK is of the utmost concern. Examples of accidents around the UK include the *Torrey Canyon* in March 1967 and the *Amoco Cadiz* in March 1978. In 1979 there were some 500 incidents involving oil spillages in UK waters alone.

The effects of oil on marine organisms vary, but they are usually harmful. The most obvious and most publicized effect is that of covering the feathers of sea

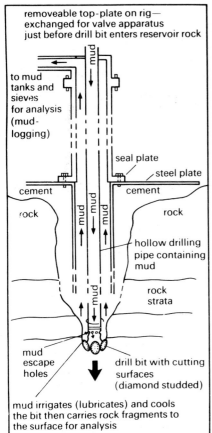

removeable top-plate on rig—
exchanged for valve apparatus
just before drill bit enters reservoir rock

to mud
tanks and
sieves
for analysis
(mud-
logging)

mud

seal plate

steel plate

cement   cement

rock

rock

mud

hollow drilling
pipe containing
mud

rock
strata

mud
escape
holes

drill bit with cutting
surfaces
(diamond studded)

mud irrigates (lubricates) and cools
the bit then carries rock fragments to
the surface for analysis

Fig. 2.2   *Drilling for oil*

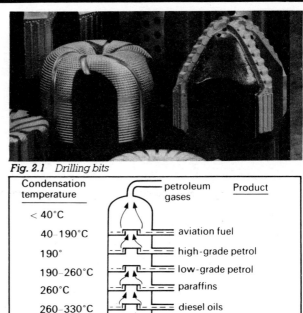

Fig. 2.1   *Drilling bits*

Condensation temperature		petroleum gases	Product
< 40°C			
40–190°C		aviation fuel	
190°		high-grade petrol	
190–260°C		low-grade petrol	
260°C		paraffins	
260–330°C		diesel oils	
330–400°C		lubricating oils	
450°C		furnace fuel oils	
450–500°C		waxes	
> 500°C condensed vapours		bitumen	
		outlet pipes	
hot crude oil vapours →		bubble valves	

Fig. 2.3   *Fractionation column for crude oil*

birds in a coat of oil. This prevents the birds from flying and, because the oil makes the feathers lie flat along the body, the birds cannot trap an insulating layer of air next to them, with the result that they may die of cold. As the birds attempt to clean the oil off by preening themselves, so they may swallow quantities of oil which may be sufficient to kill them. It is estimated that some 250000 birds died as a result of the *Torrey Canyon* accident mentioned above.

Perhaps the next most visible environmental effect of oil spillage occurs when the oil is washed onto beaches. This is not only extremely unpleasant to look at, but also spoils the beach for bathers. More important in the long term is that many of the organisms living in the sand are destroyed as their breathing structures become covered in oil.

Perhaps not so obvious, but certainly of equal concern, is the harmful effect of oil that is allowed (or made) to sink at sea. It has been suggested that this oil might destroy the breeding grounds of a variety of species of fish and thus seriously reduce our food reserves. Finally, the oil kills the plankton present in the sea that forms the basis of all the food relationships in the sea (see the section on food chains in Chapter 3).

Detergents are often used to disperse oil—particularly oil that is washed onto beaches. However, most research evidence now indicates that the detergents are, if anything, even more toxic to marine organisms than the oil they are designed to remove, even though the detergents used now are many times less toxic to wildlife than those used ten years ago. Detergents cause the burrows of burrowing animals to collapse so destroying their habitat. Detergents also destroy the breathing structures of aquatic animals.

Fig. 2.4 *An oiled guillemot stranded on the beach*   **Fig. 2.5** *Containing an oil spillage by means of a boom*

Finally, if oil escapes from a drilling rig on land, or from a lorry during transit, the oil will kill life in the soil but will cause less damage than oil in water because the oil will not spread as far. If the oil reaches a stream or river then, of course, animals in the water will be killed unless the oil is quickly contained.

Extracting Coal

The coal industry in the UK is one of the most technologically advanced extractive industries in the world, and during the last twenty years or so has become very mechanised and efficient. Coal is extracted in two main ways: **deep mining** and **open-cast quarrying.**

Deep mining

Once a suitable shaft has been dug to reach the coal, it is removed from the rock-face by means of a rock-cutting machine (see Fig. 2.6) that automatically throws the loose coal onto a conveyor belt operating alongside it. The conveyor belt takes the coal to the mine shaft ready to be taken to the surface.

A communication tunnel is kept open to the coal-face by means of jacks supporting the roof, and hydraulically-operated jacks support the roof above the coal-face as coal is removed. As the coal is cut away from the face, so the hydraulic jacks are moved forwards to support the roof, and the roof behind the jacks is allowed to collapse. This process, which results in surface subsidence, is shown in Fig. 2.7.

Fig. 2.6 *Coal shearer and hydraulic jacks at the coalface*

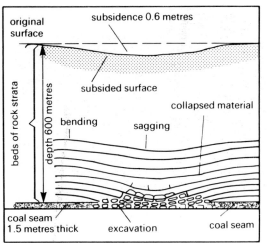
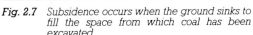

Fig. 2.7 Subsidence occurs when the ground sinks to fill the space from which coal has been excavated

Fig. 2.8 Spoil heap from Parkhouse Colliery, Derbyshire

The most obvious environmental effects of this form of coal extraction are:

1 the possibilities of subsidence,
2 The visual impact of the pit head construction—(the most apparent perhaps being the winding gear, if only because it is most often the tallest piece of equipment);
3 the waste heaps made up of the material that is separated from the coal.

The subsidence that might occur as a result of mining cannot readily be avoided. The only practical steps to be taken are either for mining operations to be halted when subsidence may affect buildings that are important, or by only building in areas not likely to be affected by subsidence. Subsidence may of course be dangerous if it occurs in areas where the public may fall down the shafts that appear.

Open-cast quarrying

This form of coal excavation uses some of the largest earth-moving machines in the UK. Before the coal can be extracted, the material lying above the coal (the **overburden**) has to be removed and stored so that it can be returned later. Once the overburden has been removed, the coal can be gouged out of the ground by mechanical shovels.

The problem of unsightly constructions can be partially overcome by suitable planning measures. Where it is possible, constructions are placed in natural hollows where they will be partly hidden. Failing this, the waste that is produced can be used to form artificial hills that can then be suitably planted with shrubs and trees to make them look attractive. This will also help to overcome the problem of disposing of the waste.

Officially it is estimated that there is more than 45×10^3 hectares of derelict land in the UK, though this value excludes workings and tips that are still being used. Of this, the National Coal Board accepts responsibility for some 10×10^3 hectares, containing approximately 2000 spoil heaps—a total of about 2.5×10^9 tonnes of waste. In some areas, such as Newcastle-on-Tyne, the waste land has been converted into recreational areas (e.g. city parks). Other areas have been planted with trees or converted back into agricultural land.

Since the Coal Board became nationalized, and therefore, perhaps, became more subject to public pressure than private industries, it has made greater efforts to reduce the dereliction it causes. Though the problem is still a very big

Fig. 2.9 *Opencast quarrying for coal in Nottinghamshire*

one, the Coal Board claims to have restored 40×10^3 hectares of derelict land since 1947. This has been achieved in various ways. A great deal of material from waste heaps (estimated at 9×10^6 tonnes) has been used as foundation material in the building of roads. Often the reclamation of pit heaps is linked to the reclamation of open-cast quarries. The 'heap' material is used to fill in the quarry and then a final covering is made with the original subsoil and topsoil, so that the area is rendered fertile again.

Fig. 2.10 and 2.11 *An open-cast coal site before and after land reclamation*

BURNING FOSSIL FUELS

The materials released when fossil fuels are burnt can be classified as either **particulate** or **gaseous.** In either case, they are generally considered to be pollutants.

Particulate Pollutants

The particulate material which may be released from these fuels may either be material that could be burnt, but which does not get burnt, or may be mineral matter present in coal which will not burn. It is usually visible as 'smoke', but may be greatly reduced if the conditions under which the fuel is burnt are more strictly controlled. It is estimated that about 1×10^6 tonnes of particulate material are released in the UK annually. The environmental effects are given below.

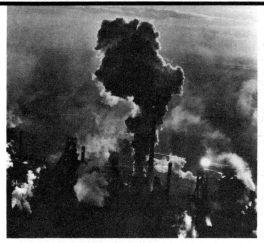

Fig. 2.12 *Particulate pollution in Scunthorpe*

Fig. 2.13 *Cleaning a building by dry-grit blasting (Crown copyright)*

1 The material may become deposited on buildings and make them look dirty and unpleasant. Often, particularly when the buildings have some historical, architectural or other particular value, large sums of money are spent cleaning them.

2 Plants are damaged by the deposits on their leaves. They often suffer a reduction in their rate of **photosynthesis** (see Chapter 3). This is partly because the particles fall on the leaves and reduce the amount of light reaching them, and light is necessary for photosynthesis. Also, if they block the **stomatal pores** in the leaf, through which gases for respiration and photosynthesis pass, the plants will suffer and will not grow as well as normally (see Fig. 2.14). It has been realized for many years that throughout the UK the likely loss to agriculture as a result of these effects runs to hundreds of thousands of pounds each year. Many evergreen perennial plants are incapable of growing in heavily industrialized areas because the deposits build up on their leaves until it leads to their death.

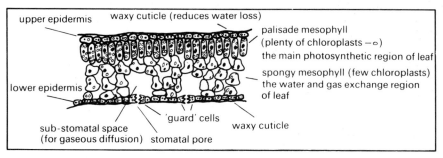

Fig. 2.14 *Vertical section through a leaf. Particulates may cover leaf surfaces or block stomatal pores*

3 The particles mainly affect animals (including man) by entering the lungs and preventing them from working efficiently (see Fig. 2.15 and Fig. 2.16). However, the effect of particulate pollution on breathing is difficult to determine, because this form of pollution is usually associated with sulphur dioxide. As such, this topic is discussed more fully later.

4 There has been some concern over the effect that particulates might have on global climates, although there is some controversy over the way they might act. Some scientists suggest that the particles will form a 'blanket' over the globe so that heat will be trapped in the atmosphere instead of passing out into space.

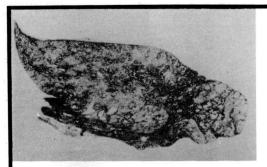 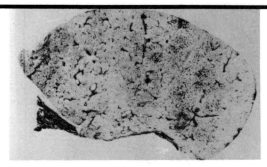

Fig. 2.15 *Lung section of a middle-aged town-dweller* **Fig. 2.16** *Lung section of a countryman of the same age*

This would tend to lead to an increase in world mean temperatures and a melting of the polar ice caps. If this were to happen, the levels of the Earth's oceans would rise sufficiently to flood much of the planet's coastal regions. Many of these regions contain the world's largest cities and much of its richest agricultural land. Other scientists suggest that the particles will act as nuclei around which water droplets will collect. These droplets will eventually join together (coalesce) to form larger droplets, leading eventually to increased cloud cover. If this happens, the clouds will increase the amount of the Sun's heat that is reflected back into space and the global climate will become cooler. One obvious effect of this could be an increase in the areas of the Earth covered by ice—in other words, another ice age.

Gaseous Pollutants

The nature of the gases released when fossil fuels are burnt depends upon the conditions in which they are burnt and the impurities present in the fuel.
1   If there is an adequate supply of air, the carbon material in the fuel is oxidized to **carbon dioxide.**

$$C + O_2 \longrightarrow CO_2$$

Since the amount of carbon dioxide in the atmosphere is increasing (Fig. 2.24) it is important to consider the possible consequences. The gas might have two effects. Firstly, because it is the starting point for photosynthesis (see Chapter 3), the rate of photosynthesis in many plants may increase. This might tend to be thought of as a beneficial effect, since the plants upon which man depends for his food would become more productive. On the other hand, it might benefit some plants more than others, thus leading to a change in the relationships that exist at the moment between different plants. Secondly, the gas might lead to an increase in world temperatures. The radiation from the Sun that passes through the Earth's atmosphere contains short wavelength (**ultra-violet**) radiation, but the radiation that is radiated from the Earth back into space is long wavelength (**infra-red**) radiation. Because carbon dioxide (and water vapour) is able to absorb infra-red radiation, any increase in the concentration of carbon dioxide in the atmosphere would tend to raise world mean temperatures with the same effect as described previously under particulate pollution. (This effect of carbon dioxide of increasing global temperatures is often referred to as the 'greenhouse effect', because greenhouses have a similar effect. The short wavelength radiation from the Sun passes through the glass and warms up the path and staging, etc. in the greenhouse. The heat that is given off by the path and staging cannot pass back out through the glass so the greenhouse temperature increases).
2   **Carbon monoxide** is produced when fossil fuels are burnt in a limited supply of oxygen.

$$2C + O_2 \longrightarrow 2CO \quad \text{or}$$
$$C + \tfrac{1}{2}O_2 \longrightarrow CO$$

Under normal circumstances, carbon monoxide is unlikely to reach concentrations that will affect man. When this does happen, the carbon monoxide forms a chemical compound with haemoglobin in the blood (**carboxyhaemoglobin**) and reduces the efficiency with which it transports oxygen around the body. On rare occasions people have died as a result of carbon monoxide poisoning when they have left their car running in a closed space. Some concern has been expressed about policemen on point duty and traffic wardens in large cities when traffic is at its heaviest. In Tokyo exhaust fumes are so bad that policemen on point duty have access to oxygen masks.

3 All fossil fuels, except very pure natural gas, contain sulphur impurities. When these impurities are burnt in air they are converted to **sulphur dioxide** (1) or **sulphur trioxide** (2).

$$S + O_2 \longrightarrow SO_2 \qquad (1)$$
$$2S + 3O_2 \longrightarrow 2SO_3 \qquad (2)$$

Approximately 4×10^6 tonnes of sulphur dioxide are released annually in the UK from fossil fuel combustion.

Sulphur dioxide readily dissolves in water to produce sulphurous and sulphuric acid. Very often rain contains quantities of these acids.

$$SO_2 + H_2O \longrightarrow H_2SO_3 \qquad\qquad SO_2 + \tfrac{1}{2}O_2 \longrightarrow SO_3$$
$$H_2SO_3 + \tfrac{1}{2}O_2 \longrightarrow H_2SO_4 \quad \text{or} \quad SO_3 + H_2O \longrightarrow H_2SO_4$$

In some instances sulphur compounds in the atmosphere may be beneficial. Sulphur is an element that is often in limited supply in the soil and this restricts the growth of plants. Increasing the supply of sulphur in these circumstances will tend to increase plant growth. It has also been shown that some pests (e.g. rose mildew) are less common in areas that suffer from sulphur pollution.

Use has been made of the sensitivity of some plants to sulphur (e.g. lichens) to measure the levels of sulphur dioxide in the atmosphere.

Despite these occasions when sulphur compounds might have a beneficial effect, it has generally been shown that they are very detrimental. The acids falling in rainwater are very corrosive and structures containing iron or limestone are particularly sensitive to them (see Fig. 2.17).

Even more important is the effect of sulphur dioxide on the breathing organs of animals, including man. Together with smoke particles, with which this pollutant is usually associated, it has been linked with chronic bronchitis,

Fig. 2.17 *Sulphur dioxide pollution has caused the stone of Bristol cathedral to 'peel'*

asthma and emphysema (see Fig. 2.18). In the case of emphysema, the air sacs in the lungs (**alveoli**) fuse together to make a smaller number of large air sacs. This reduces the area for gas exchange so the sufferer gets short of breath more quickly.

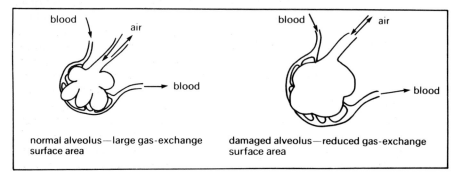

normal alveolus—large gas-exchange surface area

damaged alveolus—reduced gas-exchange surface area

Fig. 2.18   *A normal alveolus and one that has been damaged by atmospheric pollution*

Another problem with sulphur dioxide and particulates is that they paralyse the **cilia** that line the **trachea** (see Fig. 2.19). These cilia are important in removing material that becomes trapped in the mucus lining the trachea by wafting the mucus into the throat. If the cilia fail to work, the particulates and other pollutants are more able to enter the lungs and damage them. The body attempts to remove the material by making the sufferer cough. This problem leads to bronchitis. For old people, people with weak hearts, or bronchitis sufferers, sulphur dioxide is a killer, particularly when combined with particulates.

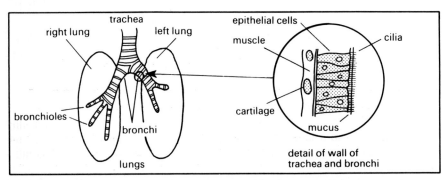

detail of wall of trachea and bronchi

Fig. 2.19   *Sulphur dioxide and particulates paralyse the cilia lining the trachea*

A value of ten parts per million (10 p.p.m.) is quoted as being a safe limit for sulphur dioxide pollution, but in one of the most publicized and most catastrophic incidents of air pollution (the London smog of 1952) when sulphur dioxide was combined with smoke, people were dying of respiratory diseases at 0·1 p.p.m. of sulphur dioxide. It is estimated that up to 15000 people die prematurely every year in the UK because they breathe in gases such as sulphur dioxide from the air.

Another important aspect of gaseous air pollution is caused by burning petrol in cars, etc. Lead, in the form of **tetra-ethyl lead**, is added to petrol to improve the performance of petrol-burning engines. As the exhaust fumes from the engine are released into the atmosphere, so the lead is released. This will then be deposited in the street or inhaled directly in air. Approximately 9×10^3 tonnes of lead are released into the atmosphere annually in the UK. Lead is a cumulative poison, which means that it is not removed from the body, and so its concentration will increase over a period of years. For many years lead has been known to affect the nervous system and cause headaches, over-activity, irritability and retard brain development. Some experts recently have even suggested that the increase in vandalism in inner-city areas is because of the increased lead in the atmosphere.

Scientists in London in 1976 measured the concentration of lead present in street dust in a number of areas. Estimates based upon their research suggest that children (who are the most at danger because they will transfer dust to their mouths via dirty fingers) might absorb 10–15 micrograms of lead per day from this source alone. A recommended maximum intake from all sources (including food, drink and inhalation) for adults is given as 12 micrograms per day. It would seem, therefore, that the growing generation of children in London (and perhaps other large cities) might well be absorbing twice this level. An indication of the increase in the amount of lead in the environment is presented in Fig. 2.20. In particular, the increase in lead levels can be related to the industrial revolution and the increase in car ownership and mileage covered. At present in the UK 0·40g of lead is allowed in a litre of petrol but the Government have introduced measures to reduce this to 0·15g by 1985, to fall in line with EEC regulations. Some countries are attempting to ban lead in petrol altogether and Japan has already done so.

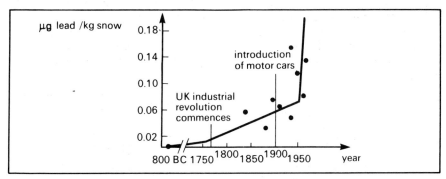

Fig. 2.20 *Lead content of samples of snow from the Greenland ice-cap (Source: Murozami, Chow and Patterson)*

5   A final problem related to gaseous pollutants is that involving the formation of **photochemical smog**. This is caused by reactions between a number of gaseous pollutants under particular environmental conditions. The gases required for its formation include oxides of nitrogen and hydrocarbons, both of which are present in car exhaust fumes. The environmental conditions required

Fig. 2.21 *Formation of a temperature inversion*

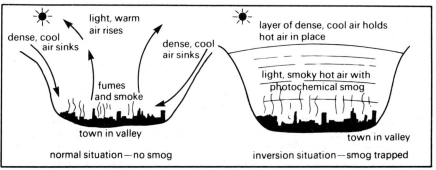

include a high level of ultra-violet (short wavelength) light and a **temperature inversion** (see Fig. 2.21). A temperature inversion occurs when a layer of cold air is trapped next to the ground by a layer of warm air above it. This condition is often found in valleys or basins with little wind and a high temperature, such as in Los Angeles which is notorious for photochemical smog and suffers a temperature inversion on average every alternate day.

The precise reactions occurring in the formation of these smogs is not known for sure. One possibility is that nitrogen dioxide (NO_2) is made to split in the presence of ultra-violet light to produce nitric oxide and atomic oxygen.

$$NO_2 \longrightarrow NO+O$$

The oxygen atom then reacts with atmospheric oxygen to produce ozone (O_3).

$$O+O_2 \longrightarrow O_3$$

The ozone and nitric oxide then react with hydrocarbons to form the smog.

These smogs reduce visibility and irritate the eyes and lungs. People in Los Angeles have to reduce drastically their levels of activity when the area suffers from these smogs.

In the UK, conditions are not suitable for the formation of these smogs because there is not enough ultra-violet light and rarely a temperature inversion. However, the initial stages of its formation were detected at the motorway complex in Birmingham known as 'Spaghetti Junction', and also in London, in the summer of 1976. The weather was good that summer so there was more ultra-violet light than usual and temperature inversions occasionally occurred.

Reducing Air Pollution

The unpleasant effects of pollution have been appreciated in the UK for many years, though very little has been done to reduce them. Often, it has been a question of moving the cause of the pollution to somewhere else. The first major move towards reducing air pollution in the UK was a direct result of the 1952 London smog—the 1956 Clean Air Act. This Act reduced the amount of thick, black smoke that industries are allowed to release, and empowered local authorities to introduce smokeless zones in which private house-dwellers are prohibited from burning fuels that release smoke (i.e. coal).

Fig. 2.22 *London in the 1950s*   *Fig. 2.23* *London today*

As a result of the Act, home-owners who were within a designated smokeless zone changed their fuel to gas, electricity or a solid 'smokeless' fuel. Industries took measures to reduce the level of smoke released by fitting electrostatic precipitators inside the flues. These are sheets of metal that run vertically up the flue and which carry an electric charge. As solid particles move up the flue, they are attracted to, and 'stick' to, the plates. Vibrators operate at intervals to remove the compacted particles from the plates. The particles fall to the bottom of the flue to be removed as necessary.

Since the Act the level of particulate pollution in the UK has dropped considerably despite the increase in fuel burnt. However, the Act did not prevent the release of gaseous pollutants and these have continued to increase. Nevertheless, because of public pressure, many industries are attempting to reduce the amount of these types of pollutant they release.

The problem of carbon monoxide removal can be solved by improving the air supply during burning—the fuel is then oxidized to carbon dioxide. Carbon dioxide, however, cannot easily be removed from emissions.

A lot of work has been done on measuring the concentration of carbon dioxide in the atmosphere. It has been noted that the level of concentration that would be expected as a result of burning fuels, is much higher than that actually present (see Fig. 2.24). Several suggestions have been made to account for this. Two such suggestions are: that plants remove carbon dioxide during photosynthesis and that much of it is absorbed by sea water (see Fig. 2.25). Concern has been expressed, however, that the removal of tropical forests to supply agricultural land will greatly reduce the number of plants able to remove the carbon dioxide. It is also suggested that the seas will perhaps reach a saturation point when they will not be able to absorb sufficient carbon dioxide

Fig. 2.24 *Expected and measured concentration of carbon dioxide in the Earth's atmosphere*

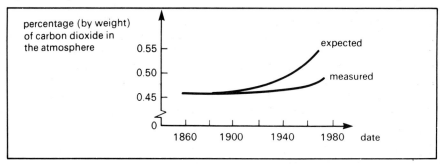

Fig. 2.25 *The carbon cycle and how man affects it*

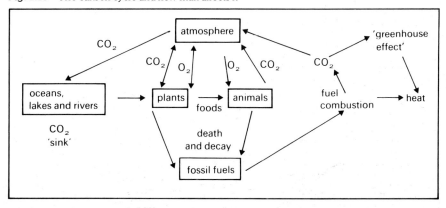

Fig. 2.26 *Tall chimneys ensure that sulphur dioxide is released as high as possible in the atmosphere*

to keep the atmospheric increase in check. If these fears should be realized, then the increased carbon dioxide concentration may increase any 'greenhouse effect' that might be affecting the planet. One should bear in mind that as fossil fuels become depleted, so the production of carbon dioxide will fall.

Finally, though sulphur dioxide cannot easily be removed from emissions, steps have been taken to reduce ground level concentrations by releasing the gases from tall chimneys (up to 200 metres) at high velocity. This measure was thought to disperse the gas quite effectively (see Fig. 2.27), but countries such as Sweden and Norway claim that the sulphur dioxide produced by us is falling as rain in their countries and causing their rivers to become acidic (see Table 2.1). They claim that this is killing their wildlife, especially fish, but also a range of different plants including forest trees. The UK accepts responsibility for about 25% of the sulphur dioxide falling on Scandinavia.

It is also possible to spray the waste gases with water. This removes sulphur dioxide by changing it into sulphuric acid which is collected at the bottom of the flues. Alternatively, the gases may be passed through a slurry of calcium oxide or calcium carbonate (limestone). This technique produces a lot of waste that has to be disposed of.

Location	pH
Scotland (1962)	5·0
Scotland (1974)	4·2
Scotland (1978)	3·5
Scandinavia (1974)	4·2
Scandinavia (1978)	3·3

Table 2.1 *The level of acidity in rain since 1962. The pH of normal rain is 5·6–6·0.*

Fig. 2.27 *Emission and ground concentration of sulphur dioxide in the UK*

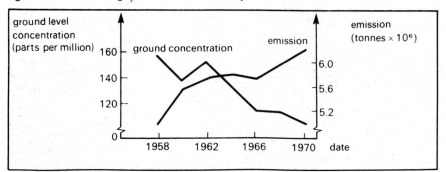

POLLUTION FROM NUCLEAR FUELS

The pollutants that arise during the operation of nuclear powered generating stations are mainly gaseous. They occur because as the neutrons released by the fission processes pass through the air, so some gases present in the air become radioactive. The most important of these (**radionuclides**) are carbon-14 (^{14}C), nitrogen-16 (^{16}N), oxygen-19 (^{19}O), and argon-41 (^{41}Ar). Of these, the nitrogen-16 and oxygen-19 quickly become harmless and carbon-14 is only present in very small quantities. Argon-41 is rather more dangerous because it has a **half-life** of 110 minutes and so has to be released in small quantities from very tall chimneys. (Half-life is a measure of the time it takes for half the number of atoms in a radioactive substance to become non-radioactive. A radionuclide having a half-life of 110 minutes will remain harmful for a much longer period of time than one having a half-life of just a few seconds or minutes.)

The problems arising from the use of nuclear fuels, however, do not end when the chain reaction in a reactor stops. At this time, the used fuel rods are removed and more fuel is put in. The 'spent' fuel is then reprocessed to extract the useful material that remains (e.g. plutonium) and remove unwanted radioactive material that has been formed. At this stage the waste radioactive material may be gaseous, liquid or solid. Some examples of the materials produced in the nuclear reactor include strontium-90 (half-life 28 years), caesium-135 (half-life 2×10^6 years), cerium-142 (half-life 5×10^{15} years), iodine-129 (half-life 16×10^6 years), and plutonium-239 (half-life 24×10^3 years).

The precise effect of specific radioactive materials is often not really known, but it is accepted that no amount of radiation is good for you. All forms of nuclear radiation can harm living tissue, the amount of harm depending upon the dose of radiation received. Nevertheless, exposure to even one radioactive particle may disrupt the working of some molecule in the body (by removing one or more electrons from it). This may cause it, perhaps, to synthesize (make) a wrong substance or, perhaps, to prevent a sufficiently rapid breakdown of toxic substances such that they accumulate in the body.

One of the major problems in studying the effect of exposure to radiation is that the effect may occur much later than the cause, so no relationship is seen to exist between the two. For instance, exposure to small doses of radiation (less

Fig. 2.28 *Examining spent fuel rods from a nuclear reactor*

Fig. 2.29 *Spent fuel rods under water about to be reprocessed*

than 50 rads) may cause leukaemia to appear up to five years after exposure. A **rad** is a measure of the energy absorbed by tissue, 1 rad $= 10^{-5}$ Jcm^{-2} or 10^{-2} Jkg^{-1} Other cancers may not become apparent for up to twenty years after exposure. Of greatest concern is the possibility that radiation may affect the reproductive organs in such a way that any offspring produced may be **mutated** (genetically changed).

Despite these areas of doubt, something is known about the effect of some radioactive substances on living systems should they be released into the environment. Strontium-90, for instance, behaves biologically in much the same way as calcium and may replace calcium in the bones. Because blood cells are manufactured in the long bones, blood cancer (**leukaemia**) may result from strontium-90 intake. Iodine is essential to the working of the **thyroid gland**—a gland which helps to control the rate of activity of the body. In 1957 a leak of radioactive iodine at Windscale generating station in Cumbria seriously contaminated grass around the station and, to prevent it from entering humans, the milk produced by cows in the area had to be thrown away. On several occasions, concern has been expressed about the safety of samples of sea food eaten by people along the Cumbrian coast where low-level radioactive waste is released into the sea.

Plutonium is a particular problem in that it is purposely stock-piled as a future energy source and for atomic weapons. It is one of the most toxic substances known to man and if a piece the size of a pollen grain were inhaled it would probably be lethal. Very great fears have been expressed about the possibility of terrorists acquiring this substance. There are over 7 tonnes of plutonium stored at Windscale and only 10 kg are required to construct a crude but effective atom bomb.

Having noted the problems created by nuclear fuels, however, it is necessary to state that very great care is exercised in the handling of these dangerous materials, though scientists are still investigating means of disposal. At present, besides mixing gaseous materials with air and pumping it into the atmosphere, some liquid wastes are diluted and pumped into the ocean. Highly radioactive wastes are currently stored in liquid form in stainless steel tanks which are continually cooled. Some 1000 m^3 of highly toxic waste are stored at Windscale. One possibility being investigated is the conversion of these wastes into a glass which is inert and can be buried in rocks in areas where there is no earthquake activity.

Despite the potential dangers it has never been proved that any member of the public has been harmed as a result of nuclear power generation. However, radiation has been accepted as the probable cause of death of a worker involved in fuel processing at Windscale. He died in 1971 of leukaemia. Also, it is statistically expected that up to 100 people may die each year in the UK as a result of the increased radiation in the air. (Compare this with the 15000 who are thought to die from breathing in pollutants from burning fossil fuels!)

THERMAL POLLUTION

A final problem of using the fuels mentioned as energy sources is the heat given off. The heat that is given off as waste heat is released into the environment and is called **thermal pollution**. Though the term is usually used to describe the heat released into rivers and the sea, the temperature in the vicinity of large industrialized areas is measurably higher than in rural areas.

The greatest concern has been expressed over the waste heat from generating stations. When the steam produced in the boilers has been used to drive the turbines, it needs to be condensed into water again. Once it has been condensed into water it can be fed back into the boilers so that the cycle is continued. The water is condensed by transferring its heat either to water alone or to a combination of the atmosphere and water by means of cooling towers. In either system, water is taken from a river (or the sea) and returned to it at a temperature 10°C–12°C higher. From Fig. 2.30 it can be seen that as the temperature of water is increased it is less able to contain dissolved oxygen. This creates the problem that there is less oxygen available for aquatic organisms at high temperatures. Because the body works faster at high temperatures, this is just the time when animals need as much oxygen as they can get. Contrary arguments suggest that by warming the water slightly the plant life and animal life in the water increases. This is because the normal temperature is below the most favourable temperature for plant and animal growth. Also, it is suggested that as the cooling water enters the river, the turbulence that is created causes enough oxygen to dissolve into the water to make up for any loss caused by the increase in temperature.

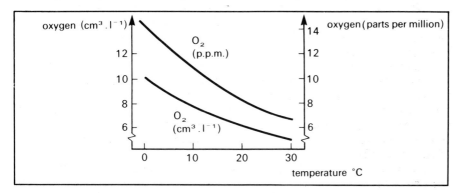

Fig. 2.30 Concentration of oxygen dissolved in water at various temperatures

ENERGY CONSERVATION

The impact of the energy crisis can be temporarily reduced by using energy conservation techniques. The savings that could be made by using such conservation techniques are quite considerable. The main areas are space-heating of buildings, reducing the inefficiencies in car and lorry engines and the recycling or recovery of 'waste heat'.

Thermal Insulation and Waste Heat Recovery

In this category we find loft and cavity wall insulation, draught excluders, tank and pipe lagging, double glazing and under-floor insulation. More recently, techniques have also come about to recover waste heat in industry and the home by passing hot, but dirty, water through water tanks in sealed copper pipes, so allowing the heat to be captured by the water in the tank.

   All insulation techniques rely on placing a barrier of material of low thermal conductivity either between the interior and exterior of the house or on pipes or hot-water tanks. Such materials include air (as in double-glazed windows), rock wool (rock that has been spun like candy-floss at high temperature), glass wool, wood fibre and polystyrene foam (both of these are fire-risks unless fire-proofed). Urea formaldehyde foam is used for cavity wall insulation and wool fibres for pipe lagging. Various foamed plastics and rubber are also used. All of these materials contain pockets of air, which makes them excellent insulating materials. Fig. 2.38 shows the extent of the heat losses one can normally expect from an uninsulated dwelling. Figures vary of course, depending on the type of house and its size. Terraced houses have the lowest heat losses, detached houses the highest.

If insulation technology was applied liberally in the UK to homes, industry and public buildings we could reduce our energy consumption by about one-third. Many scientists feel we would be better to spend more money in this way and less on developing nuclear power.

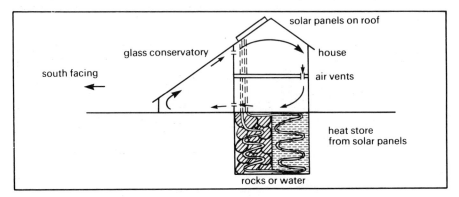

Fig. 2.31   *Passive solar house with underground heat source*

House Design

Fig. 2.31 and Fig. 2.32 illustrate some of the possibilities for improving house design so as to incorporate the maximum use of direct solar heat from the sky. The principle is to enable warm air from south-facing windows (or a conservatory) to circulate through the property and afford warming during the day. At night the use of flaps to close off air ducts prevents the warmth being lost to the outside. The most famous example of this type of design in the UK is the extension built in 1961 to St George's School, Wallasey, Cheshire. The solar energy trapped in this building, the heat of the occupants and the high level of insulation mean that no central heating is needed even in the coldest winter. Other low-energy houses can be found in Milton Keynes and at the National Centre for Alternative Technology at Machynlleth in mid-Wales.

Some houses in countries with warmer climates, such as parts of the USA and Israel, store heat trapped during the day in rocks or water under the floor of the house. These then re-radiate the heat at night and so keep the houses warm. Similar developments can also be seen in Denmark, Japan, Holland, W. Germany and Austria. These could probably be used in the UK too.

Fig. 2.32   *Passive solar house with 'trombe wall'*

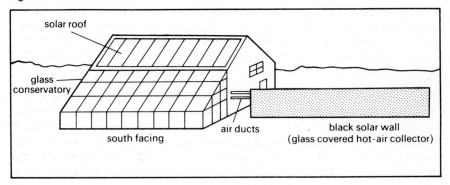

Heat Pumps

Heat pumps are often combined with the energy conservation measures discussed above. A heat pump works on the same principle as a refrigerator. In both, heat is transferred from one place to another by a moving fluid (usually an easily liquified gas called **Freon**). The gas is circulated through two radiators connected 'in series' (see Fig. 2.33). In a refrigerator one radiator is located in the freezer compartment and the other is at the back of the unit on the outside. Heat is transferred by the motion of the fluid from inside the refrigerator to the outside.

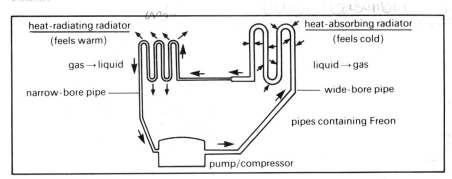

Fig. 2.33 Principle of heat pump and refrigerator

One radiator (called the collector) absorbs heat energy, the other gives out heat energy. In the refrigerator, the unit in the ice-box absorbs heat because the piping is of a wide bore, allowing the liquified gas to change into a vapour. All liquids absorb heat energy from their surroundings to achieve this change of state. The other radiator has very narrow piping and when the gas is forced through it the pressure is sufficient to liquify it. As it does, so heat energy is released. (Both these changes of state illustrate the 1st law of thermodynamics; see Chapter 1.)

A heat pump absorbs heat energy from the outside air, a stream, the soil or the house loft and transfers this heat, via the moving fluid, to the house air, or into the hot-water tank or central heating system. The great advantage of heat pumps is that for a relatively small energy input, required by the pump/compressor to move the liquid, quite large amounts of heat energy can be transferred from one place to another. The Festival Hall in London (built 1951) is heated entirely by heat pumps.

Transport

Transport consumes about 21% of Britain's fuel. This is mainly in the form of petrol and diesel oil, though an increasing number of cars are being converted to run on propane gas. Because oil is the first fossil fuel that will run out it is vital for us to develop a restructured transport policy to conserve rather than squander our oil reserves. Various suggestions have been made to achieve this.

Railways

The electrification of the railways continues and this reduces, very sensibly, their dependence on diesel oil. Even though power stations are notoriously inefficient at producing electricity (only 25–35% of the energy in the fuel is converted into electricity, as explained in Chapter 1), they rely mainly on coal. Around 70–80% of electricity is coal-generated. Britain has extensive coal deposits which could last for several hundred years. Electrification of the railways reduces our dependence on oil and enables us to use a resource that we have plenty of. Nuclear power or some of the alternative sources of power, described in Chapter 1 could produce the electricity when the coal becomes unavailable at some time in the future.

Engine and vehicle design

Cars can be made with much smoother-running and more efficient engines. The design and performance of the carburettor is particularly to be considered as this controls the rate at which the fuel enters the engine cylinders. Improved engine design, streamlined bodies and lighter engines and bodies have enabled manufacturers to produce cars that will travel 60 miles on a gallon of petrol and further improvements are sure to follow.

Canals

We in Britain have a very extensive network of inland waterways. Though some are still in use, most notably the Manchester Ship Canal, most have fallen into alarming disuse and decay. This became particularly apparent in the winter of 1962–3 when extensive lengths were frozen for long periods making the transport of goods impossible. However, the re-vitalization of the canal system for freight is seen by many as a sound alternative to heavy lorries. Heavy lorries not only consume fuel very inefficiently, pollute the air and make a lot of noise, they are also very damaging to road surfaces and inconvenient in towns and small villages. However, canals could not be used for perishable goods and conflicts would occur on the small number of canals currently used solely for recreational purposes such as fishing and pleasure boating.

Alternative fuels

These include methane, ethanol and hydrogen, which can be produced by the anaerobic decay of animal and plant wastes, by fermentation of plant and food wastes and by the electrolysis of water, respectively. These fuels are ideal for use by cars and lorries. Details of the production of methane and ethanol have been dealt with (page 24).

Though hydrogen is the simplest and lightest of all substances, it is possible to use it as a fuel. Unfortunately it is expensive to make, because it involves passing an electrical current through water. The molecule of water is split to produce hydrogen gas and oxygen gas.

$$2H_2O \longrightarrow 2H_2 + O_2$$

The large-scale production of the gas would require electricity that could be produced cheaply or from renewable sources, such as HEP, tidal, wave or wind power. Hydrogen is easily liquified and stored in metal bottles (like 'Calor gas') and would be suitable in this form as a transport fuel. Though the only waste product from its combustion would be water (the oxide of hydrogen), one major problem would be the volume of hydrogen a vehicle would need to carry. Vehicles might have to be designed to accommodate large storage tanks.

Electric vehicles

Much interest has been shown in the development of completely electric cars. The electric milk-float is the most familiar example. The 3 main problems involve the maximum speed of the vehicle, the distance the batteries would allow one to travel on one 'charge' and the size and weight of the batteries. The latest figures suggest 50 miles per hour as the top speed, 200 miles as the maximum journey, and batteries the equivalent weight and size as 5–6 normal car batteries. Electric vehicles produce no pollution and little noise, but their development on the scale required to replace oil-powered vehicles, is still a long way in the future.

Heating Schemes

As mentioned earlier, a power station or industrial process that produces more heat than it can use sees the disposal of this heat as a problem and calls it waste heat. On average 60–70% of the coal energy going into a power station is lost as waste heat to the atmosphere or to rivers. This heat can be used to heat homes, offices, schools, hospitals or swimming baths. Some parts of Paris, for example, are heated in this way. The process is called **combined heat and power** (CHP) if the heat comes from a power station, or **district heating,** if the heat comes from industry. There are already several examples of district heating in Britain. For example, the Bournville swimming Baths in Birmingham are heated by waste heat from Cadbury's chocolate factory and waste incinerators in Nottingham and Norwich provide heat to offices and flats. The only CHP scheme in the UK is at Hereford, but the Government is funding a further scheme in which 18 local authorities will participate. Each authority will connect a power station to a local housing estate. It is expected that more such schemes will follow, if the experiment is a success. It is thought that by using these schemes up to 80% of the chemical energy of the fossil fuel used by the power station can be usefully exploited.

Integrated Systems

Integrated systems rely on the idea of bringing together on one site many diverse processes of industrial society and making enormous savings in the process. No such schemes exist as yet, though some prototypes are in operation abroad.

The best example of such a scheme involves bringing together sewage treatment, a power station, a fish-farm, waste reclamation, refuse incineration and liquid fuel production. Waste heat from the power station and incinerator is used to heat methane digestors which can produce the gas from the sewage sludge. Any excess heat can be used to heat offices, homes, etc. and also the fish tanks in the fish farm. Some of the heat can also be used to warm the fermentation chambers for producing ethanol from food and forestry wastes. After digestion and fermentation any remaining wastes can be used as a fertilizer or dried and pelletized for fuel for the power station. Some paper and plastics from the waste reclamation works can also be pelletized and used as fuel. Brighton power station, for example, already uses such pellets as a fuel-additive. Finally, plastics, metal, paper and glass can be recovered from refuse and recycled in the usual way.

These schemes bring together all the low-impact, recycling and resource-conservation ideas that environmental science could be seen as trying to encourage. Examples of similar schemes include a sewage-fired power station in W. Germany and a combination of fish-farming, sewage treatment and methane production in Florida, USA. India and China also have large methane production industries. Methane is now being tapped (1981) from decomposing refuse in the disused quarries of the London Brick Company in Bedfordshire. Some of the gas is used in the brick ovens and the rest enters the gas grid. Finally, several power stations in Britain already use a fraction of their waste heat for fish-farming.

ACTIVITIES

Fossil fuels

The most important fuels today are the fossil fuels. These are coal, oil and gas. This series of experiments investigates some of the characteristics of these fuels.

1   This experiment shows that crude oil is a complex mixture of chemicals that can be separated by heating the oil to different temperatures and collecting and condensing the vapours that are released. (This process is known as **fractional distillation**).

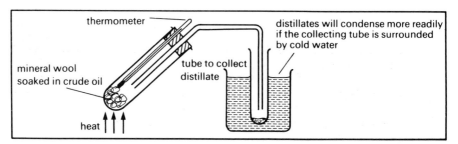

Fig. 2.34   *Fractional distillation of crude oil*

a) Set up the experiment as in Fig. 2.34 and place some crude oil to a depth of 2·5 cm in the bottom of the boiling tube. Add sufficient mineral wool to completely soak up the oil.

b) Arrange four test tubes to receive the distillates (the vapours that you will condense).

c) Place the delivery tube in the first test tube and raise the temperature of the oil to 70°C. Maintain this temperature for 5 minutes.

d) Remove the delivery tube and place it in the second test tube. Raise the temperature of the oil to 120°C and maintain this temperature for 5 minutes.

e) Repeat this process to collect samples of oil in the temperature ranges 120°C–170°C and 170°C–220°C.

f) Pour each fraction in turn onto a piece of mineral wool resting in a tin lid and try to light the liquid. Note also which mixture is the least viscous (most runny).

From these tests you should be able to suggest which of the mixtures most resembles petrol, which most resembles paraffin and which most resembles fuel oil. (If the experiment is continued with a longer-range thermometer, liquids which are collected at about 300°C are similar to wax.)

In a commercial fractionating column, the temperature ranges from high at the bottom to cool at the top so you should now be able to suggest the position in the column at which the different mixtures of chemicals are collected.

The environmental effects of energy production

2   Set up the apparatus shown in Fig. 2.35. You are going to investigate gaseous and particulate pollution from coal.

a) Crush a 4 g sample of coal in a pestle and mortar and place it mid-way down the combustion tube.

b) Loosely place a piece of cotton wool of known weight in the top half of each limb of the absorption tube.

c) Pour sufficient dilute potassium permanganate into the boiling tube so that the longer of the two tubes passes into the solution to a depth of about 2 cm.

d) Clamp the apparatus and connect it together as shown in the figure. Clamp

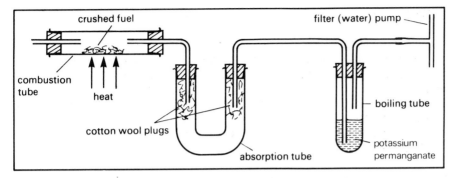

Fig. 2.35 *Investigating gaseous and particulate pollution from coal*

the combustion tube at one end so that the heat from the Bunsen burner does not burn the rubber (or cork) on the clamp.

e) Turn on the filter (water) pump until you see a steady stream of bubbles passing through the potassium permanganate. This will draw air through the apparatus which will help to oxidize (burn) the coal.

f) Heat the coal strongly for 5–10 minutes and note any changes in the cotton wool and the lime water.

g) Re-weigh the cotton wool (dry it first).

You should find that the cotton wool increases in weight and that the potassium permanganate turns brown or clear. The cotton wool will also look dirty.

It is possible to conclude from this that when coal is burnt it releases particulates (unburnt carbonaceous material and grit, etc.) and sulphur dioxide (sulphur dioxide is the only gas to change potassium permanganate in this way).

3   Compare particulate pollution in different areas of your town.

a) If a piece of filter paper is placed on a flat surface and held down, then over a period of a few days it will become covered in particulate pollution. The amount of particulate pollution could be measured if the weight of filter paper is known beforehand and it is dried and weighed again at the end of the experiment. Also, if you know the area of your filter paper (πr^2 where r is measured in centimetres), you can calculate the mass of particulates that fall on one square centimetre or on one square metre.

$$\frac{\text{mass of particulates}}{\text{area of paper}} = \text{mass cm}^{-2}$$

$$\frac{\text{mass of particulates}}{\text{area of paper}} \times \frac{10000}{1} = \text{mass m}^{-2}$$

By placing a piece of filter paper in different areas of the town (be sure to place them where they will not be disturbed) you will get an idea of which area of the town is most dirty.

b) The experiment can be done another way without weighing the filter paper. Place your pieces of filter paper in different parts of your town. After a suitable period (when they look dirty) collect them and take them to the laboratory. (Remember to label where you have taken them from.)

Take a piece of tracing paper and place it over one piece of filter paper. Note if you can still see the dirt. If the dirt is still visible, place a second piece of tracing paper over the filter paper and continue until no dirt is visible. Repeat this for all your pieces of filter paper.

The paper that needs most tracing paper to cover the dirt is the dirtiest piece and the cleanest piece is the one that needed least tracing paper.

c) If you cannot leave your filter paper out without it being disturbed, try this next technique.
Select an area of your town you wish to investigate and take along a piece of filter paper and a 100 g mass. Choose a spot that has not been cleaned in any way and place your filter paper onto it with the 100 g mass on top of the paper. Pull your paper along the surface for a certain distance.
The paper will pick up dirt and different pieces of paper can be compared as described under (b) above.
Note that the 100 g mass is used to make each experiment as nearly the same as possible.

Oil spillages

When oil spillages occur, one of the most obvious effects is that birds are found with their feathers covered in oil. When this happens, the oil is removed with detergents and the bird is released after a period of 'convalescence'.

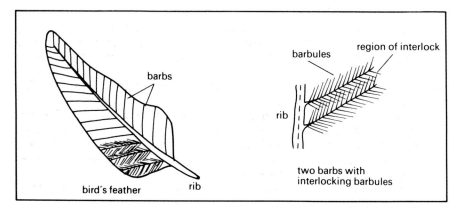

Fig. 2.36 Investigating the effect of oil on birds' feathers

4 You are to investigate the effect of oil and detergent on birds. Use the following procedure as a guide but make any other observations you think might be important.
a) Obtain a feather, view it under a microscope and draw its structure. (It should be similar to that in Fig 2.36.)
b) Weigh your feather.
c) Place a drop of water on the feather from a drop pipette and note what happens.
d) Soak your feather in water, allow excess water to drain off and weigh your feather again.
e) Soak your feather in oil.
f) View and draw your feather under a microscope.
g) Remove the oil using cotton wool soaked in detergent or by swilling the feather in a container of detergent (washing-up liquid will do).
h) Repeat stages (a), (b), (c) and (d) using the feather treated with detergent.
Record your results carefully and write a conclusion, which should describe the effects of oil, and the effect of detergent to remove oil, on birds feathers.
Finally use your results and conclusion to write down the possible effects of oil and detergent on birds.

Biological effects of nuclear radiations

5 Investigate the effect of nuclear radiation on the growth of barley seeds.
a) Obtain 5 sets of 10 barley seeds that have been irradiated by the following

amounts: (i) no radiation (control); (ii) 10 kilorads; (iii) 25 kilorads; (iv) 50 kilorads; (v) 100 kilorads.

b) Sow each set of 10 seeds into a suitable container and leave them to germinate.

c) After each set has had time to germinate count how many seeds have germinated in each set and calculate this number as a percentage of seeds sown. You should use the following equation:

$$\text{percentage of seeds germinated} = \frac{\text{number of seeds germinated}}{\text{number of seeds sown}} \times \frac{100}{1}$$

d) Allow the seeds to grow and, for each set, measure the tallest leaf of each plant in the set each week for five or six weeks. For each set of seeds find the average length of the tallest leaf by using the equation:

$$\text{average length of tallest leaf} = \frac{\text{total length of tallest leaves}}{\text{total number of leaves measured}}$$

e) Draw a bar graph of the information collected about percentage germination. The best way to draw your graph will be to have percentage germination on the vertical axis and amount of radiation on the horizontal axis.

f) Write down any conclusion you can make about the effect of nuclear radiation on the germination of barley.

g) Draw graphs of the information collected about length of leaves. The best way to draw your graphs will be to have average length of leaves on the vertical axis and time on the horizontal axis. The information collected from each set of seeds can then be drawn separately as a line graph to produce 5 lines on the one sheet of graph paper.

h) Write down any conclusion you can make about the effect of nuclear radiation on the length of leaves in barley seeds.

i) Finally, state whether or not you feel nuclear radiation is harmful to barley seeds at the levels with which you have experimented. Give reasons for your statement.

Generating electricity

6 Find out where your nearest electricity generating station is and try to obtain answers to the following questions.

a) How much electrical power can it produce?

b) What fuel does it use and how much?

c) How efficiently does it convert the chemical energy in the fuel (or nuclear energy) into electrical energy?

d) How much cooling water does it use?

Energy losses and conservation

It is in the interest of everybody that we should avoid wasting energy. There are three major reasons why this is so:

1 Wasting energy now will bring the time when energy sources (fuels) run out much sooner. Even as we use it now, oil and gas will run out when you are aged between 35 and 50.

2 Wasting energy means that we are polluting our environment with the waste from energy production much more than we need.

3 As fuels become in short supply, so they will become more expensive. By wasting energy, the time when we shall no longer be able to afford fuels will come very much sooner.

7   The following experiment investigates the effect of insulation on heat loss.
Method 1. Heat a beaker of water to 80°C. Use a paper towel to place the beaker on a bench. Record the change in temperature every minute for 12 minutes. At no time remove the thermometer from the water.
Method 2. Repeat the experiment above using the same volume of water. When you have placed the beaker on the bench, insulate it and record the temperature change every minute for 12 minutes. Graph your results as shown in Fig. 2.37.
a) What can you say about the effect that insulation has on heat loss?
b) Is the heat that is lost, lost most quickly when temperatures are high or when they are low?

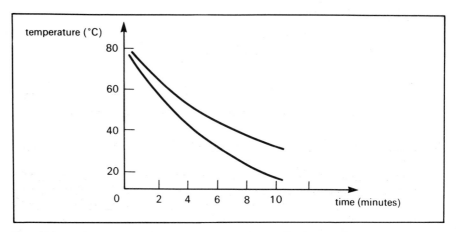

Fig. 2.37   *Graph showing energy losses from a beaker under different conditions*

8   The two forms of energy that are most obvious in the home are light and thermal (heat) energy. Each of these may, of course, be converted from electrical energy. The home owner is probably most conscious of thermal energy because it is providing sufficient heat in the home that cost is so much money—particularly during the winter. The energy losses that occur in a house are indicated in Fig. 2.38. The values given refer to the percentage of thermal energy losses that occur through the walls, roof, windows, etc. of a typical house. The information given in Fig. 2.38 might vary from one house to another depending upon the area of wall and glass in the house, etc. The information relates to an uninsulated house.
Copy Fig. 2.38 and answer the following questions.
It is assumed that the heating bills for this house total £200 per year.
a) How much money is lost as heat through the roof?
b) How much money is lost as heat through the walls?
c) How much money is lost as heat through the windows?
d) How much money is lost as total heat lost in a year?
e) By using a 100mm depth of glass fibre roof insulation, losses through the roof can be reduced by 80%. How much money would this equal?
f) By insulating the cavity walls with urea-formaldehyde foam the heat losses can be reduced by 40%. How much money would this equal?
g) By double-glazing all windows, heat losses can be reduced by 60% (through the windows). How much money would this equal?
h) How much money could be saved in total in a year?
i) Assuming loft insulation could be done for £40, how long would it take to repay itself?

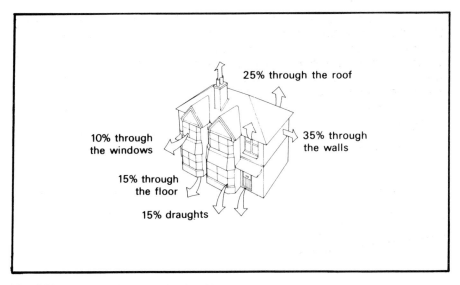

Fig. 2.38 *Heat losses from an uninsulated house*

j) Assuming wall insulation could be done for £200, how long would it take to repay itself?

k) Assuming double glazing costs £760, how long would it take to pay for itself?

l) As fossil fuels become depleted, will they cost more or less? What effect will this have on the period of time that must pass for the insulation to pay for itself?

m) Explain how fibre glass, cavity wall insulation and double glazing each help to reduce energy losses.

9   Try setting up a series of simple experiments to investigate the principles of cavity wall insulation and double glazing by using the ideas presented in Fig. 2.39.

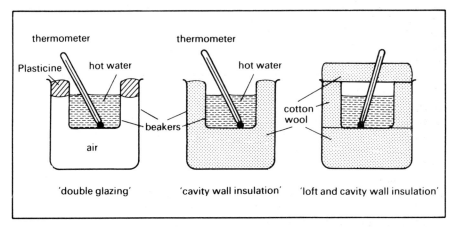

Fig. 2.39 *Investigating the effects of insulation*

3 Natural Systems

THE FLOW OF ENERGY IN LIVING SYSTEMS

The source of energy present in any living system is the Sun. This energy enters living systems by the process of **photosynthesis.** This is a process that occurs in the green parts of plants. During this process light energy from the Sun is absorbed by the chlorophyll in plants. The energy is used to split water molecules which produces molecular oxygen and hydrogen ions. The hydrogen ions are used to convert carbon dioxide to organic materials (mainly sugars). The overall chemical equation given to describe this process is:

$$6CO_2 + 6H_2O \xrightarrow[\text{chlorophyll}]{\text{light}} C_6H_{12}O_6 + 6O_2$$

$C_6H_{12}O_6$ is the chemical representation of the **glucose** molecule. Sugars are the most commonly made (synthesized) material formed by photosynthesis and the simplest of these is glucose. Because only green plants are capable of using the energy from the Sun in this way, they are called **producers** (or **autotrophs**). Without them, life as we know it could not exist.

Some of the chemical energy now stored in the glucose molecules of the plant is used by the plant itself for the internal transport of chemicals and absorption of nutrients from the soil. Much of it, however, is used to build larger molecules such as cellulose, starch, oil and protein. As the plant synthesizes these materials, so it increases in size or mass and an increasing amount of energy is stored within it.

Fig. 3.1 *Cereal crops*

Fig. 3.2 *Herbivores (primary consumers) eat producers*

Fig. 3.3 A common buzzard (secondary consumer) eating a rabbit (primary consumer)

This energy stored in the structure of plants is available to animals (**heterotrophs**) which eat them. These animals are, by definition, **herbivores.** They are also termed the **primary consumers.** They use the energy present in the plant material for two purposes:

1 To perform life processes such as movement, the internal transport of materials, internal communications by the nervous system, production of heat in warm-blooded animals and the removal of waste products from the body.

2 To synthesize materials necessary to keep the animal healthy or for it to increase in size.

Finally, the primary consumers may be eaten by **secondary consumers** (these must by definition be **carnivores**). These in their turn may be eaten by other consumers. The final consumers in a relationship such as the one described are termed the **tertiary consumers**. The organisms present in such a food relationship are said to form a **food chain** and rarely number more than four or five for the reasons discussed in the next section. (Food chains are summarized in Fig. 3.4.)

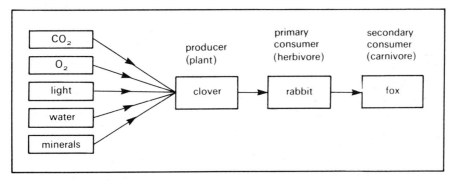

Fig. 3.4 A simple food chain

The Efficiency of Food Chains

When plants (the producers) convert light energy into chemical energy, only some of the light energy is converted to chemical energy. Most of the energy that falls onto the plant is reflected again. Also, some of the energy is used by the plant itself to maintain its life processes.

When herbivores (primary consumers) eat the plant, energy is lost from the food chain for a variety of reasons.

1   As described above, the animal uses much of the energy for its own life processes.

2   Some of the chemical energy present in the food is converted into other forms. (Examples include: electrochemical energy for the nervous system and kinetic energy for movement.) During these conversions some energy is 'lost' as heat. This is a consequence of the second law of thermodynamics explained in Chapter 1.

3   Some of the food is not digested by the animal but is **egested** (egested food is that which passes through the alimentary canal without ever being absorbed into the blood.) Also, some of the food that is digested by the animal is eventually excreted.

4   Finally, when the primary consumer is eaten by secondary and subsequent consumers, more energy is lost from the system for the same reasons.

In general, of the energy present in the producers, only 10% is used by the primary consumer for growth. Similarly, of the energy present in the primary consumers, only 10% is used by the secondary consumer for growth. Another way of looking at the situation is to say that 90% of the available energy is 'lost' from the food chain at each link in the chain. Because of this, food chains have an efficiency of about 10% across each link. The situation is illustrated in Fig. 3.5. Simple values for the energy in an average square metre of pasture have been chosen. As a result of these energy 'losses' any producer can only produce enough chemical energy to support a small number of organisms in the chain.

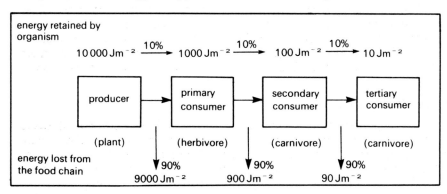

Fig. 3.5   *How enery is lost from a food chain*

At this stage it is important to note that the energy 'lost' from the food chain, because of excretion, egestion and death, becomes available to **decomposers** (organisms that feed on these materials). These organisms are themselves important (as described in the section on cycling of matter) but may also form a part of other food chains.

Having considered the simplified food chain above, it is now necessary to consider the more realistic situation described by the **food web**. The unnatural state described by a food chain can be appreciated by a simple model. Look at the food chain:

grass ⟶ rabbit ⟶ fox

This chain represents the fact that foxes eat rabbits and that rabbits eat grass. Obviously, however, this represents only a part of the truth. The fox feeds on animals other than rabbits, the rabbits eat plants other than grass, and grass is eaten by animals other than rabbits. The rather more complex pattern that results from this is represented by a food web. Such a web might be as described in Fig. 3.6.

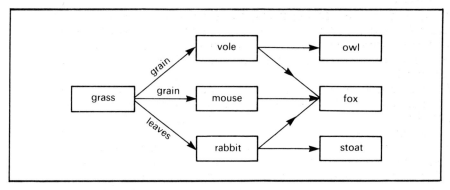

Fig. 3.6 *A food web*

As you can appreciate, food webs are rather more complicated. However, they are a more realistic means of describing the energy flow (or food) relationships between different organisms. Even so, they are often incomplete because of a lack of knowledge. To complete the above web in full, it would be necessary to know the feeding habits of each of the organisms listed in it. We would also need to know the feeding habits of each successive organism included in the web. Also, as you may be aware, many wild animals and plants have **parasites** and these would also have to be included in the web.

Because diagrams representing food webs are very complicated, much of the meaning of a food (energy flow) relationship can be represented more simply by **pyramids of number, pyramids of biomass** or **pyramids of energy**.

Pyramids of Number

In these diagrams, the organisms are grouped into **trophic (feeding) levels**. Though in practice some animals occupy different feeding levels during their life cycle, it is generally possible to assign each organism to either the producer level or one of the consumer levels. Having grouped the organisms in this way, the number that occupy each trophic level are noted for a unit area of the system (e.g. each square metre). Having obtained this information, the number of organisms present at each trophic level is represented by a rectangle. The area of the rectangle is proportional to the number of organisms. An example is shown in Fig. 3.7. In most relationships the pyramid takes the form shown—the largest rectangle appears on the bottom of the pyramid and successively

Fig. 3.7 *A pyramid of number*

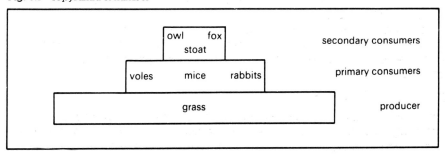

Fig. 3.8 *Large cabbage white caterpillars on a cabbage*

smaller ones appear on top of it. Exceptions to this occur when a large number of small herbivores feed on a large plant (e.g. caterpillars on a cabbage) and in food chains that involve parasites. In these cases the bottom rectangle (representing the producer level) will be smaller than the rectangle representing the primary consumer level. The other stages in the relationship will be represented by increasingly small rectangles as before. An example of this is shown in Fig. 3.9.

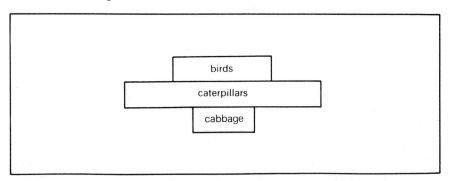

Fig. 3.9 *Pyramid that results when a large number of small herbivores feed on a large plant*

Pyramids of Biomass

Pyramids of biomass largely overcome the problem mentioned under pyramids of number. The diagrams representing these pyramids are constructed in much the same way. However, in this instance instead of measuring the **number** of organisms in a unit area, a measure is made of the **mass** of organisms. Because a small mass of organisms cannot support a larger mass of organisms, the pyramid almost always takes the expected shape—a larger rectangle at the bottom of the pyramid than at the top. Nevertheless on occasions, if measurements are taken over a short period of time, it can appear as though a small mass of organisms is supporting a larger mass. Because of this **pyramids of energy** are used.

Pyramids of Energy

In order to construct a pyramid of energy, the quantity of energy present in a unit mass (e.g. a kilogram) of each organism in a food relationship must be known. This must then be multiplied by the total mass of organisms involved. As in each of the other pyramids, the energy value of each trophic level is represented by a rectangle whose area is proportional to the energy value. Because there is *always* a decreasing quantity of energy present in successive trophic levels, the pyramid will *always* take the expected form. The largest rectangle will always be on the bottom with smaller ones on top. (Values should be recorded over a year to obtain satisfactory values.)

The quantity of energy present in an organism is found by using a **calorimeter** (see Fig. 3.10). The apparatus allows a known mass of material to be burnt in a crucible. The heat produced passes through a copper coil and heats a known volume of water the temperature of which is recorded. An oxygen supply is required to ensure complete burning of the fuel, and waste gases are removed by using a filter pump.

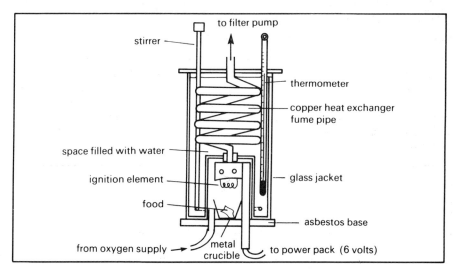

Fig. 3.10 A food calorimeter

The energy in the material is calculated in calories. One calorie is the heat required to raise the temperature of 1 g (1 cm³) of water by 1°C. If 4 g of material raise the temperature of 600 g of water by 5°C, the energy value of the material is found from the equation:

$$\text{energy value} = \frac{\text{mass of water} \times \text{temperature rise}}{\text{mass of food}}$$

$$= \frac{600 \times 5}{4} = 750 \text{ calories per gram (cal g}^{-1})$$

(In S.I. units this would be $750 \times 4 \cdot 2 = 3 \cdot 15 \times 10^3$ Jg^{-1}.)

THE FLOW OF ENERGY IN NON-LIVING SYSTEMS

The various flows of energy in non-living systems are found mainly in the movement of air and water on the Earth, and are a result of the Sun's heat energy. Other flows of energy that are of importance to the environment are concerned with the thermal (heat) energy present in the Earth's crust and mantle.

The Movement of Air

The movement of air is affected by the Sun and the spin of the Earth. The effect of these on air is described in some detail in Chapter 1. In that chapter we saw the means by which man can use the energy present in air movement. Here it is intended to outline some other important effects of these movements.

The wind is important in the weathering and erosion of rocks and soils. When winds blow across areas of soil (particularly sandy soils) that lack material such as organic matter to bind the particles together, the soil gets blown away (eroded). If this occurs excessively, then fertile areas may become infertile. The classic case of this effect is the American 'dust bowl' (Oklahoma, 1930s). Here the soils were depleted of organic matter as a result of poor management. The shifting soils made it uneconomic to continue to grow crops in the area.

Fears have been expressed about East Anglia. Because of agricultural intensification (Chapter 7), hedges that previously acted as wind-breaks have been removed, and organic material in the soil is becoming depleted. This is leading to an increase in the rate at which the wind is removing topsoil in much the same way as the American example quoted above.

When the air-borne soil particles are blown against rocks, the rocks become **weathered** (worn away). The weathered material so formed is itself important in soil formation as this is what the mineral part of soil consists of.

Fig. 3.11   Weathered rocks

Wind has a considerable influence on the organisms present in an area. Plants growing in sites that are open to the wind must be able to withstand an increase in **transpiration** (See the section on the hydrological cycle in Chapter 4.) because water evaporates more quickly from their leaves. They must also be able to withstand the physical damage caused by the wind. In extreme cases, the effect of wind can be seen on trees and shrubs. Occasionally they can be seen with their main growth facing away from the direction of the prevailing winds and with their height severely restricted. In severe winds, trees are commonly blown over and crops destroyed.

Fig. 3.12   *Trees uprooted by severe gales*

The Movement of Water

Apart from being a potential source of energy, the movement of water is also extremely important in its ability to erode rocks and soil. The eroding effects of water on rocks are particularly noticeable in two ways. Firstly, because rain is invariably acidic, it is able to dissolve such rocks as limestone. Secondly, and more importantly, water in streams and rivers carries material in suspension. This material rubs and knocks against the sides and bottom of the stream or river and so makes the water-course larger. The material that is removed may be deposited when the river loses its speed (kinetic energy), for instance at river bends and at the estuary of a river. This material may help to form soil.

Fig. 3.13   *River deposition—the River Spey, Inverness-shire*

Water that flows over the surface of soils that have a limited amount of plant cover and organic matter in them may remove large quantities of soil and make them infertile. Also, water flowing down through soil will tend to remove soluble substances, including minerals that plants need, and make the soils less fertile. This has proved to be a particular problem when tropical forests have been felled to provide increased areas for cultivation. The removal of ground cover combined with heavy rainfall rapidly results in the materials being removed from the soil. (See also the formation of bauxite ores in Chapter 6.)

The Sun

The Sun provides the major input of energy to the Earth, and its importance has been described in its relation to fossil fuels, energy in living systems and the movement of air and water, elsewhere in this book.

The different quantities of solar energy reaching various parts of the Earth's surface also have an extremely important effect. This effect can be seen by looking at the world's **biomes**—those areas of the world having similar climate and vegetation cover (see Table 3.1, Table 3.2 and Fig. 3.14).

Biome	Rainfall	Summer temperature	Winter temperature	Some typical plants	Some typical animals
savannah	low	warm–hot	warm	eucalyptus	lion
tundra	very low	cool	very cold	dwarf trees lichens mosses	arctic fox reindeer
desert	very low	very hot	hot	cacti creosote bush	lizard snake gerbil
temperate forest	medium	very warm	quite cold	oak beech dandelion	fox rabbit hedgehog owl
tropical forest	high	no real seasons—very hot		mahogany mangrove	parrot monkey tiger
coniferous forest	low–medium	warm	cold	pine	wolf bear
chapperal	low	hot	warm	olive 'cacti' rosemary	lizard
grasslands	low–medium	warm	cool	grasses shrubs	bison horse

Table 3.1   *Major world biomes.*

Biome	Geograpical areas
savannah	Africa, Asia
tundra	Arctic, Antarctic, N. Russia, Siberia, Alaska, Alps, Himalayas, Andes
desert	Sahara, N. America, Central and S. Asia, SW USA, Mexico, Australia
temperate forests	Britain, NW Europe, Eastern, Central and Western USA, Central USSR, New Zealand
tropical forests	Tropical Africa, America, India, Indonesia, Malaysia, Borneo
coniferous forests	N. Canada, Sweden, Norway, Russia
chapperal	Mediterranean countries, Middle East, Afghanistan, N. Africa, California
grasslands	Plains of Asia, N & S America

Table 3.2   *Major world biomes—geographical areas.*

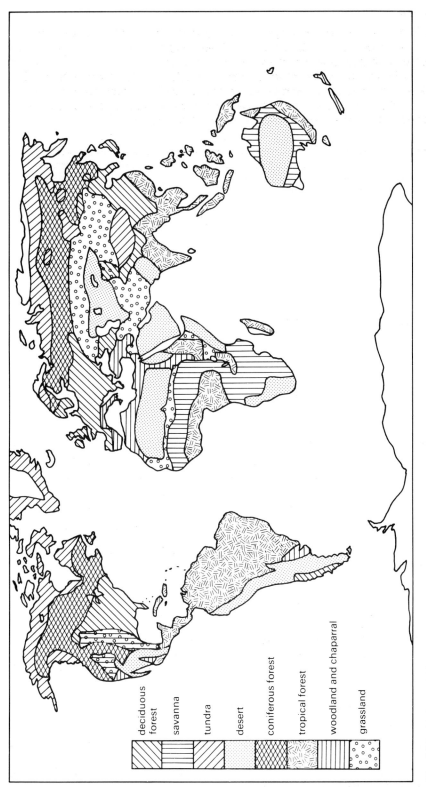

Fig. 3.14 Major world biomes: geographical areas

deciduous forest

savanna

tundra

desert

coniferous forest

tropical forest

woodland and chaparral

grassland

Fig. 3.15   *The volcanic Mount Etna on the island of Sicily*

Energy in the Earth's Crust

The energy present in the Earth's crust and mantle affects the environment in many ways. The presence of hot geysers indicates that some of this heat is relatively close to the surface. Its importance as an energy source is considered in Chapter 1.

The most obvious sign of the heat present in the Earth's crust and mantle is that of volcanic activity. Occasionally, weaknesses in the Earth's crust appear close to concentrations of heat energy present in the mantle. This energy may be released by heat and **magma** (the molten lava of volcanoes) flowing to the surface and 'erupting'. This mechanism is important in the formation of **igneous** and **metamorphic** rocks, together with many of the world's largest land features such as mountain ranges. Igneous rocks are those formed from the cooling, crystallization and solidification of magma. Metamorphic rocks are sedimentary rocks that have been changed from their original form as a result of the very great heat and pressure associated with energy flows of this type. Examples of metamorphism include the transformations: shale into slate, limestone into marble, or graphite into diamond (see Chapter 6 for further details).

A rather less obvious effect of volcanic activity is the quantity of particulate matter released into the atmosphere. This quantity is possibly greater than that produced by burning fossil fuels. Because of this, it will probably aggravate any changes in the global climate as a result of particulate pollution (see Chapter 2) produced by man.

Finally, the flow of energy present in the crust and mantle is responsible for the 'drifting' of continents. It is now an accepted fact that the Earth's surface can be divided into a number of sections (**plates**) which move slowly across the surface of the world. Naturally, because these plates are moving, the surface land masses and seas situated on them must move. Because of this, the areas suffer changes in climate over hundreds of thousands of years. This will lead to changes in the plants and animals living on the land and in the sea. (See Chapter 6 for more details about crustal plates).

CYCLES OF MATTER

Unlike energy, which is constantly being received from the Sun, the elements found on our world are present in a fixed quantity. However, although the total quantity of any element is fixed, the form in which it is present varies with time.

This variation frequently has a cyclic nature. This is readily appreciated from a consideration of the cycling of two elements—carbon and nitrogen.

The Carbon Cycle

This is represented diagrammatically in Fig. 3.16. The carbon might be thought of as beginning as part of the compound carbon dioxide (CO_2) in the atmosphere. This gas is taken in through the leaves of green plants and is converted into carbohydrates, the simplest of which is glucose ($C_6H_{12}O_6$) (see 'The flow of energy in living systems'.

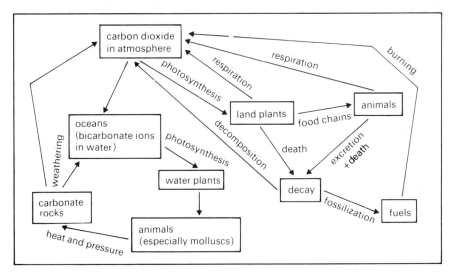

Fig. 3.16   *The carbon cycle*

The carbohydrates may be used by the plant as a source of energy for its life processes. In this case, the carbohydrate will be oxidized by a process known as **respiration**. This process releases energy—and carbon dioxide and water as waste products.

$$C_6H_{12}O_6 + 6O_2 \longrightarrow 6CO_2 + 6H_2O + energy$$

In this instance, the carbon dioxide will have completed one cycle.

Alternatively, the glucose formed by the plant may be built up into larger carbohydrate molecules. An example of this is starch which is used as an energy store in tubers like the potato. Another example is cellulose which is used as part of the general plant structure such as in plant cell walls. In these cases the carbohydrate may well be held stationary in the cycle for many years—perhaps for hundreds of years in the case of trees. Eventually, however, the plant may either be eaten or it will die. In both cases the carbohydrates will be broken down.

1   Plants that are eaten will pass through the digestive system of a herbivore. Much of the carbohydrate will be absorbed into the animal's blood system. From here it may be used to provide energy (by respiration) or it may be stored in the body after being converted to fat. The oxidation of carbohydrate during respiration will end in the carbon entering the atmospheric stage of the cycle again as carbon dioxide. The fat that is stored may remain in the animal for many years. The carbohydrate that is not absorbed from the digestive system will be egested as waste. Eventually the herbivore may die or be eaten by a carnivore (in which case the same process may operate).

2   The material that is egested from animals, or that which is present in dead plants and animals, will generally enter a food chain consisting of decomposers. These organisms will use the carbohydrates present in the material as an energy source (by respiration) and so carbon will be released as carbon dioxide into the atmosphere. In some cases micro-organisms involved in decomposer food chains release the gas methane (CH_4) which can be used as a fuel (see Chapter 1):

$$C_6H_{12}O_6 \longrightarrow 3CH_4 + 3CO_2 + energy.$$

3   More rarely, the remains of living organisms may be fossilized and perhaps used as a fuel for man (see Chapter 1). In this instance man will obtain energy from the fuel by burning it, and carbon dioxide will again be released.

$$CH_4 + 2O_2 \longrightarrow CO_2 + 2H_2O$$

4   The carbon dioxide may dissolve in water and produce bicarbonate ions which are available to aquatic plants. The shells of aquatic animals may be converted into carbonate rocks (e.g. limestone and chalk). These rocks may eventually be weathered to release the carbon again as bicarbonate ions in water or as CO_2 gas.

The Nitrogen Cycle

The nitrogen cycle is shown in Fig. 3.17. The nitrogen gas present in the air cannot be used directly by plants but may gain entry to them in one of three main ways.
1   In the presence of lightning or ultra-violet light, nitrogen may be converted into oxides of nitrogen. These are washed out of the atmosphere in rain and so enter soils as nitric acid (HNO_3). The nitric acid reacts with materials in the soil to produce **nitrates**. In this form, the nitrogen can enter the roots of plants. The conversion of nitrogen to nitrates in this way is termed **nitrogen fixation**.
2   Some free-living bacteria in the soil are able to convert atmospheric nitrogen into nitrates. These are then available to plants via their roots. These bacteria are called **nitrogen-fixing bacteria**.

Fig. 3.17   The nitrogen cycle

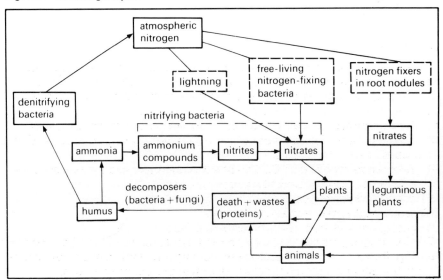

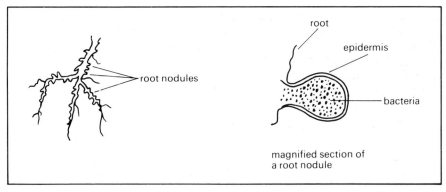

Fig. 3.18 Root nodules on a leguminous plant

3   The roots of some plants form a very close relationship with similar nitrogen-fixing bacteria. Of particular importance in this respect are the group of plants known as **legumes**, such as peas, beans and clover. In these relationships the bacteria produce nitrates from the air in the soil for use by the plants, and the bacteria obtain carbohydrates and other materials from the plants. (The presence of these bacteria on the roots of leguminous plants can be noted from the presence of swellings or nodules—see Fig. 3.18.) Relationships that exist between different organisms where *both* organisms benefit are known as **symbiotic** relationships.

Having entered the plants as nitrates, the nitrogen is built into larger molecules of amino acids and proteins which may be eaten by herbivores. These may in their turn be eaten by carnivores. Eventually, the proteins may return to the soil as plant or animal debris (following death) or animal excreta. This protein material will generally be broken down by micro-organisms (mostly bacteria such as **nitrobacter**) which use it as an energy source. As a result of their activities, the nitrogen present in the protein material will be oxidized to nitrites and nitrates and thus be available to plants again.

Another alternative is that **denitrifying bacteria** may use the nitrites and nitrates in the soil and in doing so release nitrogen to the atmosphere again.

ACTIVITIES

Questions

1   Name two effects of the absence of decay organisms in the environment.
2   In what way are the carbon and water cycles related to each other in nature?
3   What is the primary energy source for the manufacture of foods in all food chains?
4   Name a form of carbohydrate that is important in the structure of plants.
5   Name a form of carbohydrate that is commonly found in plants and is a source of energy for animals.
6   Rearrange each of the following lists of organisms into a 'food-chain order':
a) polar bear, herring, seal, plankton;
b) corn, hawk, field mouse;
c) shark, seal, sprat, mackerel, plankton;
d) caterpillar, oak tree, carnivorous beetle, bird.
7   Construct a possible food web from the list of organisms in 6(a) and 6(c).
8   Fig. 3.19 is a simplified ecosystem that might be typical of a tundra biome. Copy the diagram into your books and answer the following questions.

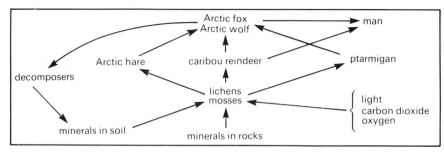

Fig. 3.19   *A typical tundra ecosystem*

a) List the producers.
b) Name three primary consumers.
c) Name two carnivores.
d) Name one herbivore.
e) Name two secondary consumers.
f) Construct a food chain from the ecosystem to include four organisms.
g) Copy a pyramid into your book and place each organism in its correct trophic level.
h) Name two groups of organisms that could be included in the group labelled 'decomposers'.

9   By using the population sampling techniques described in Chapter 8, investigate the plant and animal populations in an environment such as a hedgerow. Find out whether each organism is a producer, primary consumer or secondary consumer and construct a pyramid of number.

10   Ten Indian Moon Moth caterpillars were kept in a container over a period of time. During two consecutive 24 hour periods, detailed records were taken and these are summarized in Table 3.3.

Date	Total mass of moths (g)	Mass of food present (g)	Mass of excreta produced (g)
10.12.81	158	341	
11.12.81	176	235·3	51·5
12.12.81	197	100·4	67·0

a) Calculate the following:
 i) The mass of food eaten in the first 24 hour period;
 ii) The mass of food eaten in total;
 iii) The mass of food used for metabolism in the first 24 hour period;
 iv) The mass of food used for metabolism in total;
 v) The growth (increase in mass) of the caterpillars in the first 24 hour period;
 vi) The growth (increase in mass) in total.
b) Use the values calculated above, and given in the table, to answer the following questions.
 i) What percentage of the food was used for each of growth, metabolism and excretion during the first 24 hours?
 ii) What percentage of the food was used for each of growth, metabolism and excretion in total?
 iii) To what extent did the growth efficiency of these animals compare with theoretical food-chain efficiencies?
 iv) What happened to most of the food consumed by the moths?
If these animals were to be harvested for food how could you reduce the amount of food fed to them?

Water 4

WATER IN THE NATURAL ENVIRONMENT

Water is one of the few naturally occurring liquids on this planet and is very important in the life of all organisms. The importance of water can, in part, be appreciated from the fact that many organisms contain a very high proportion of water. Animals such as jellyfish are made up over 90% water and man himself is made up of approximately 60% water.

Organisms in Water

Water is often referred to by scientists as being a 'universal solvent'. The ability of water to dissolve a large number of different substances means that organisms living in water have sufficient materials to live. Both oxygen and carbon dioxide dissolve into water from the atmosphere. The minerals required by aquatic organisms are dissolved from the soil and rocks by rainwater which eventually finds its way into rivers, streams and lakes.

The great majority of organisms that live in water are **cold-blooded**. This means that they have very little control over their body temperature. Because of this they are strongly influenced by changes in the temperature of their environment. An important property of water is its **high thermal capacity**. This means that a body of water is able to gain or lose relatively large quantities of heat without suffering correspondingly large changes in temperature. Because of this, animals living in water do not have the problem of their own body temperatures changing all the time.

When the surface layers of water do begin to freeze, ice is formed. This is less dense than water and so floats on the surface. This is extremely important because ice is a poor conductor of heat and so tends to prevent further loss of

Fig. 4.1 *Fish are cold-blooded animals*

heat to the atmosphere. As the ice becomes thicker, so its insulating properties improve and this reduces the risk of the whole body of water freezing—a condition that would lead to the death of many organisms living in it.

Finally, water is relatively dense and so is able to support the many organisms that have developed with little skeletal support. Also, however, it has a sufficiently low viscosity to make it quite easy for animals to move through. (A liquid with high viscosity would be like treacle.)

Organisms on Land

Many terrestrial organisms still require a film of water around them if they are to avoid drying out (**dessication**) and possible death. An even greater number of organisms require a film of moisture round their respiratory surfaces (e.g. lungs and skin) before gas exchange can take place.

All terrestrial organisms depend to some extent on water to transport materials around their bodies (e.g. blood and sap). In general, the larger they are, the more dependent upon this form of internal transport they become.

Because air offers much less support to an organism than water does, many terrestrial organisms (particularly among the plant kingdom) which have not developed a firm skeletal structure still rely upon water as a means of support. In plants this support works by keeping the cells in the organisms in a state of **turgidity** (cells that are full of water are kept rigid by the pressure of water in the cells forcing outwards against the cell membranes and cell walls. If each cell is in this condition it makes the whole plant rigid—the plant is then said to be turgid).

The Hydrological Cycle

This term is used to describe the way in which water circulates through the environment, and illustrates very clearly the way in which water passes from physical to biological systems and back again (see Fig. 4.2). As water increases in temperature, the water molecules may gain sufficient kinetic energy to escape from a body of water into the atmosphere. At the same time the water changes from a liquid to a vapour. As the vapour moves upwards through the atmosphere, it passes through increasingly colder air until a point is reached when the vapour condenses back into water. The water droplets so formed tend to collect around dust particles (which act as nuclei) and then coalesce or join together. When the droplets become sufficiently large they fall as rain which can follow one of several routes.

Fig. 4.2 *The hydrological cycle*

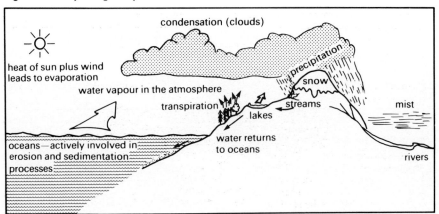

Fig. 4.3 *Reservoirs can be used for leisure activities*

1   It can run along the surface (run off), enter streams and rivers and flow to the sea. This water may be used to provide power (hydro-electric power) for man, or a basis for leisure activities. It will contain habitats for many aquatic organisms.

2   It can become trapped in reservoirs or lakes where water authorities may use it for distribution to domestic and industrial users. Again it may provide amenity value and offer habitats for organisms.

3   It can soak into the soil where it may enter biological systems, or it may pass down through porous rocks to form **aquifers** (undergound reservoirs). These may again be used by water authorities for distribution to its customers. This water is called **groundwater**.

Water that is used by man for industrial and domestic purposes will eventually pass back into rivers or streams and flow back to the sea. At all stages where water is in contact with the atmosphere, molecules may absorb sufficient energy to change back into vapour and enter the atmosphere.

Vast quantities of the water that enters the soil passes through plants. It enters plants through root hairs which are found at the ends of root sytems (see Fig. 4.4). The external covering to the root hair is permeable to many substances in the soil. Inside this outer covering is a semi-permeable membrane which separates the cell contents (containing a relatively strong solution of salts) from the soil water. Under these conditions, water passes from the weak to the strong

Fig. 4.4 *Transverse section of a root hair showing the passage of water*

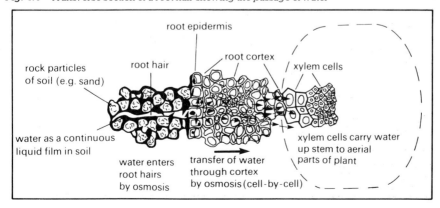

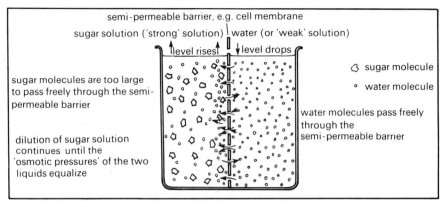

Fig. 4.5 *Diagrammatic representation of osmosis*

solution through the semi-permeable membrane. This process is called **osmosis** (see Fig. 4.5 and Activity 9). As water enters the root hair it dilutes the cell contents so that the concentration in the cell becomes less than that in the adjacent cell. Because the cells are separated by semi-permeable membranes, water passes from the root hair to the adjacent cell as a result of osmosis. Thus a chain of events occurs that causes a flow of water through the plant. (Cells towards the centre of the plant, called xylem cells, are long and narrow to assist the flow of water from the roots to the leaves of the plant.) As the water enters the leaves of the plant, it may pass through the cell membranes into the atmosphere and vapourize. At this point the vapour may pass out through the **stomatal pores** and enter the atmospheric stage of the cycle—a process called **transpiration**.

WATER AS A RESOURCE FOR MAN

Man uses water for a range of purposes, including domestic uses, industry, agriculture, waste-disposal and leisure. Of the total water present in the environment, only a relatively small proportion is readily available for the first three of these uses, as can be seen from Table 4.1

Water source	Approximate percentage
oceans	97·5
snow and ice fields	1·9
groundwater	0·5
lakes and inland seas	0·1
water vapour	0·0001
rivers	0·0001

Table 4.1 *Water in the hydrological cycle. Source—G. E. Hutchinson*

Water for Domestic Uses

Each person in the UK uses on average approximately 150 litres of water per day. (Domestic use accounts for approximately 40% of the total water consumption in the UK.)

All this water is of the same level of purity. In future it may be necessary to provide water of different levels of purity for different uses. (It is not really necessary, for instance, to have pure water to flush the WC.) At the moment, all

Purpose	Amount (litres)
WC flushing	55
personal washing	50
laundering	20
dishwashing and cleaning	10
drinking and cooking	10
car washing	5

Table 4.2 *Daily domestic use of water (per individual).*

domestic water should have no smell, no colour, no unpleasant taste and no pathogenic bacteria. The Public Health Act of 1956 also states how much suspended solids are allowed and how much possibly toxic material such as copper, lead and zinc is allowed to be present.

Water for Industrial and Agricultural Uses

Industry and agriculture use about 60% of the water consumption in the UK (see Table 4.3). Industrial uses of water fall into three broad divisions.

For power production

With the exception of hydro-electric power, water has to be converted into steam before it can produce power. On evaporation, any substances dissolved or suspended in the water are left behind as a residue and could eventually damage or 'clog' boilers and pipes. For this reason water used for producing steam must have as few suspended and dissolved solids as possible.

For cooling purposes

Examples of water used in this way would include the iron and steel industry for cooling the hot metal (approximately 200×10^3 litres per tonne of steel), and the electricity generating industry for condensing steam. (A 2000 megawatt generating station will use about 185×10^3 litres of water per hour.) Water is of particular value as a cooling agent for two reasons. Firstly, it has a high **thermal conductivity**. This means it quickly transfers heat away from its source.

Consumer	Amount ($m^3 \times 10^6$)	Percentage of total	Comments
public water	5610	40·36%	increasing
CEGB	5204	37·4%	decreasing
other industry	2995	21·53%	decreasing
agriculture—$(A+B)$	98	0·71%	fairly constant but fluctuates
A spray irrigation	41	—	variable
B other than A	57	—	decreasing
totals	13907	100·00%	decreasing

Table 4.3 *UK water consumption—breakdown of consumers.
Source—Water Data, 1975, D.o.E.*

Secondly, its high **thermal capacity** allows it to store relatively large quantities of heat for small increases in temperature. Water for this purpose need not be of high quality.

Fig. 4.6 Irrigating crops

Crown copyright

Agricultural uses

Agricultural uses of water include drinking water for stock; for cleaning apparatus and machinery; and for irrigation. This last use for water claims the greatest quantity of agricultural water and is extremely important in the south-east of England in particular, where transpiration can be twice as high as rainfall. (On average, in the south-east of England, water will be below optimum for crop production in nine seasons out of ten.)

Miscellaneous

Various industries require water for a range of different purposes. Because of this, the required purity of the water will differ. Industries manufacturing food and drink will require water of equal purity to that used for domestic distribution (sugar refineries require approximately 125×10^3 litres of water per tonne of sugar), while industries using rivers as a means of disposing of waste can use water of very low quality.

Fig. 4.7 'Fur' caused by temporary hard water

Fig. 4.8 A pipe almost completely blocked by 'fur'

Of particular importance to the various cleaning industries (and to the housewife) is the ability of water to form a lather with soap. Water having this ability is termed **soft water**, while that which forms a scum with soap is called **hard water**. The compounds responsible for forming hard water are mainly sulphates and bicarbonates of calcium and magnesium. A distinction is made between water containing bicarbonate salts of these substances and water containing sulphate salts. Water containing calcium and magnesium sulphate is termed **permanently hard** because the hardness is relatively difficult to remove. **Temporary hard** water is caused by calcium and magnesium bicarbonates and is readily cured by boiling. This property of temporary hardness, however, can prove to be a problem. When the water is boiled, insoluble carbonates precipitate out. These form a 'scale' that can cause blockages in pipes or form a covering on boilers.

Permanent hardness may be removed by adding sodium carbonate (washing soda) or by passing the water through Permutit (sodium aluminium silicate). In both cases the calcium or magnesium is exchanged for sodium which does not cause hardness.

The salts that cause hardness become dissolved in water as the water passes over and through rocks. Hard and soft water are characteristics of different parts of the country and depend upon the geology of the area (see Fig. 4.9.)

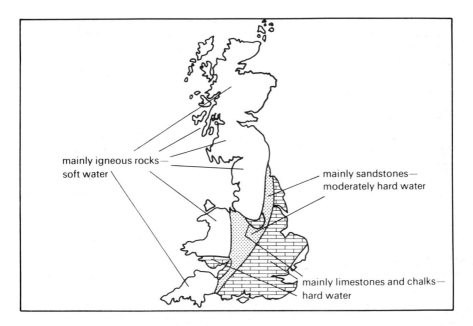

mainly igneous rocks—
soft water

mainly sandstones—
moderately hard water

mainly limestones and chalks—
hard water

Fig. 4.9 *UK geology and water types*

WATER AS A WASTE DISPOSAL MEDIUM

Water is used for this purpose by both domestic and industrial users of water, and in the past this has led to a lowering of the quality of river water in the UK (see Fig. 4.10). More recently, there has been a reversal in this trend; the situation in 1975 regarding water quality in England and Wales is given in Table 4.4.

Fig. 4.10   *River pollution—the River Tame at Tamworth*

	Total length (km)	Percentage unpolluted	Percentage doubtful	Percentage poor	Percentage grossly polluted
England and Wales total	41 432	74·0%	17·3%	4·9%	3·8%
Non-tidal rivers	36 154	77·6%	15·3%	4·0%	3·1%
Tidal rivers	2 865	49·7%	25·1%	14·8%	10·4%
Canals	2 413	50·7%	38·3%	7·3%	3·7%

Table 4.4   *Water quality—river classification.*
Source—Water Data 1975, D.o.E.

Waste Disposal by Industry

Industries are charged for the water they use, not only on the basis of how much water they use, but also on the extent to which the water is degraded (or polluted). Because of this, firms are encouraged to clean any dirty water before releasing it. There are two types of industrial waste—inorganic and organic. (Disposal of waste heat into rivers is discussed in Chapter 2 and the problem of detergents is discussed under 'Waste disposal from domestic sources'.)

Inorganic wastes

These may be either in the form of a solution or as particulate matter, and each may have a different effect. Solutions of inorganic materials might include copper, zinc and lead from a variety of industries and mines. Chromium may come from the electroplating industry and such chemicals as cyanides from the chemical industry. Many such substances, if present in sufficient quantities (often less than one part per million), are toxic to a number of organisms. The release of water by firms is controlled by water authorities but even so some rivers in the UK carry substantial quantities of these substances (in excess of 2–3 p.p.m.). Often these materials prevent the use of the water for domestic purposes and seriously reduce the range of aquatic organisms present.

Particulate matter may arise from such industries as the china clay industry and the sand and gravel industry. Much of the material extracted by these industries is treated with water to remove unwanted matter, and the waste obtained is released into rivers. The most obvious effect is that the water becomes coloured. This reduces the amount of light entering the water so photosynthesis is slowed down. A less obvious effect occurs when the particulates begin to settle. They may fall onto plants and again reduce photosynthesis, or they may block the respiratory membranes of animals. Finally, they may sink to the bottom and cover the natural substratum of the river. In this case, the habitats will be spoilt for animals living in the gravel, those feeding from the organisms normally found there, or those using it as a breeding ground. Many animals found in the gravel are **detritus** feeders (decomposers) and are extremely important in re-cycling nutrients (see Chapter 3).

Organic wastes

Organic wastes may come from a range of sources, including the paper-making industry, the textile industry, breweries, sugar-refineries and the chemical industry.

Small quantities of organic material may be benefincial. The **aerobic** (oxygen requiring) bacteria present in the water oxidize many of the materials present in organic matter to a form that is beneficial to plants. Examples of these are nitrates (NO_3), phosphates (P_2O_5 and PO_4) and sulphates (SO_4). An increase in the plant growth will tend to increase the overall productivity of the water. (This increase in nutrients and thus productivity is called **eutrophication**.)

However, in order to oxidize the material, the bacteria remove oxygen from the water. If the organic material is present in sufficient quantities, the quantity of dissolved oxygen in the water may fall to a level where it makes it difficult for plants and animals to live. If the process continues, there may be a complete removal of dissolved oxygen. In this case only animals such as the rat-tailed maggot (which can use atmospheric oxygen) and **anaerobic** bacteria (bacteria

State of water	Animals present	Volume of oxygen (cm³)/litre of water	
		at 5°C	at 20°C
clean, unpolluted water	stonefly nymph, mayfly nymph, salmon, trout, grayling, good coarse fishing	6·5–9·0	4·5–6
doubtful	caddis fly larvae, freshwater shrimp good coarse fishing —trout rarely	6·0–6·5	4·0–4·5
poor	water louse, 'blood worm' (midge larvae), leech, roach, gudgeon, moderate to poor fishing	3·5–6·0	2·5–4·0
grossly polluted	sludge worm, rat-tailed maggot, no fish life	0–3·5	0–2·5

Table 4.5 *The biotic index.*

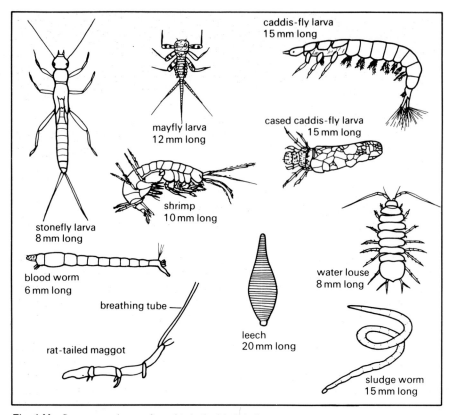

caddis-fly larva
15 mm long

mayfly larva
12 mm long

cased caddis-fly larva
15 mm long

shrimp
10 mm long

stonefly larva
8 mm long

blood worm
6 mm long

breathing tube

water louse
8 mm long

leech
20 mm long

rat-tailed maggot

sludge worm
15 mm long

Fig. 4.11 Some organisms referred to in the biotic index

not needing oxygen) can survive. (A standard American example of this process is Lake Erie.) When this condition is reached, anaerobic bacteria continue to use the organic material as an energy source. However, they do so by **reducing** the material rather than **oxidizing** it. These processes tend to form inflammable or unpleasant gases, such as methane (CH_4), ammonia (NH_3) and hydrogen sulphide (H_2S). (This has, of course, been important in the past in the formation of natural gas and oil from swamps, which indicates why gas and oil often contain so much sulphur—see the section on sulphur dioxide pollution in Chapter 2.)

The amount of dissolved oxygen in a river can be estimated from the **biotic index** (see Table 4.5). This relates various communities of organisms to the quality of water in which they might be expected to be found (see Fig. 4.11).

Waste Disposal from Domestic Sources

Generally, water disposed of from domestic sources contains organic material. This may be in the form of food particles, excreted or egested food, which may contain **pathogenic** (disease-causing) bacteria, or in the form of detergents. If released into a river the food particles would have an effect similar to that described in the previous section under organic wastes. Before considering the effects of detergents on water systems, it is necessary to explain the term as used here.

Strictly used, the term detergent describes *any* cleaning agent, or an agent that reduces surface tension. Detergents form two groups, the **soapy detergents** and **soapless detergents**. The first of these groups, the soapy

Fig. 4.12 *The River Mersey at Warrington. The large quantity of surface foam suggests pollution by 'hard' detergents*

detergents, includes all the detergents that are made from animal fats or vegetable oils. In general, these detergents are not troublesome in water systems because they are rapidly broken down by bacteria to simple compounds, in much the same way as the organic material described previously. Nevertheless, in large quantities they may lead to a reduction in dissolved oxygen.

In the 1950s, soapless detergents made from the waxes produced from the fractional distillation of crude oil quickly became popular in the UK. At this time, the detergents that were produced were **hard** or **non-biodegradable** and were not broken down to any extent by bacteria present in water (or sewage works). This led to the formation of large quantities of foam, particularly where water disturbance occurred such as over weirs. This was not only very unsightly but often carried pathogenic organisms. The foam was often blown into towns and cities on the wind and became extremely unpleasant.

In an attempt to prevent this problem, **soft** or **biodegradable** detergents were produced, which were far more easily broken down by bacteria in the water. The detergents on the domestic market in the UK are now almost totally of the biodegradable type, and although industry still uses a majority of the non-biodegradable type it is obliged to treat effluents before they are released into water systems.

Waste Treatment

It has been stated earlier that the overall quality of rivers in the UK has improved. This has been achieved mainly by treating waste before it is allowed to enter rivers. Many industries now treat their own waste prior to its release, but large volumes of waste are treated in sewage works (see Fig. 4.13).

The preliminary treatment process is to screen the inflowing waste to remove large objects such as wood or sacking. It is then allowed to pass along grit channels (detritus tanks) where material of a size and/or density similar to that of grit or gravel is removed.

From the grit channels, the sewage is passed to **primary settlement** (primary sedimentation) tanks where the sewage flows with a sufficiently slow speed to allow particles of greater-than-microscopic size to settle out. The sediment so formed is called **sewage sludge**.

From the primary settlement tanks, water passes either to **percolating filters** (trickling filters) or to **activated sludge tanks**. Percolating filters consist of a bed of broken stone or clinker through which sewage is passed from overhead

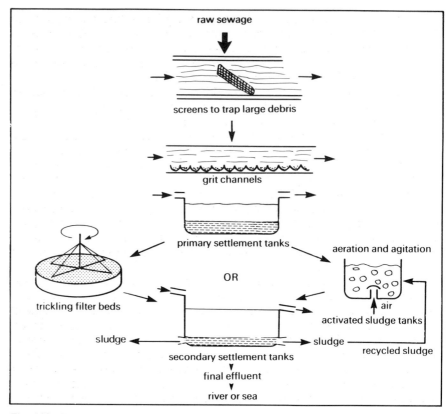

Fig. 4.13 *Treatment of sewage in a sewage works*

trickle or spray bars. The upper layers of the filter are colonized by algae, together with a range of animal organisms (particularly worms and insect larvae) and aerobic bacteria. These organisms feed on the organic material in the water, so converting them into inorganic compounds such as nitrates, phosphates, and sulphates. Activated sludge tanks contain aerobic bacteria. The liquid present in the tanks is continually aerated either by mechanical agitation of the surface or by 'forcing' air in at the bottom. The bacteria present remove the organic compounds by converting them into simple, inorganic compounds as in the percolating filters.

Fig. 4.14 *Activated sludge tanks at a sewage works*

Material from these two systems passes to **secondary settlement tanks** where any material still present is allowed to settle out. This material is called **sludge** or **humus** depending on which process it has passed through. The cleaned water that is passed into rivers is called **effluent**. The effluent may need to be chlorinated (disinfected) if it contains too many bacteria.

The humus that is formed in sewage works is rather different from the sludge, but may be treated in much the same way. The first attempts at using the material produced was to spread it on the ground in its crude state as a fertilizer. Often, however, the ground eventually became 'sick' and there was the possibility of disease being transmitted with the crops if they were not washed properly before being eaten. More recently the sludge has been dried, either naturally or artificially, before being spread onto the ground, and rather more success has been achieved. There are still problems to be overcome, however, concerning the presence in it of very hardy seeds (e.g. tomato), the presence of toxic chemicals (notably metals), and the presence of a number of pathogenic bacteria. Though each of these problems can be overcome, it is expensive and makes the use of the sludge, which is not high in nutrients, a much less economical practical possibility.

A final use of the sludge involves its digestion under anaerobic conditions and at about 37°C. Under these conditions, certain bacteria (including methanogenic bacteria) chemically reduce the material to produce a range of gases. After a suitable period the gases produced include a large proportion of methane, which after removing unwanted gases, can be burnt as an energy source. This technique is rapidly becoming standard practice in the large modern sewage works in the UK, where the gas is used for space heating or for producing electricity to power the pumps used in the works. In some of the larger sewage works it is liquified and used to power sewage works' vehicles.

WATER SUPPLY AND TREATMENT FOR HUMAN CONSUMPTION

The sources of water for human consumption are two-fold—surface sources and underground sources. The quantity of water supplied from these sources is given in Table 4.6.

	Consumption ($\times 10^6 \text{m}^3\text{yr}^{-1}$)	Percentage
Surface water	11512	82·8%
Ground water	2389	17·2%

Table 4.6 *UK water consumption by source.*

Surface Sources

The three major types of surface source are rivers, natural lakes and reservoirs. River water may occasionally be pumped directly to a water treatment works for purification. Usually, however, a storage reservoir is used in conjunction with the river. To operate without a storage reservoir avoids the cost of constructing the reservoir and of flooding the land, but means that low water levels in the summer cannot readily be catered for and this may lead to water shortages. Also, unexpectedly high levels of pollution may render the water temporarily unusable.

Natural lakes and reservoirs help to compensate for periods of low rainfall

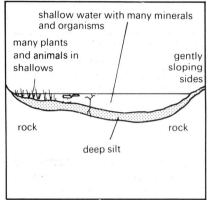

Fig. 4.15 *Eutrophic lake, e.g. Windermere*

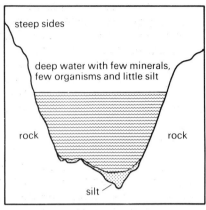

Fig. 4.16 *Oliogotrophic lake, e.g. Wastwater or Ennerdale*

and also allow natural purification processes to operate on the water. By allowing the water to stand, much of the suspended material will settle to the bottom and much of the organic material will be decomposed by bacteria present in the water.

Natural lakes can be sub-divided into two types—**eutrophic** (see Fig. 4.15) and **oligotrophic** (see Fig. 4.16). Eutrophic lakes are usually shallow and have gently shelving sides which, because of the wide range of habitats so produced, allows for the build-up of organic material. This encourages the presence and growth of a wide variety of animals and plants in the water and so these lakes are relatively highly productive. Oligotrophic lakes, on the other hand, are much deeper and have more steeply shelving rocky sides which do not readily allow for colonization by plants. These lakes are much less productive. Of the two, the oligotrophic lake is preferred for water abstraction. Reservoirs generally have characteristics somewhere between the two.

Underground Sources

Underground sources, or aquifers, may form wherever water is able to percolate down through permeable rock and become trapped by an impermeable barrier. Often the water in aquifers is under pressure because it is trapped between two impermeable rock strata. A well or bore hole sunk down into the Earth's crust to penetrate the permeable rock allows the water to

Fig. 4.17 *A confined aquifer and an unconfined aquifer*

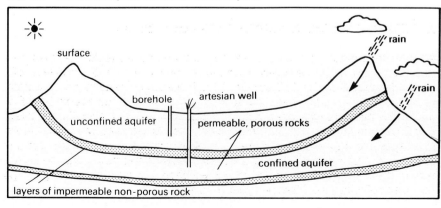

be raised to the surface by this natural pressure (**confined aquifer**). Wells in this type of aquifer are known as **artesian wells**. Alternatively, the water may have to be pumped out of the rock and in this case the aquifer is an **unconfined aquifer**.

Though aquifers, at present, produce less than 20% of the UK water supply, they are often favoured by water authorities. This is because as water percolates down into the Earth's crust it is naturally purified. It is also usually out of reach of polluting agents. Underground water may be 'hard' because of the minerals being dissolved out of the rocks through which the water percolates.

Water Treatment

Water from both surface and underground sources is usually pumped to a water works for treatment, where several processes operate. (The number and type of processes required depend, in part, on the source of the water.)

Firstly, the water passes through a **screening** process using either bars, to remove large objects (as in river abstraction), or fine screens or microstrainers, to remove algae (as perhaps in eutrophic lake abstraction). From here, the water passes to **settlement tanks** where the larger materials settle out. After this, the water passes either through a **slow sand-filter** or a **fast sand-filter**, linked to a **flocculation process**.

Slow sand filtration works by allowing water to pass through a bed of graded sand (finest particles at the top) at a rate of about 100 litres per square metre per hour. Algae inhabit the upper layers of the sand, together with animals such as fly larvae (e.g. *Chironomids*). Bacteria live in a layer below this. As water passes down through the filter, the organic matter present is oxidized to simple compounds (such as carbon-dioxide, water and nitrates). The bacteria also remove some inorganic substances such as copper, and the sand acts as a physical barrier to particulate material.

Flocculation involves the formation of a chemical 'floc' (a fine meshwork of material) which, as water passes through it, removes suspended material and some water colour. Water flocculants include aluminium sulphate and some borates. Water passes from the flocculation tank to a sand filter, which allows water to pass at a rate of about 800 litres per square metre per hour.

The final form of treatment involves the addition of chlorine to destroy pathogenic bacteria. Generally, the chlorine is applied as liquified chlorine gas, at a concentration of less than 1%. Some water authorities in the UK also add fluoride. At 1 p.p.m. it has been known to reduce the incidence of tooth decay. Some concern has been expressed about the possible harm to man that results from this treatment, but some areas in the UK have water that naturally contains up to five times this level and it has not shown itself to be toxic.

ENSURING FUTURE, ADEQUATE WATER SUPPLIES

Though, in general, people expect water always to be available whenever they turn on the tap, any excessively hot summer, even in the UK, leads to fears of a water shortage (see Fig. 4.18 and Fig. 4.19). In the very hot summer of 1976 many areas could only obtain their water from stand-pipes in the streets (see Fig. 4.20). This measure was taken to allow water authorities to ration the relatively small quantities of water that were available. At present, of course, these shortages are only seen during periods of excessively dry weather, but it is anticipated that if we were to rely upon our present water supplies alone, by the turn of the century, England and Wales will face a water shortage of perhaps hundreds of millions of litres per year (Fig. 4.21).

Fig. 4.18   *Reservoir depleted by drought*

Fig. 4.19   *The effect of severe drought on soil*

Fig. 4.21   *Drought-susceptible areas of the UK*

Fig. 4.20   *Queuing at a standpipe for water*

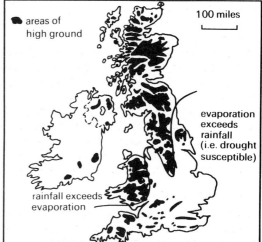

If this state of affairs is to be avoided, a great deal of thought and effort must be given to increasing the quantity of water available to us. Many of the steps that can be taken can only be implemented by water authorities, but there are a number of water-conserving measures that can be taken by individuals.

Water Authority Measures

Reservoirs

The most obvious measure that could be taken is to construct more reservoirs. However, though this will undoubtedly be necessary, there are a number of

Fig. 4.22 *Lake Vyrnwy—built in Wales to supply water to Liverpool*

environmental objections. Naturally, when a reservoir is constructed it is necessary to build a dam and to flood the area of land behind it. Unfortunately, the most suitable sites for a reservoir tend to be in upland areas of great scenic beauty and though it is possible to construct dams from natural stone, many people feel that a dam spoils the scenery. The land behind the dam that has to be flooded is generally agricultural land, though it is not unknown in the UK for a village to be 'drowned' to allow a reservoir to be formed. (Examples of such sites include Lake Vyrnwy in North Wales, Fig. 4.22; and Blithfield in Staffordshire.) Obviously this creates considerable social problems for people who have to move.

The land that is flooded also loses its value as a habitat for the organisms that lived in the area, though it is arguable that a new habitat has been formed in its place. Because the reservoir will flood slowly, large animals are able to escape without harm, though many smaller organisms may die.

Apart from attempting to blend dams into the environment by constructing them from natural stone, water authorities display their concern for the environment by providing such structures as fish 'ladders' to allow migrating fish to negotiate the dams. These problems, of course, are much the same as those associated with hydro-electric power schemes.

Estuary barrages

Estuary barrages have much in common with reservoirs, in that a barrier is constructed to hold a body of water. The principle is to construct a barrier at the mouth of a river. Several sites for estuary barrages have been suggested, such as the Solway Firth, River Dee, Morecambe Bay and the Wash. (This last named area receives $2.5\text{-}3 \times 10^6$ litres of fresh water daily and at present it flows into the sea and is thus 'wasted'.) Barrages of this nature have the advantage of being relatively large and of being sited close to areas of high population density, where the water is in greatest demand. There are, however, severe environmental objections to these schemes, as much of the shallow, salty marshlands found in these areas would be destroyed. Being of no direct use to man, they do, however, support a very wide range of animals and plants specially adapted to these habitats, and these would perish. Also, rivers are important in the natural recycling of nutrients from land to sea and the discharge of water in say, the Wash, might affect fishing grounds in the North Sea. These problems are similar to those connected with tidal power projects.

Recharging aquifers

The principle of this method is to ensure that the water in aquifers is replaced at least as quickly as it is being extracted. Recharging aquifers may occur either by injecting water through bore-holes, or by diverting rivers into lagoons excavated into permeable rocks, overlying the aquifers. The benefits of this technique include the possibility of storing large quantities of water without using areas of valuable land. Also, because the water will become naturally cleaned as it filters down through the permeable rocks, low quality river water can be used, which would otherwise be unusable or would require very expensive treatment. (Experiments in Nottinghamshire suggest that a lagoon covering about twenty hectares would allow recharge to occur at over 100×10^6 litres per day.)

Redistribution of water

To some extent this practice already occurs. The Midlands receives much of its water from Wales, and Manchester obtains much of its water from the Lake District. It has been suggested, however, that a similar scheme should operate to pipe water from Scotland into England: it is estimated that potential water supplies from Scotland could be several times larger than the deficit forecasted for England and Wales by the turn of the century. The greatest objection is that of cost, which would be very large indeed.

Desalination

This process involves the large-scale distillation of sea water to produce fresh water. The practice is not, of course, a new one (it has been used on board ships since the 19th century), but it is only relatively recently that serious consideration has been given to this process as a means of supplying domestic and industrial water as an alternative to the conventional aquifer or reservoir storage schemes. To date, in the UK, some 9×10^6 litres per day are produced by desalination techniques from several plants, e.g. at Scunthorpe and in the Channel Islands. The cost of water from this process can compare quite favourably with the cost from reservoir storage shemes, and in cases where a cheap source of heat is available (for instance, the 'waste' heat from a generating station) the cost may be even less.

The environmental advantages of these schemes are obvious when it is realized that the structures required to desalinate water cover only a fraction of

Fig. 4.23   *The UK's largest desalination plant, on Jersey*

the area of a moderately large reservoir. The largest desalination plant in the UK at Jersey, capable of producing some 6×10^6 litres of water each day, is built in a disused quarry! Practical advantages of the system include the fact that the sea is capable of providing all the water that we could possibly want, and the water that is produced is of a consistently high quality.

Individual Measures

Many of the measures that can be taken by individuals are those that we are all familiar with and that have been taken during periods of drought. Some simple possibilities include:
   i) Having a shower instead of a bath.
  ii) Having a shallow bath instead of a deep one.
 iii) Using a bucket and sponge for washing cars, rather than a hose-pipe.
  iv) Using water from washing machines to wash cars or water gardens.
   v) Mending leaking taps.
   Finally, it is possible to have toilet systems installed that operate by vacuum action, sucking the waste away, rather than simply allowing it to be washed away as occurs in conventional systems. The vacuum systems use only a fraction of the amount of water, though they may not be as efficient in removing harmful bacteria from the porcelain, of which toilets are made.

ACTIVITIES

River water

1   Investigate the amount of suspended solids in river water.
a) Obtain a sample of river water (at least $150 \, cm^3$).
b) Shake your sample of water (the suspended material in a river would not normally be allowed to settle out because of the water movement).
c) Pour $100 \, cm^3$ of your sample into a measuring cylinder.
d) Weigh a piece of filter paper and then filter your $100 \, cm^3$ of river water through it.
e) Dry your filter paper and weigh it again.
f) Calculate the amount of material on your filter paper. This is the amount of suspended solid in your $100 \, cm^3$ sample.
g) Calculate how much solid is present in one million parts of water from the formula:

$$\text{amount of suspended solids (parts per million)} = \frac{\text{mass of suspended material in } 100 \, cm^3 \times 1 \times 10^6}{100}$$

2   Investigate the amount of dissolved solids in river water.
a) Obtain 25 or $50 \, cm^3$ of *filtered* river water.
b) Weigh a clean, dry evaporating dish and pour your filtered water into it.
c) Evaporate the water to dryness. Be careful not to lose any of the solids as the water evaporates.
d) When the water has completely evaporated and your solids are dry, re-weigh your evaporating dish and calculate how many solids are present. This gives a value of how much dissolved solids there are in $25 \, cm^3$ (or $50 \, cm^3$) of your water.
e) Calculate how much dissolved solids would be present in one million parts of water from the equation below:

$$\text{dissolved solids in river water} = \frac{\text{mass of dissolved solids in } 25\,\text{cm}^3 \text{ (or } 50\,\text{cm}^3\text{) of water} \times 1 \times 10^6}{25 \text{ (or } 50)}$$

3   List any possible effects on aquatic life, domestic users or industrial users of a high value of suspended and dissolved solids in river water.

Drinking water

4   Drinking water should have a total value for suspended and dissolved solids of less than 500 p.p.m. Water that has too many suspended solids can have them removed in a water works by settlement and by sand filtration. The following experiment (see Fig. 4.24) shows how efficient sand can be in removing suspended solids. You will need about 400 cm³ of river water.

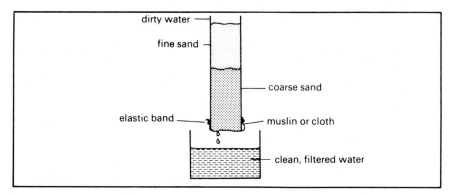

Fig. 4.24   *A simple sand filter*

a) Obtain a big cylinder of about 3 cm diameter and 40 cm or more in length. The cylinder must be open at both top and bottom.
b) Obtain some washed coarse sand and some washed silver sand.
c) Tie a piece of fine muslin over one end of your tube and put a 15 cm depth of washed coarse sand into it.
d) Put a 15 cm depth of washed silver sand on top of your coarse sand.
e) Pour sufficient river water into the tube to allow you to collect 100 cm³ of filtered water.
f) Carry out experiment 1 using both untreated and sand-filtered river water.
g) Comment on the extent to which your sand filter has removed suspended solids.
h) Suggest ways in which your sand filter could be made more efficient. Try some of your suggestions.

5   No amount of physical cleaning will remove the bacteria in water. If these were left in drinking water they could cause disease. This experiment investigates the efficiency with which chlorine kills bacteria. The means of treating your water (preferably river or pond water) will be by adding a solution of sodium hypochlorite containing 14% of chlorine.

The sterile water you will need can be obtained by boiling the water. The remainder of your apparatus *can* be sterilized in an autoclave or by whatever other technique your teacher suggests.

For this experiment you will need:

1 sterile bottle into which you will put sterile water;
7 sterile test tubes labelled 1–7;
1 test tube rack;
1 beaker of *filtered* river water;

1 sterile syringe to measure 2 cm³;
4 sterile petri dishes containing nutrient agar.
a) using your syringe:
 i) into tube 1 put 2 cm³ of sodium hypochlorite;
 ii) into tube 2 put 2 cm³ of sterile water + 2 cm³ of sodium hypochlorite;
 iii) into tube 3 put 1 cm³ of sterile water + 1 cm³ of solution from tube 2;
The three tubes will now contain sodium hypochlorite in 3 different strengths.
Tube 1 contains full strength solution containing 14% chlorine. Tube 2 contains
half strength solution containing —— % chlorine. Tube 3 contains —— strength
solution containing —— % chlorine. (Calculate the missing values yourself.)
b)
 i) Place 1 cm³ of filtered river water into each of the tubes 4–7.
 ii) into tube 4 add 1 cm³ of solution containing 14% chlorine.
 iii) into tube 5 add 1 cm³ of solution containing 7% chlorine.
 iv) into tube 6 add 1 cm³ of solution containing 3·5% chlorine. Tube 7 will contain
 no chlorine.
 v) Using your syringe, remove 1 cm³ of solution from test tube 4 and place it in
 one petri dish. Swirl gently and tip out all the excess solution.
c) Repeat this procedure for tubes 5 to 7 putting each solution into different
 petri dishes every time.
d) Finally, label your dishes and sellotape the lids on.

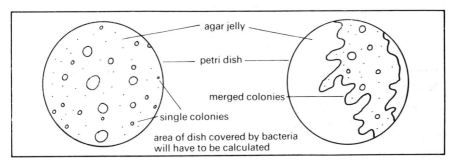

Fig. 4.25 *Colonies of bacteria*

e) Record results after 4–7 days incubation at about 37°C by counting the
 number of bacteria colonies (each colony is assumed to come from one
 bacteria). If the colonies run together you could estimate the area of petri
 dish covered by bacteria by using a quadrat divided into centimetre
 squares.
f) You could graph your results by plotting percentage chlorine present on
 the horizontal axis and number of colonies present on the vertical axis.
g) Write down what conclusion you can make about the effect of chlorine on
 water.

Properties of water

6 Porosity is a measure of the pore space in rock or soil.
In this experiment (see Fig. 4.26) you will measure the percentage porosity for
clay and sand.
a) Collect a 20 cm³ sample of sand and a 20 cm³ sample of dry powdered clay
 (the clay can be ground in a pestle and mortar).
b) Obtain 2 measuring cylinders and pour 40 cm³ of water into each one.
c) Pour the 20 cm³ sample of sand into one cylinder and the 20 cm³ sample of
 clay into the other cylinder.
d) Each cylinder should theoretically contain 60 cm³ of material (40 cm³ of

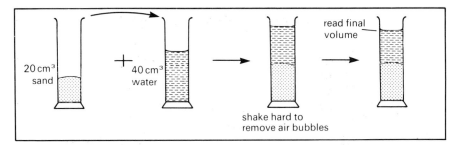

Fig. 4.26 *Finding the porosity of sand*

water + 20 cm³ of sand or clay). In fact, each cylinder will contain less than 60 cm³ because air will have been forced out of the sand and clay.
e) Calculate how much air has been displaced by subtracting the actual total volume found in each cylinder from 60 cm³.
f) Calculate the percentage porosity of each sample by using the calculation:

$$\text{percentage porosity} = \frac{\text{volume of air}}{\text{volume of sand/clay}} \times \frac{100}{1}$$

7 Permeability is a measure of the ease with which liquids or gases will pass through a rock or soil. You are going to find out which is more permeable: sand or clay (see Fig. 4.27).
a) Place a wad of cotton wool *loosely* into the neck of a filter funnel and add enough sand to fill the funnel to within 2 cm of the rim.
b) Pour 60 cm³ of water onto the sand and allow the water that drains through to be collected in a beaker or measuring cylinder.
c) Measure how much water came out and calculate this as a percentage of the amount you put in. Use the formula:

$$\text{permeability} = \frac{\text{volume put on}}{\text{volume collected}} \times \frac{100}{1}$$

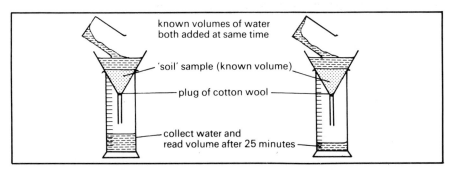

Fig. 4.27 *Comparing the permeability of sand and clay*

d) Repeat the experiment using dry, powdered clay. Remember to use exactly the same quantity of clay and the same volume of water.
e) Which was the most permeable, sand or clay?
8 Investigating the process of osmosis (see Fig. 4.28).
In this experiment visking tubing is used to represent the semi-permeable membrane of root hairs. It could also represent the semi-permeable membrane which separates the cell contents of most microscopic aquatic organisms from their environment.

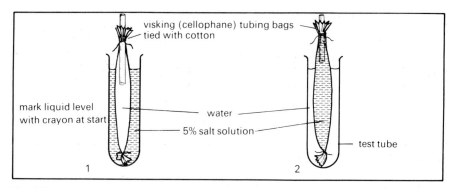

Fig. 4.28 *Investigating osmosis*

a) Take an 8 cm length of visking tubing and tie a piece of thread round one end to seal it (there must not be any leaks).
b) Pour a 5% solution of salt water into the visking tubing until the tubing is full.
c) Place a 6 cm length of narrow bored (or capillary) glass tubing into the open end of the visking tubing. The glass tube should have about 2 cm of its length inside the visking tubing.
d) Tie the thread round the visking tubing and the glass tubing so that the visking tubing is sealed. The salt solution should be visible inside the glass tubing. Mark the level to which it reaches.
e) Place the visking tubing into a boiling tube containing distilled water.
f) Note the level of salt water in the glass tubing every 2 minutes until an obvious change in level takes place.
g) State whether the level in the tube has gone up or down. Can this result be explained by the process of osmosis? To remind you, osmosis is said to have occurred when water flows from a weak solution to a strong solution through a semi-permeable membrane.
h) Set up the experiment again but with distilled water in the visking tubing and with a 5% solution in the boiling tube.
i) State what has happened and explain your results.

5 Food and Man

THE NUTRITIONAL REQUIREMENTS OF MAN

Foods are needed for two main reasons:
1 for growth and repair;
2 for providing energy for the work the body does.

In terms of the need for food, man is as much a part of nature as any other animal. The food substances he needs are the same as most other animals, and like them he is part of many food chains. However, man differs from all other animals in the way that he is able to control natural systems, for example, he can increase the food he obtains from a given area of ground.

The food materials needed by man and other animals are generally thought of as falling into five major groups or classes. These are: **carbohydrates, fats, proteins, vitamins** and **minerals.** Note that water, although the main constituent of protoplasm and essential for life, is excluded here as it cannot be considered to be food.

Carbohydrates

As explained in Chapter 3, carbohydrates are the first materials to be made (synthesized) by plants during the process of photosynthesis, the equation for which is:

$$6CO_2 \quad + \quad 6H_2O \quad \xrightarrow[\text{chlorophyll}]{\text{light}} \quad C_6H_{12}O_6 \quad + \quad 6O_2$$

$$\text{Carbon dioxide} \ + \ \text{water} \quad \longrightarrow \quad \text{carbohydrate} \ + \ \text{oxygen}$$

Fig. 5.1 *A four-month-old child suffering from starvation*

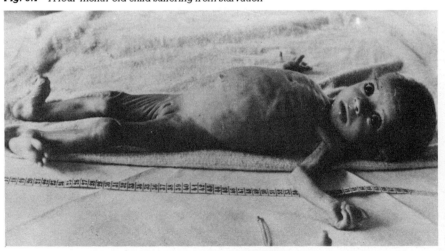

Fig. 5.2 *How many of the five major classes of food can you see in this picture?*

(Light and chlorophyll are both needed for the reaction to take place.) Carbohydrates, therefore, are food substances containing the elements carbon, hydrogen and oxygen. The carbohydrate shown in the chemical equation is glucose, one of the simplest of all sugars.

Two groups of carbohydrates are recognized, these are **sugars** and **starches.** Sugars are the simplest of carbohydrates and inlude such substances as **sucrose** (the white sugar we put in our tea), **fructose** (the brown sugar we put in our coffee) and **glucose.** Starches are substances made up of many sugar units linked together.

The major role of carbohydrates in the body is to produce energy. To do this they are oxidized during the process of respiration as shown in the equation below.

$$C_6H_{12}O_6 + 6O_2 \longrightarrow 6CO_2 + 6H_2O + \text{energy}$$

glucose + oxygen $\longrightarrow$ carbon dioxide + water + energy

Carbohydrates are also important in the structure of the body. They combine with proteins to form such things as cell membranes.

Fats

These substances are also made up of carbon, hydrogen and oxygen but are larger, more complex molecules. In the same way that some carbohydrates (e.g. starches) are made up of many sugar units, so some fats are made up of many **fatty-acid units.** Fats serve several functions in the body:

1 During the process of respiration they can be oxidized to release large quantities of energy.

2 They can be stored under the skin so that they insulate the body against cold. This is particularly apparent in the blubber of whales and seals.

3 They are stored round body organs so that the organs gain extra protection against damage if the body is hurt. The kidneys in particular are protected in this way.

4 Many vitamins that are needed by man are fat compounds and are therefore 'fat soluble'. In effect, this means that these vitamins are present in the fats that we eat, e.g. vitamins A, D and E.

5 Many fats are also involved in the structure of the body, such as **lipoproteins** and **phospholipids** in cell membranes and the nervous system.

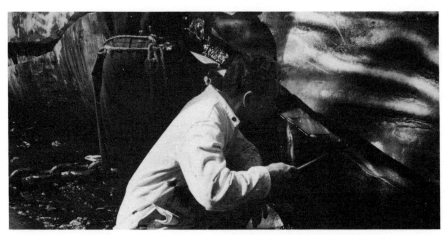

Fig. 5.3 *Whales have a thick layer of blubber to provide insulation against the cold*

Proteins

These substances are the most complex of all food substances. Like carbohydrates and fats they also contain carbon, hydrogen and oxygen but they also contain nitrogen; some also contain phosphorus or sulphur.

Proteins are made up of **amino acids**, of which there are approximately twenty. By combining these twenty or so amino acids together in different ways, many thousands of different proteins can be formed containing possibly thousands of different combinations of amino acids. Unlike fats or carbohydrates, proteins cannot be stored and so must either be used in the body or broken down and excreted.

Because the body's structure is made mainly of protein, the major role of proteins is that of growth and repair of the body. However, the carbon, hydrogen and oxygen parts of them can be oxidized to produce energy while the nitrogen part is released in water. The waste may appear as the urea in urine.

Vitamins and Minerals

The functions and sources of supply of some major vitamins and minerals are summarized in Table 5.1 and Table 5.2. If someone is to grow and develop fully, and then to maintain himself in a healthy condition, he must have a **balanced diet.** This means that he must receive the correct amount of each of the different classes of foods. The actual amount of each class of food required by a person depends upon several factors. These include: climate (people in warm climates require less energy-giving foods); age (children require more energy-giving foods and protein per unit mass of body than adults); sex; occupation; size of body; etc. (see Table 5.3).

A person suffering from an unbalanced diet may *either* be suffering from **undernourishment** or from **malnutrition.** Undernourishment is a term used to describe the condition of being underfed, or receiving an insufficient supply of food material to maintain a healthy body. Often, undernourishment is referred to as being a lack of energy (calories or joules). A satisfactory daily intake of calories is generally considered to be 2300–2700 kilocalories for an average adult (9·6–11.34 MJ). Although many adults in Western Europe and North America receive over 3000 kilocalories per day (12·6 MJ), many adults in underdeveloped countries receive less than 1500 kilocalories a day (6·3 MJ).

Vitamin	Source	Deficiency diseases
A	milk, butter, cheese, liver, eggs	Night blindness (this vitamin is essential for seeing in poor light)
B1 (thiamin)	green vegetables, seeds of plants such as peas and beans, most dairy products	Beriberi—a disease affecting the nervous system leading to paralysis
B2 (riboflavin)	green vegetables, eggs, liver, milk	Deficiency leads to a cracking of the skin round the mouth
C (ascorbic acid)	fresh fruit, fresh vegetables especially broccoli and cabbage	Scurvy—leads to a lowering of resistance to infection, bleeding gums and loosening of teeth
D (cholecalciferol)	fish-liver oils egg-yolk, butter. Made in the skin when exposed to ultra-violet light	Softening of bones in children (rickets) and deformed bones in adults. The absorption of calcium (a major component of bone) is not possible without this vitamin

Table 5.1   *Some major vitamins.*

Fig. 5.4   *Oranges are a good source of vitamin C*

A lack of, or excess of, particular classes of food in the diet leads to malnutrition. The first recognized causes of malnutrition were related to a lack of vitamins. The deficiency 'diseases' of some vitamins and some minerals are given in Table 5.1. However, more recently publicity has been given to malnutrition caused by protein deficiency or an excess of fats and carbohydrates.

Mineral	Function
calcium	Required for the formation of bones and teeth
phosphorus	Required for the formation of bones and teeth but also important in many chemical reactions in the cells of the body
iron	An essential part of the blood
sodium potassium chloride	Important for maintaining the correct concentration of body fluids .
fluoride	Important in the structure of tooth enamel

Table 5.2   *Some important minerals and their functions.*

Age (yrs)	Sex	'Activity'	Energy requirements (kJ Kg^{-1})
1	—	—	452
5	—	—	1030
10	Male	—	329
	female	—	290
15	male	—	191
	female	—	171
20	male	sedentary	173
	female	sedentary	167
20	male	very active	232
	female	very active	190
50	male	sedentary	167
	female	sedentary	162
	male	very active	232
	female	very active	190

Table 5.3   *The varying daily energy demands of people.*

Protein deficiency is particularly common in Asian and African countries and leads to conditions such as **kwashiorkor** and **infantile polycarencial syndrome** (see Fig. 5.6). Kwashiorkor results in discoloured hair and skin and a swollen abdomen (pot-belly). Both physical and mental development is restricted. High starch and low protein diets cause infantile polycarencial syndrome. The skin pigmentation that is characteristic of this 'disease' disappears if protein-rich foods are given. Some estimates suggest that up to 50% of the children aged 1–4 in these countries suffer from protein deficiency. Children suffering from severe food deficiencies may never fully recover even if they receive a balanced diet later in life. Deficiencies in the pregnant mother may even affect the foetus (unborn baby).

In the developed countries, particularly North America, malnutrition arises as a result of too high an intake of fats. A diet containing large quantities of fat (and animal fat in particular) is now thought to be closely linked with coronary thrombosis (heart attacks) and is now regarded as causing a high proportion of deaths in many of the world's developed countries.

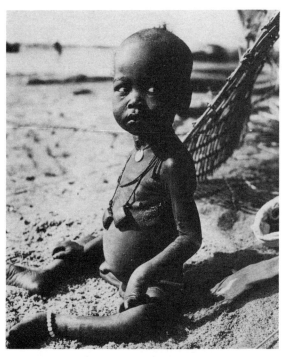

Fig. 5.5 *A child suffering from rickets. This disease is caused by a lack of vitamin D in the diet*

WHO photo

Undernourishment and malnutrition are thought to be major factors in 50–75% of all deaths in Latin America. Throughout the world, up to 30% of all deaths are thought to be associated with these factors.

Fig. 5.6 *These children are two years old yet weigh only 4.5kg. The discolouration and straightening of the hair is a symptom of kwashiorkor*

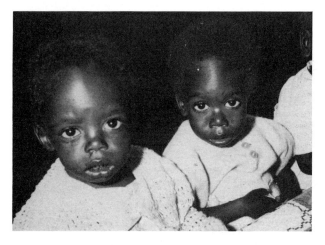

FOOD PRODUCTION

In an effort to produce sufficient food for his requirements, man attempts to control food-producing systems so that the production from them is as large as possible. However, even though Britain has one of the most highly productive agricultural systems in the world we still have to import 40% of our food requirements. If only those foods that we can grow in the UK are considered, we are still only 75% self-sufficient. However, because of his interference, man often adversely affects the environment in a number of ways that are described below.

Plant Production

Because all food is initially dependent upon plant production (see Chapter 3), man's first efforts must be to obtain the maximum plant production from each area under cultivation. Factors that control plant productivity that are external to the plant include the availability of carbon dioxide, water, light and mineral nutrients. Also important is a lack of competitors such as weeds, herbivorous animals, parasites or disease.

Carbon dioxide and light can be controlled under greenhouse conditions but it is not practicable to control them on a large scale. Water availability, however, is controlled on a large scale by means of either drainage (if the quantity of water present is too much) or irrigation (see Fig. 5.7). The commonest form of irrigation in the UK is by spray irrigation lines. This technique is particularly important in east England where rainfall is low, but can also be found in many other parts of the country.

The major mineral nutrients of plants can either be introduced in an inorganic or an organic form. Organic food materials include animal and plant waste and sewage sludge (see Chapter 4 for more information on sewage sludge). These materials have several advantages. Firstly, the minerals that are of major importance (nitrogen as nitrates, phosphorous as phosphates and potassium) are released in small quantities over a long period of time. This ensures that the plants obtain maximum benefit from them. As well as providing food, however, these organic materials also improve the texture of soils. Clay soils are made more 'open' in texture improving drainage and aeration. Sandy soils treated with organic material are better able to retain moisture. In general, soils are also very much improved as a habitat for the many organisms that live there. Finally, organic materials tend to 'bind' light soils together into aggregates so that there is less tendency for them to blow away (become wind eroded). See Chapters 3 and 7 for more information on wind erosion.

Inorganic fertilizers containing the major minerals may be supplied by a variety of compounds. Nitrogen (N) necessary for the healthy growth of the green parts of leaves is generally supplied as ammonium sulphate, sodium nitrate or ammonium nitrate (Nitram). This last mentioned fertilizer contains the

Fig. 5.7 *Drainage lines under construction*
Crown copyright

Fig. 5.8 *Organic material being spread on a farm*

greatest quantity of nitrogen but its use has to be carefully controlled. Too much nitrogen results in large leaves and long stems and plants that tend to have thin-walled cells. These thin-walled cells are quickly invaded by disease-causing organisms (pathogens). Phosphorous (P) is often supplied as Superphosphate or less frequently as basic slag. This element is important in healthy root growth and is of particular importance in satisfactory root growth in cereals and all young plants. Finally, potassium (K) can be supplied as potassium sulphate. This is important in the ripening process of such plants as fruits and tomatoes, and the swelling of storage organs. More generally, potassium is required for healthy growth and strong plants. Too much potassium may make the cell walls of plants tougher than normal so that animals have difficulty in digesting them.

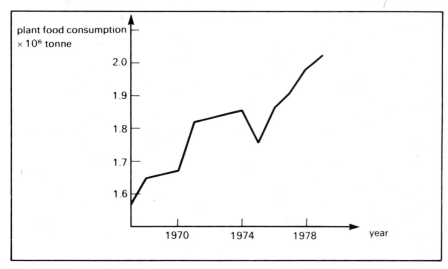

Fig. 5.9 *Consumption of plant foods (N, P, K) in the UK. Source—UK Mineral Statistics, 1975.*

The use of inorganic fertilizers has increased greatly over the last 30 years or so, for two major reasons. Firstly, in an attempt to improve the productivity of plants, plant breeders have produced strains of plants (in particular cereals) which will grow far more rapidly than their predecessors. It is the development of these plants that has been the basis of the 'Green Revolution'. In order for these plants to perform with maximum efficiency, however, they require very high quantities of fertilizer and water. Secondly, again in order to improve efficiency, farmers have tended either to specialize in producing plant crops or animals. Different regions in the UK favour one type of farming rather than another. A situation arises, therefore, where there are no animals in some areas and so no animal waste is available. (Transportation charges make it uneconomic to transport animal waste from one region to another.) The necessary nutrients therefore have to be provided by inorganic fertilizers.

The result of this reliance on inorganic fertilizers is a tendency for soils to lose their structure. Because of this they also lose fertility and suffer more from erosion. Also, as more inorganic fertilizer is applied to the land, so more of it finds its way into water systems. This tends to cause eutrophication (see Chapter 4). A particular problem occurs in relation to nitrogen fertilizers because high nitrate levels in drinking water are harmful to man—particularly to infants. The nitrates in water may be converted into nitrites by bacteria in the gut and these reduce the ability of blood to carry oxygen round the body. (The bacteria responsible for this are not present in the adult gut.) Groundwater in some areas in the UK is giving cause for concern because of nitrate levels.

Water authorities are having to spend considerable amounts of money to ensure the protection of consumers.

Fig. 5.10   *Inorganic fertilizer being applied to a grass crop*

The competitors of crop plants in the form of weeds are generally controlled today by herbicides—chemicals designed to kill plant life. (see Fig. 5.11). Herbicides may either be **contact** or **systemic**, **total** or **selective**. Contact herbicides are those that are designed to destroy those parts of plants that the herbicide falls on. For this reason, they are most effective against annuals that have no structures below ground that can regenerate the aerial parts that are destroyed. Examples of this type of herbicide are DNOC and Dinoseb. Systemic herbicides, on the other hand, are transported round the plant (translocated). This ensures that they reach and destroy the undergound structures of plants as well as the aerial parts that they contact. Examples of these herbicides are MCPA, 2,4–D, Dalapon and Simazine.

Fig. 5.11   *Competitors of crops are reduced by means of herbicides and pesticides*

Many of the first herbicides to be used were generally 'total' in their action; they destroyed all of the plants that they contacted and so could not be used on growing crops unless great care was taken to ensure that the herbicide made no contact with the crop plants (e.g. sodium chlorate, Simazine.) However, scientists have developed selective herbicides which can be used in an area of mixed plants and only kill those plants that they are intended to kill. MCPA for instance will select the broad-leaved dicotyledons in a field of cereal or grass (narrow-leaved monocotyledons).

The environmental effects of herbicides

Initially, the environmental effects of many herbicides were unknown because it was uncertain how toxic (poisonous) they were to many organisms. Some, however, are extremely toxic to both mammals and other animals. DNOC for example may be absorbed through the skin and has caused the deaths of a range of animals including man. Paraquat has also caused the death of humans as a result of its misuse, for example, it has been drunk in mistake for lemonade. The effects of herbicides as direct poisons, however, are fortunately limited because their toxicity rapidly decreases after they have been applied.

Rather more concern has been expressed about the use of herbicides to kill particular species of plant. It has been suggested that killing off, or even greatly reducing, many of the wild flowers (weeds) in the environment will destroy the food source or habitat of a range of insects and birds. Many of these animals may be beneficial to the farmer. An example of this is the nettle. Though it would appear to be a nuisance and of no value, the nettle plant is a food source for the larvae of ladybirds. This is an insect that helps to control the number of aphids by preying on them. If nettles are destroyed so are the ladybirds, and aphids will become even greater pests than at present.

It is equally argued that our wild flowers add beauty to the countryside and that their destruction will remove a great deal of pleasure for a great number of people. Finally, it is suggested that the continued use of herbicides in an area (even those that are rapidly broken down in the environment) might eventually destroy the small organisms in the soil that are necessary to maintain its fertility.

Insects and insecticides

Insects are responsible for destroying many plants that are a food source to man and so chemicals have been designed to kill them. The most important of these chemicals (**insecticides**) fall into two major groups: **chlorinated hydrocarbons** and **organophosphates**. The chlorinated hydrocarbons include such chemicals as DDT, Aldrin, Dieldrin and Endrin. These insecticides (in common with the organophosphates) began to be used extensively after the Second World War. The chlorinated hydrocarbons were thought at first to have little or no toxicity to mammals, birds and fish but to be very toxic to insects. For this reason their introduction was hailed as a great breakthrough in the fight against insects. However, within a decade of their wide-spread use, serious doubts were being expressed about their safety. It is now appreciated that these chemicals are very persistent in the environment. Up to 40% of DDT, for instance, may be present in the soil up to twenty years after its application. Unfortunately, more often than not, the remaining insecticide is no longer harmful to the insect for which it was intended. This is because it occupies a different place in the environment, perhaps in the soil instead of on plant leaves for example. As a consequence, it is necessary to keep repeating the doses of insecticide. This means its concentration in the environment increases.

Another disturbing fact concerning these chemicals is that they are very mobile in the environment. This means that they do not stay at the site of their application. They can be transported great distances in streams and groundwater, they may become attached to dust particles that are blown by the wind and may even be present in water as it evaporates and condenses again in the atmosphere to fall as rain.

The fact that these chemicals are so persistent and so mobile is all the more worrying when it is appreciated that they also tend to enter the bodies of animals. This has led to them now being present in the bodies of most animals, including man, throughout the world. The animals that are most affected by these chemicals are the animals at the top of food chains (see Fig. 5.13). As the chemicals enter the bodies of animals at the base of the food chain, so many of these animals are eaten by animals in the next trophic level (see Chapter 3). In this way their concentration increases. This process repeats itself until the chemicals reach such concentrations in the top carnivores that the animals are killed. In the UK alone, the deaths of thousands of individual animals occupying the tertiary consumer levels of food chains have been traced to poisoning by chlorinated hydrocarbons. Before the strict control of the use of these chemicals in the UK there was a great danger of many of our rarer predatory birds becoming extinct.

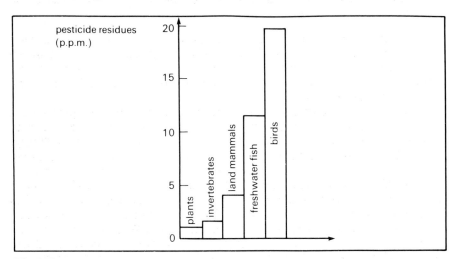

Fig. 5.12 *Pesticide accumulation in food chains. (Source—C. H. Walker, 1964)*

The organophosphorous insecticides were developed from Second World War nerve gases and so are obviously highly toxic to man and other mammals, as well as to birds, fish and of course insects. Examples of this group include Parathion and Malathion. Because of their great toxicity to man, their introduction was viewed with great concern. Indeed, in the early years of their use these chemicals were responsible for the deaths of many people who used them. However, despite their obvious dangers, they are very quickly broken down into non-toxic forms in the environment. They are said to be rapidly **degraded**.

A final problem that has become apparent with insecticides is that insects tend to become immune to them. Occasionally it has been shown that this immunity has developed because of a mutation on the part of the insect. This process is rare, however. In the great majority of instances, immunity in a population of insects has developed from the natural resistance of a few individuals within the population. It is to be expected that within any large population of insects some individuals will be naturally immune. These will breed and pass on their immunity to their offspring. Eventually, a whole

Fig. 5.13 *Birds of prey, like this goshawk, fall victim to poisoning by pesticides*

population of insects becomes immune and so larger doses of insecticides must be used or new chemicals developed. It is now known that there are over 300 species of insect and mite that are resistant to one or more pesticides. This compares with about 50 just after the Second World War and none at the beginning of the century.

Other pests such as nematodes, fungi and rodents also cause problems in varying degrees, and various pesticides have been developed to combat them. These pesticides have also created problems. Seeds treated with mercury-based fungicides have caused the deaths of large numbers of seed-eating birds, and many rodents have become immune to a range of rodenticides.

In conclusion to this section it must be pointed out that the insecticides that have been developed have greatly reduced the amount of human food that has been lost to insects. They have also helped to control a number of diseases that are spread by insects such as the malarial mosquito. What perhaps could be done to enable the quantity of insecticides and herbicides to be reduced is to lay greater emphasis on biological control and on cultivations that tend to make conditions less favourable to weeds and insects.

Non-poisonous and other techniques for controlling pests

A variety of cultivation techniques are possible to reduce the incidence of pests. One example includes the removal of the tips of broad bean plants as the first flowers 'set' to reduce the colonization of the plants by aphids. Removing the tips removes the softest tissues that the aphids prefer to attack and it tends to lead to a toughening of the remaining parts of the plants.

Another example is the practice of 'earthing-up' or ridging potatoes. This not only automatically reduces competition from weeds but also reduces the risk of potato blight. The organisms that cause **potato blight** (leading to discolouration and eventual rotting of the edible tuber) fall from the leaves of the plant during its growing season onto the soil. By ridging the potatoes, the organisms tend to fall to the bottom of the ridge, below the level of the tuber, to a position where they are unable to affect it.

Two further interesting techniques used to combat pests are aspects of biological control. These are the release of pest predators and the introduction of sterile male pests.

Fig. 5.14 *The effect of nematodes on field beans*   **Fig. 5.15** *Pea aphids feeding on a broad bean leaf*

The release of pest predators as the title suggests, involves finding a natural predator to control the numbers of the pest in question. More often than not, however, the predator has to be imported from abroad because if the predator was naturally present the pest population would have been less likely to reach numbers that created the problem in the first place. It is often very difficult to find a suitable predator. Not only does it have to be capable of surviving in our country but must also be capable of catching the pest. It is also necessary that the imported predator should only eat the pest. If this were not the case, the predator itself could become a pest by eating harmless or even useful organisms. The control of pests using this technique has been successful for many years and has been used in several countries including America, Britain and Australia. Though instances of great success can be found in the natural environment, it is most easily accomplished under greenhouse conditions. In these cases, the predator is unlikely to survive and prove to be harmful if it leaves the greenhouse conditions. An example of pest control using this technique is the use of the mite *Phytoseiulus persimites* to prey on red spider mite *(Tetranychus urticae)* in greenhouses. Plants at risk from the red spider mite include cucumbers, tomatoes, peppers and strawberries. Another example is the chalcid wasp *Encarsia formosa* which lays its eggs in the larvae of whitefly. The wasp larvae then develop as parasites in the whitefly larvae and eat them as they develop. One further problem with the technique is the number of predators required. It may be necessary to have some 10–12 000 Phytoseiulus per hectare, for instance, to combat an infestation of red spider mites.

The technique of releasing sterile male pests is still in its infancy but in outline the idea is to rear and sterilize male insects which are regarded as pests and then release them into the environment. (The insects are sterilized by means of nuclear (ionizing) radiation.) The intention is that when they are released they will mate with normal females. These females will only mate once before they lay their eggs and die. Any eggs that are layed will be infertile and so of course will not develop. Difficulties include the rearing and releasing of sufficient sterile males and the fact that the normal females tend to select out normal males in the environment and mate with them. New research is in progess to develop chemical sterilants which can be sprayed from aircraft.

Finally, the practice of crop rotation tends to reduce the problem of pest organisms. If the same crops are grown in the same area of ground every year, any pest that affects the plants will have the opportunity to increase rapidly in number. If on the other hand the crop is rotated, then in the absence of a suitable food material or habitat over a period of three of four years, the pest organisms will tend to die out. Unfortunately, in an attempt to become more efficient, farms now tend to specialize in growing either one or two crops, and so rotating crops is no longer practicable. The practice of repeatedly growing only one type of crop is known as **monoculture**. This practice tends not only to lead to increased problems with pests but also leads to the need for heavier applications of fertilizers. This is because the plants remove specific mineral salts in large quantities and so there is a general loss of fertility.

Control of production

Man exercises the greatest control over plant production under glasshouse conditions, and this control is apparent if we consider the growth of tomatoes.

The tomato seed can be sown in January or February in a temperature of about 18–20°C. There is a very great range of composts that can be used to sow seeds in, but the loamless composts are now the most favoured. These are based on peat (with perhaps sand added) and nutrients in the form of inorganic fertilizers. The peat will generally need the addition of limestone to reduce its acidity, and composts for sowing seed will contain a high proportion of phosphate to encourage rapid root development.

A major advance in the growth of tomatoes under glass is the development of **hydroponics**. This is a technique whereby plants are grown in a nutrient solution so that maximum control can be maintained over the root environment. If this technique is used, when the seeds have developed their first pair of leaves they can be 'pricked out' into fibre pots and these can be placed directly into the hydroponics system. This will involve placing the pots in a rigid or semi-rigid trough along which the nutrient solution flows. A 'spreader mat' some 2–3 mm thick ensures that the whole base of the trough (some 15–20 cm wide) is equally supplied with solution. There is no appreciable depth of solution in the trough though the mat is kept permanently wet. Six major environmental factors affect the plant's productivity. These are oxygen supply, nutrient concentration, level of acidity, light, humidity and temperature (occasionally the carbon dioxide concentration may be increased in an attempt to increase photosynthesis, though this tends to be expensive). Of the factors listed above, the first three of these achieve maximum control in hydroponics, while all techniques demand close attention to the last three.

A satisfactory supply of oxygen to the roots is ensured by providing sufficient solution to wet the matting but not swamp the roots. A growing trough with a slope of approximately 1:50 and water supplied to it from a 'stock' tank by means of a small pump will accomplish this. A uniform trough gradient ensures that no static pools of solution form that might become de-oxygenated. If this were to occur, roots would die and a serious loss of productivity would result.

The nutrients used will include the major nutrients such as nitrogen, phosphorous, potassium, calcium and magnesium, together with minor nutrients (trace elements) such as iron, manganese, boron, copper and molybdenum. The exact quantity of each nutrient tends to vary between different advocates of the system, but Table 5.4 gives some typical values.

Nutrient	Amount (parts per million)
nitrogen	90 000
phosphorous	93 000
potassium	225 000
calcium	170 000
magnesium	33 000
iron	7 300
manganese	1 300
boron	200
copper	45
molybdenum	30

Table 5.4   *The main nutrients used in hydroponic cultivation.*

The lack of a particular nutrient in the solution will show itself by a 'deficiency symptom'. For instance, if nitrogen is deficient a general yellowing throughout the green parts of the plant will be seen; if manganese is deficient, the leaves will turn white, starting at the margins and progressing to the centre (this is called **chlorosis**). Those nutrients that prove to be in short supply can quickly be made available to the plant by dissolving the required amount of nutrient into the 'stock' solution.

The concentration of nutrients can be checked regularly by using a conductivity meter. This is because the concentration of ions (dissolved nutrients in the solution) is proportional to the conductivity of the solution (the ease with which electricity will pass through it). A conductivity value of between 2×10^{-3} and 3×10^{-3} mho is normally regarded as being satisfactory. (The unit mho is the reciprocal of the resistance between opposite faces of $1 m^3$ of a substance.) The pH of the solution (level of acidity) should be maintained at between 6·0 and 6·5. The pH tends to increase and can be corrected by the addition of phosphoric acid.

If the nutrient solution is heated, then the air temperature of the glasshouse can be allowed to fall. This is important when it is appreciated that the solution can be heated for a fraction of the cost of the total volume of the whole unit. A suitable solution temperature would be around 15–18°C. Apart from the attention to the nutrient solution, the production of tomatoes in hydroponics is the same as in other systems. The plants are supported by being tied to canes or wires and the side shoots removed as they develop. As the flower 'trusses' form, the pollen is transferred from the male sex organs (the **anther** of the **stamens**) to the female sex organs (**stigmas**) to assist in pollination and fertilization. Keeping the atmosphere humid helps in this, and the pollen can be made airborne by knocking the supporting wires. Alternatively, in smaller systems, pollination can be ensured by touching each flower daily with a wad of cotton wool on a stick. The pollen sticks to the cotton wool and so is easily transferred from one flower to the next.

Soil-borne pests and weeds are not a problem in hydroponics systems, though the plants are just as likely to be attacked by airborne pests. However, because they grow very strongly, they are perhaps rather less susceptible to their effects. Such pests as thrips, leafhoppers, and whitefly can be controlled by chlorinated hydrocarbon insecticides such as Lindane or by organophosphate insecticides such as Malathion. Fungal diseases are generally associated with to much humidity which is most easily controlled by reducing the amount of water used and by increasing ventilation.

Fig. 5.16 *Growing tomatoes by hydroponics*

Animal Production

However much man increases plant production there will remain a need to produce animal products, certainly in the foreseeable future. This is necessary in order to satisfy the desire of large numbers of people in the world who expect to be able to eat meat. As a result of this, man has taken steps to increase the efficiency with which he raises animals. To do this takes a great deal of effort. This effort has been devoted to improving the strain of animals used and in controlling their environment. It has been necessary to improve the strain of animals because, with the best management in the world, a poor animal will not grow and produce food material for man as fast as a good animal will. The environment is controlled to reduce energy losses.

As explained in Chapter 3, at each link in a food chain 90% of the energy available is lost from the chain. By eating animals, man must accept considerably more loss of energy than would be the case if he only ate plants. However, he is able to reduce these losses.

Fig. 5.17 *Grain drying and storage*

In general, the losses in man's food chains involving animals occur because the animals egest much of the food they eat. They also use a large proportion for their own purposes (e.g. movement, keeping warm). Obviously, therefore, this is where the losses must be reduced.

To reduce the losses caused by egestion, the plant material that is fed to the animal must be used when it is most tasty for the animal and contains most nutritional value. To ensure this, the crop must be harvested, preserved in some way (dried, cured or malted) and taken to the animals as they need it. In order to reduce the food required for the animal's own purposes, the animal must be restricted in movement and must be kept warm. To accomplish this, the animal must be kept indoors.

All of these practices lead to the process known as **intensive husbandry** or **factory farming**, and many people consider it to be cruel. However, if these practices were not followed, the cost of animal products (e.g. meat, milk and eggs) would increase very considerably.

As a result of intensive husbandry however, there are practices that are potentially harmful to man. To ensure that the animals waste as little as possible, grow as rapidly as possible, and suffer as little as possible from pest and disease organisms, the animals are fed a range of chemicals. These include growth stimulants, tranquilisers, hormones and antibiotics. If suitable precautions are not taken traces of these materials may remain in the carcase when man eats it.

To illustrate some of these points a typical intensive husbandry system is outlined below in respect of poultry.

Poultry husbandry

Usually farmers that rear poultry for egg production do not produce their own chicks. These are purchased from a breeding farm that will have selected birds from the best strains available to produce fertile eggs. These eggs will then be incubated in a carefully controlled environment. Particular care will be taken with regard to temperature and humidity. The birds may be reared at the hatchery or be sent to a rearing unit.

The chickens will be sexed and the female birds sent to the farm in question. Generally, these will be raised in a building that enables maximum control of the environment to be maintained. The walls of the building will be insulated and side ventilation will be through specially designed vents that exclude all natural daylight. Large extractor fans in the roof will remove 'stale' air. The chicks themselves will be on a 'litter' of woodshavings, peat or straw, have food and water always available, and will be kept warm by means of infra-red heaters.

The birds will be housed in their laying quarters at about eighteen weeks of age and will generally be 'in-lay' for fifty-two weeks. More often than not the birds are then killed and used for chicken soup or paste, etc. Occasionally they may be kept for a further year. The environment in the house will be controlled in terms of temperature, ventilation and lighting.

The purpose of controlling the temperature is so that the bird uses less of its food to maintain a constant body temperature. At the same time, if the temperature rises too far, the birds will eat less food and so will not produce as many eggs. An optimum temperature has been shown to be between 18·5°C and 24°C. This temperature range is maintained in several ways. Firstly, enough birds are housed to allow them to heat the building with their own body temperatures. Secondly, the walls and roof of the building are well insulated to prevent heat escaping. Thirdly, the ventilators in the roof can be controlled to increase or decrease the amount of fresh air admitted. It is not usually necessary to heat the laying house 'artificially', even in winter.

The main aim in ventilation is to remove carbon dioxide and supply an adequate amount of oxygen. Carbon dioxide should not exceed 0·5% and oxygen should not fall below 11%. In practice, these aims are easily achieved. Usually, ventilation is by means of large extractor fans in the roof removing stale air and drawing fresh air in through side vents. These vents will be specially constructed so that all natural daylight is excluded (see Fig. 5.18). The ventilation system is also important in controlling temperature. Obviously, the more air that enters, the cooler the unit becomes.

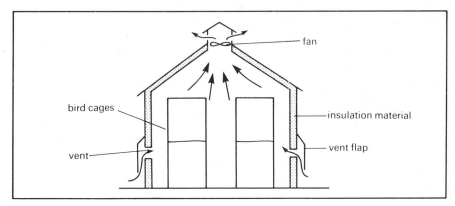

Fig. 5.18 A controlled environment poultry unit

The production of eggs in chickens is controlled by a chemical that is produced by the pituitary gland at the base of the brain. The pituitary gland in turn is stimulated by light that activates nerves at the rear of the eye. The intensity of light required to cause hens to lay eggs is as little as 0·45 lux, though maximum egg production occurs at about 5·5 lux. Usually 11–22 lux is provided so that it is not too dark for egg collecting. Also the period of light and dark that the birds receive depends upon the point in the laying cycle that the birds have reached. It is also important to know whether or not the light has been above or below 4·5 lux in intensity during their rearing period. If the chicks have been reared in a system where light intensity has been less than 4·5 lux, then a typical lighting system is the 'step down' lighting pattern. For a short period of time (approximately 2–3 days) the lights are left on for 23 hours a day. This is so that the birds are able to locate their food and water. After this the light period is reduced so that at 10 to 20 weeks of age, the birds receive 6–10 hours of light. At

Fig. 5.19 A typical battery unit

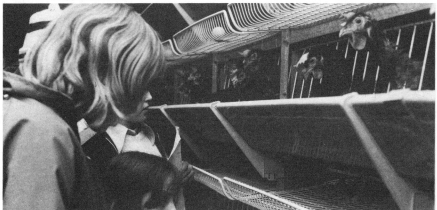

this age, the light period is increased by 20 minutes each week to a maximum of 17 hours. This is then held constant until the birds finish laying.

The chickens inside the laying house may be kept either on a deep litter system or a battery system. Most chickens now, however, are kept in a battery system. In this system the chickens are kept in cages. Each cage is occupied by several chickens so that each chicken has approximately $0.07\,m^2$ of floor space. They must also have sufficient head room to stand up. Food and water can then be supplied along the rows of cages automatically. The cages are generally stacked three high and an 'endless' belt runs between each layer of cages and over rollers at each end. The excreta from the birds falls into the belt and can be readily removed at intervals. Eggs that are laid by the birds run down a sloping floor and out beyond the front of the cages (see Fig. 5.20). This prevents the birds from eating them and makes them easier to collect.

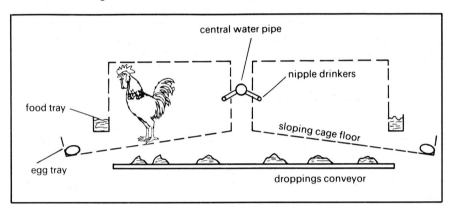

Fig. 5.20 *Side view of bird cages*

The food that is fed to poultry in battery cages is generally in the form of a mash. This ensures that the birds take as long as is practicable to eat their food so that they do not become bored. Boredom in poultry tends to lead to egg-eating and feather-pecking. This in turn might lead to cannibalism. Along with their food the chickens receive soluble calcium grit to ensure a firm shell around the egg. Insoluble flint grit is also fed to assist the bird in its digestion of the food.

Because very large numbers of poultry are kept in confined quarters, the spread of disease through a flock is very rapid. Though high standards of hygiene reduce this risk it is common practice now to include a range of preventative medicines in the food. For instance sulphamethazine is used to control a disease called **coccidiosis** caused by a parasite in the intestine which often leads to high mortality rates. A range of other antibiotics may be included to increase growth rates. Finally, mites and lice cause reduced performance from the birds and pesticides such as Malathion (an organophosphorous compound (see earlier in this chapter)) may be used on the poultry while they are in the laying house.

Some Environmental Effects of Intensive Food Production

Man's attempts to increase his food production have also affected plants and animals in the environment. In order to increase the efficiency of farms, the farms have increased in size. To make it faster to cultivate these large farms, the size of machinery (particularly harvesting machinery) has increased in size. To allow these large machines to be used most effectively, many kilometres of farm hedges have been removed. These hedges offered a habitat to countless numbers of plant and animal species, the most obvious perhaps being birds. The loss of this habitat will be appreciated when it is realized that about 70% of all birds found on farmland require trees and hedges for nesting sites. In addition to this, man has drained marshes, removed scrubland and small copses, and reduced the range of grassland species. All of these measures have reduced the value of farmland to wildlife and so have reduced the number and range of plants and animals found on farms. Also, as described earlier in this chapter, herbicides, insecticides and artificial fertilizers have had an effect on wildlife and their habitats.

Despite the measures to increase food production described in this chapter, large areas of the world (particularly the underdeveloped areas) suffer from a lack of food. Because of this, concern is being expressed about the future levels of food that will be necessary to support the increasing population even in the developed areas of the world. Much work is now being done to find ways of using food sources other than those being used at the moment and of increasing food sources that are not used as much as they might be.

NEW FOOD TECHNOLOGIES

In an attempt to supply sufficient food to his growing population, man has investigated the possibility of using less traditional, and in some cases, totally new food sources. Several things have to be considered when new food technologies are being investigated. These include such features as:

1   Is it more efficient to produce the new food than the traditional food it is to replace?
2   Is it going to be economically possible to produce sufficiently large quantities of the food?
3   Is it perfectly safe to eat?
4   Is the end product palatable and will people eat it?

Some examples of these technologies are outlined below.

Fish Farming

The UK was amongst the first countries to develop a suitable technique for rearing marine fish in 'farms'. However, these techniques have not been fully developed because the UK market demands white fish, in particular cod, which is not reared satisfactorily in farms. Also the number of sites round the coast of Britain that would provide conditions suitable for a sufficiently rapid growth of the fish are relatively few. Most of the developments in the UK are now nearly totally restricted to trout and salmon farming in the sea lochs of Scotland. In these cases protein conversion values approaching 1:1 have been recorded. (This means that if 1 kg of protein is fed, the fish increase in mass by 1 kg). Recently, investigations have been made into using the warm water from the cooling towers of generating stations to make fish grow faster. Most of these investigations, however, have used carp and these are not normally eaten in the UK.

Much more work on marine fish farming is, however, continuing in other countries. Japan has large expanses of brackish water which are sufficiently warm and productive to allow the fish to grow rapidly.

More recently, work has been started to investigate the possibility of harvesting **krill** from the oceans. This is a small shrimp-like animal which it is estimated could yield over 50×10^6 tonnes of edible material per year. A fear that

Fig. 5.21 *Rainbow trout being packed ready for transit*

has been expressed by many environmentalists, however, is that because the krill represent the base of many marine food relationships, man's interference may endanger the welfare of large numbers of marine animals.

The Use of Vegetable Protein

There is great advantage in using vegetable protein in large quantities instead of feeding it to animals and eating the animal protein produced—it automatically reduces the food chain length. As explained in Chapter 3, this will reduce losses of food that occur between the links of a food chain. Most work so far done in this field has involved the conversion of soya bean into a form that is palatable and acceptable as a food to man. Though the means of achieving this aim varies from one manufacturer to another, probably the most successful techniques involve the extraction of material from the bean under conditions of heat and pressure. This produces a rather bulky material that has a 'chewy' texture and contains up to 50% protein. Flavourings are then added to make them palatable. These materials are then referred to as **texturized vegetable proteins** (T.V.P.). Further treatment can produce **protein isolates** that are up to 90% protein, though of course the production costs are considerably higher than the texturized vegetable protein. The protein isolates can be made to taste and look like meat and are often referred to as **meat analogues**.

The Use of Micro-organisms

In principle this involves the growth of yeasts, bacteria or fungi on material such as petroleum products. Agricultural or industrial wastes can also be used. The micro-organisms multiply very rapidly under suitable conditions and are harvested at appropriate times. They must then be treated in a manner which makes them palatable.

At the present time, research is still in progress to develop a satisfactory product that will be acceptable as a food to man. However, yeast has been used for several years as a source of food for animals. These yeasts have been satisfactorily grown and harvested on the waste liquids from pulp and paper mills and also from distilleries. Bacteria have also been grown by I.C.I. (on methanol) and then processed as an animal food. This food is about the same price as fish meal which costs more than soya meal but it is more nutritious.

FOOD PRESERVATION

The period for which foods will keep their quality after harvesting varies but is always limited. Initially, food preservation was designed to extend this period. Though this is still one reason for preservation, other reasons have become increasingly important. Some of these reasons are outlined below.

1   By preserving food, it can be eaten at a time of the year when the fresh food is not available.

2   By preserving food as 'pre-packed' meals, the working housewife is now able to prepare a complete meal in a fraction of the 'normal' time.

3   Preserved foods can be bought in bulk without the fear of the food deteriorating. This can help to keep down the price of food.

Preserving Techniques

All of these techniques are designed either to kill the organisms that spoil food (or to cause the organisms to become inactive), or to destroy the chemicals that cause food to spoil. The organisms concerned are bacteria, yeast and fungi (see Figs. 5.22, 5.23 and 5.24). The chemicals include enzymes naturally present in the food.

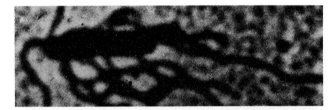

Fig. 5.22   *A food bacterium magnified 5000 times*

Fig. 5.23   *Yeast cells magnified 1600 times*

Fig. 5.24   *A mould magnified 50 times*

1   **Sterilization**—Practically any food can be treated in this way, although of course the food ends up being at least partly cooked. The food is heated to a high temperature and for a long enough period of time to kill the micro-organisms. The sterilized food is then sealed inside a sterile container—usually a glass or metal container (see Fig. 5.25).

Fig. 5.25 *Food cans emerging from a sterilizer.*

2 **Freezing**—By lowering the temperature of the food to about −18°C as rapidly as possible, the micro-organisms are made inactive. In this way they are prevented from spoiling the food. Because the micro-organisms are not dead, great care has to be taken to heat the food thoroughly before it is eaten. If this is not done, as the temperature of the food increases the micro-organisms will increase until they reach harmful numbers. Great care must also be taken to keep the food under suitable conditions when it is in storage.

Fig. 5.26 *Cod steaks on a production line. They go through a batter mix before entering the freezer in the background*

3 **Dehydration**—By removing the water in the food, the micro-organisms are made inactive or are killed.
4 **Pickling**—Food is placed in an acid solution (usually ethanoic acid/vinegar) at a pH that prevents the activity of micro-organisms, or kills them.
5 **Curing**—By adding salt to a food substance, the water is removed from the cells of the food and from the micro-organisms (by osmosis, see Chapter 4). In this way, the micro-organisms are destroyed.
6 **The addition of chemicals**—A range of chemicals may be added to foods to help in preserving them. Some of these may cause reactions in sensitive individuals and some have given general concern. These chemicals include sodium nitrate, benzoic acid and sulphur dioxide.

Food Additives

Often, the processes used to preserve the food causes the food to lose its colour or taste. For this reason, a range of 'flavour enhancers', colourings and sweeteners may be added. Several of these have created concern in the past and some have been removed from the list of permissible additives. For example, monosodium glutamate is added to many savoury foods as a flavour enhancer. Saccharine and cyclamates are two sweeteners which have given cause for concern in the past about their safe use in foods. Different countries seem to be unable to agree about which additives are safe and which are not.

ACTIVITIES

Tests for foodstuffs

1   This experiment is a test for the presence of reducing sugars (e.g. glucose, fructose and maltose) in food.
a) Add 1 spatulaful of the food being tested to a boiling tube containing a 5 cm depth of water.
b) Add one full drop-pipette measure of Benedict's solution and heat to boiling point.
c) If reducing sugars are present, a colour change will take place. If traces of sugar are present, the solution will turn green. More sugar will turn the solution through shades of yellow and eventually to orange. The more orange the solution turns, the more sugar there is present.
2   The presence of non-reducing sugars (e.g. sucrose) can be detected in the following way.
a) Add 1 spatulaful of the food to be tested to a boiling tube containing a 5 cm depth of water.
b) Add 7 drops of 1 molar hydrochloric acid and boil carefully for 1 minute.
c) Neutralize the solution with 1 M sodium hydroxide. (To do this you should add just sufficient sodium hydroxide so that when red litmus paper is placed in the solution it will turn blue.)
d) Add one full drop-pipette measure of Benedict's solution and heat to boiling point.
e) A colour change will indicate the presence of sugar as in experiment 1.
In this test, the non-reducing sugar has been changed to a reducing sugar to make it sensitive to Benedict's solution. If you use a food other than sucrose, you could find out if non-reducing sugars are present by comparing the difference in colour of the 'food solution' after completing experiments 1 and 2 on separate samples of food.
In this case, if experiment 2 shows more sugar to be present than experiment 1 (the solution is more orange) then the food must have contained some non-reducing sugar.
3   There are two techniques you could use to test for the presence of starch; both are given here.
a) Add one drop of iodine in potassium iodide to a piece of the food you are testing. If starch is present then the iodine solution (which is brown in colour) will turn blue-black.
b) Place one spatulaful of the food into a boiling tube containing a 5 cm depth of water. Heat the tube until the water boils.
Pour off the water (decant it) into another tube and add a drop of iodine in potassium iodide to it. If starch is present, the solution will turn blue-black. The deeper the colour, the more starch there is present.
This second technique could be used to compare the amount of starch in

different foods. The first technique would be more difficult to use because iodine solution is so sensitive it will turn a deep blue-black in the presence of even small amounts of starch. The difference in depth of colour would be difficult to detect. With the second technique, the solutions can be diluted until you *can* detect a difference.

4   This experiment is a test for the presence of fat.

a) Place a spatulaful of the food to be tested in a boiling tube containing a 2 cm depth of ethanol.

b) Make a water bath by placing a beaker of water on a tripod and gauze so that it can be heated with a Bunsen burner (see Fig. 5.27).

c) Place your tube of ethanol and food into the water bath and heat the water to 50°C. Be careful—ethanol is inflammable. Heat at 50°C for 2 minutes.

d) Obtain a second tube and half fill it with cold water. Decant the ethanol into the tube of cold water. If fat was present in the food the mixture of water and ethanol will give an **emulsion** (it will look milky). The amount of emulsion (cloudiness) gives an indication of how much fat is present.

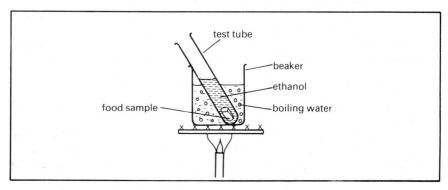

Fig. 5.27   *Heating ethanol in a water bath*

5   To test for the presence of protein:

a) Add one spatulaful of the food to be tested to a boiling tube containing a 3 cm depth of 10% sodium hydroxide solution. (Do *not* get this solution on your skin. Wash it off immediately if you do.)

b) Add a few drops of 5% copper sulphate solution until you can detect a pale blue colour in the solution.

c) Warm the solution gently over a Bunsen burner.

If protein is present, the solution will turn pink or violet. The exact colour depends upon the type of protein that is present.

6   Try testing for the amount of vitamin C (ascorbic acid) in a food. Pale-coloured fruit juices or cordial drinks are suitable for the technique given here.

a) Place 1 cm^3 of DCPIP (phenol-indo-2:6 dichlorophenol) solution into a test tube without shaking (any disturbance will affect the result).

b) Using a syringe or pipette of 1 cm^3 capacity, measure how much test solution you have to add to the DCPIP solution to remove its colour. An end result is achieved once the initial colour changes.

c) Repeat this procedure using fresh DCPIP solution and a solution of ascorbic acid (Vitamin C) of known strength.

d) Calculate the amount of vitamin C in your food in the following way. Suppose 0·6 cm^3 of test solution decolorizes the DCPIP and suppose that 0·3 cm^3 of ascorbic acid solution did the same. The test solution is then 0·3/0·6 times as concentrated as the ascorbic acid solution. If the ascorbic acid solution contains 1 mg cm^{-3}, then the test solution contains:

$$\frac{0\cdot3}{0\cdot6}\times1=0\cdot5\,\mathrm{mg\,cm^{-3}}.$$

7 An important aspect of diets in the UK and other developed countries is the amount of fat that is eaten. It is thought that if too much fat is eaten, then a substance called **cholesterol** may build up in the arteries and cause **thrombosis**. A thrombosis is a blood clot and if such a clot gets trapped in the coronary artery the blood supply to the heart muscle is impeded and the heart 'packs up'. It is thought that eating **unsaturated** fats is less likely to cause this than eating **saturated** fats. Saturated fats are most likely to be found in animal fats, unsaturated fats are more commonly found in vegetable oil and fats. The test given below indicates the amount of unsaturated fats present in a food. Suitable foods would be lard and cooking oil.

a) Place 1 g of food in a boiling tube containing a 2 cm depth of ethanol. *Carefully* heat the ethanol for 2 minutes at a temperature of 50°C in a water bath. (Experiment 4 suggests how you can set up a water bath).

b) Pour a solution of iodine in potassium iodide into a burette.

c) Allow the iodine solution to run into the ethanol 0·1 cm³ at a time until a permanent brown/yellow colour appears.

If a lot of iodine is required, the food contains a lot of unsaturated fats. If only a little iodine solution is needed, the food contains very little unsaturated fat.

Processed foods

This next experiment allows you to investigate some of the features and some of the problems concerning 'processed' foods.

8 It has been suggested that the techniques used to process certain foods may remove or alter certain classes of foodstuffs present in the food. Design your own experiments to compare the amounts of sugar, fat and starch in fresh and processed food. (To be fair, each food should be prepared to the point where it would be ready to be eaten.) Use the techniques described in experiments 1–4. Suitable foods include potatoes and milk. These can be obtained in fresh and processed form all the year round.

Food production

Whenever a crop is being considered for its suitability in an area, it is essential to take topography, climate and *soil* into account.

9 Attempt a mechanical analysis of soil.

a) Obtain a sample of soil and dry it in an oven.

b) Allow the soil to pass through a tier of sieves having mesh sizes 0·002 mm, 0·2 mm and 2 mm.

c) Weigh the material that collects in each of the sieves.

d) Calculate the mass of soil in each sieve as a percentage of the total mass of soil used. Use the formula:

$$\frac{\text{mass of soil in sieve}}{\text{total mass of soil}} \times \frac{100}{1}$$

The soil will have been divided into its four major groups: gravel (2–10 mm); sand (0·2–2 mm); silt (0·002–0·2 mm); and clay (less than 0·002 mm)—see Fig. 5.28.

Compare your results with Table 5.5 and try to classify your soil as sandy, clay or loam.

If you do not have access to a suitable set of sieves, you can try another, rather less satisfactory technique.

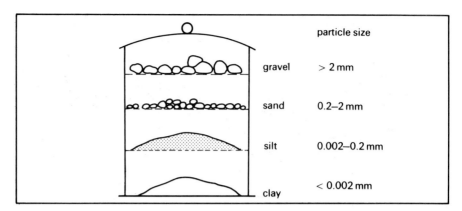

Fig. 5.28 *A mechanical analysis of soil involves separating the fractions in a tower of sieves*

a) Take 40 cm³ of oven-dried soil and add it to 60 cm³ of water in a measuring cylinder.
b) Shake the cylinder so that the soil and water are fully mixed up. Allow the mixture to settle.
   The soil will separate into layers that can be separated by their appearance into clay/silt and sand/gravel. Assume that the sand/gravel is a layer that contains individual particles that can easily be distinguished by the naked eye. The remainder is clay/slit.
c) You can calculate the percentage of each layer from the formula:

$$\frac{\text{volume of particular layer}}{\text{total volume of soil}} \times \frac{100}{1}$$

Description	Typical composition (%)		
	Sand and gravel	Silt	Clay
sand	80	10	10
loam	50	25	25
clay	30	20	50

Table 5.5 *Results obtained from a mechanical analysis of soil.*

Classify your soil using the chart given above.
10 Measure the organic content of soil.
a) Place 20 g of oven-dried soil into a tin lid.
b) Heat the soil strongly for 10 minutes using two Bunsen burners. Stir the soil occasionally so that when you finish the soil looks a uniform black colour. There should be no plant stems, etc. visible when you finish. It may be necessary to heat the soil from above and below (Fig. 5.29).
c) Allow the soil to cool and then re-weigh it.
d) The loss in weight is equal to the amount of organic matter that was originally present in the soil. Calculate the percentage of organic matter from the formula:

$$\frac{\text{mass of organic material}}{\text{original mass of soil}} \times \frac{100}{1}$$

A good agricultural soil should contain about 10% of organic matter.

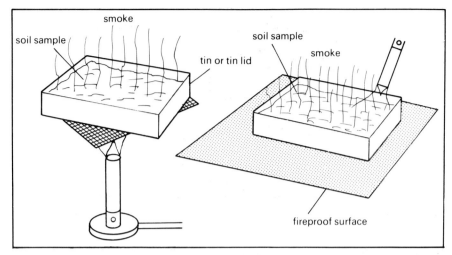

Fig. 5.29 *Burning off the organic matter from soil requires a great deal of heat*

11   Measure the pH (level of acidity) of some soil. To do this you can either use a commercially produced test kit and follow their instructions or use the techniques described below.

a) Place a 1·5 cm depth of soil in a test tube and put a small covering (1–2 mm) of barium sulphate on the surface of the soil.

b) Add distilled water to within 1·5 cm of the top of the tube.

c) Add one full teat pipette measure of universal indicator.

d) Shake the mixture and allow it to settle.

e) Note the colour and compare it with the colours on a universal indicator colour chart. Note its pH and whether it is neutral, acidic or alkaline. (If you fail to get a colour after you have allowed the mixture to settle in your tube, add another full pipette measure of universal indicator.)

The pH of a good soil should be between 6·5 and 7·0.

To complete your analysis of soil you should really measure the plant nutrients available. To do this, however, you must have access to a commercially produced kit.

12   Use the results of your soil analysis to answer the following questions.

a) Is your soil likely to suffer from water-logging in winter or from drying out in summer? Give a reason. If you are unable to answer this question try experiment 8 in Chapter 4.

b) Will your soil benefit from the addition of lime? Give a reason.

c) Is your soil likely to be lacking in nutrients? Give a reason.

d) Is your soil likely to warm up early in the spring, or is it likely to be a 'late' soil? Give a reason.

e) Make any other comments about your soil which you think are relevant.

Plant production

13   Investigate the effect of availability of carbon dioxide on plant growth. Plant growth depends upon photosynthesis and this process requires carbon dioxide. By increasing carbon dioxide availability it might be possible to increase plant growth.

This experiment uses water plants (either *Elodea* or *Nitella*) because these are convenient.

A measure of the rate of photosynthesis can be obtained by assuming it is proportional to the rate at which the plants produce bubbles. The gas is mainly oxygen produced as a by-product of the process of photosynthesis.

a) Obtain eight 10 cm lengths of Nitella or Elodea and place them in a litre beaker or a small tank.
b) Fill the beaker with water and place a filter funnel over the material. The neck of the funnel should be under the surface of the water. Arrange for a lamp to illuminate the plant to ensure that there is sufficient light for an increase in the rate of photosynthesis. It is best to leave the plants under these conditions for a few hours to allow them to settle down.
c) It is now necessary to arrange for a test tube or burette to be filled with water and inverted over the neck of the filter funnel. As bubbles are produced by the plant, they will pass up the tube. In doing so they will displace the water. The bubbles can be counted or estimated, or the amount of gas that collects can be measured (see Fig. 5.30). Measure the rate of gas produced over a period of (say) 5 minutes.

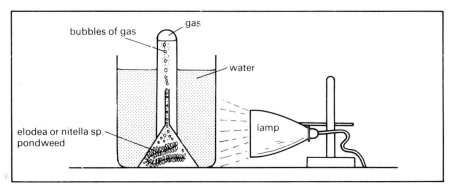

Fig. 5.30 *Apparatus to investigate the effect of availability of carbon dioxide on plant growth.*

d) Add 10 cm³ of a saturated solution of sodium bicarbonate to the water and stir. (The plant will be able to obtain carbon dioxide from the sodium bicarbonate in solution.)
e) Measure the rate of gas produced over a further period of 5 minutes. Repeat this until you have obtained 4 or 5 readings for different amounts of carbon dioxide (sodium bicarbonate).
f) Write a conclusion to include the effect that increasing amounts of carbon dioxide have on the rate of photosynthesis.
g) Write a few sentences about how practicable it would be to increase the amount of carbon dioxide in horticultural systems (including greehouses).
14 Investigate the availability of light by varying light intensity.
Photosynthesis is dependent upon light and so by varying light intensity it might be possible to vary photosynthesis.
You should be able to design your own experiment by using the information and suggestions given in the experiment above. (This experiment often works better if some sodium bicarbonate is added to the water first. This ensures that there is sufficient carbon dioxide to allow for an increase in the rate of photosynthesis.)
15 Choose one of the following investigations and design your own method.
You should not need a piece of ground any larger than about 2 m × 2 m.
a) Investigate the effect of plant density on yield.
b) Investigate the effect of different levels of fertilizer on yield. (**Hint:** it will make it less complicated to choose a 'complete' food such as phostrogen.)
c) Investigate the effect of mixed (inter) cropping on yield. (**Hint:** sow a rapidly maturing crop such as beet or lettuce between rows of a crop such as broad beans. Compare the yield of these plants with plants grown on their own.)

Raw Materials 6

The raw materials covered in this chapter can be placed into two major groups. These are organic raw materials and inorganic raw materials. The group of inorganic raw materials may be further divided into metals and non-metals.

ORGANIC RAW MATERIALS

This group of materials really includes all the substances used by man that are produced from living plants and animals. Some examples of materials in this group include cotton, wool, linen, silk, leather and timber. Strictly speaking, of course, food is also an organic raw material but is considered separately in Chapter 5.

Unlike the inorganic raw materials, this group of substances is **renewable**. In other words, provided we manage the materials in a sensible manner, we should never run out of them. This particular feature of organic materials enables us to use a **sustainable yield** policy in our management of them. This term simply means that each year we should harvest only as much of the material as can be replaced annually.

Of the materials listed in this group wool, linen and timber are considered in this chapter. These three are chosen because they are produced within the UK. The other materials listed (excepting leather) are not produced within the UK and so have to be imported.

Wool

The main producers of sheep for wool are Australia and South Africa. The breed of sheep in these countries which produces the finest wool is the Merino breed. New Zealand and some areas of Europe (including the UK) produce

Fig. 6.1   *Most sheep in the UK are dual purpose animals—their wool is marketed and they can also be sold for meat*

Fig. 6.2 Carding wool

Fig. 6.3 Spinning yarn in a wool mill

wool of coarser texture from breeds such as the Romney. There has been a move in the UK and other European countries to rear breeds of sheep that produce a marketable wool and which can also be sold for meat.

The wool is removed from the sheep once or twice a year. The soiled edges are removed and the fleeces are then sorted according to quality. The quality depends upon the breed and age of the sheep—the younger the sheep the finer the wool. Once the wool has been graded it is baled and transported to a wool mill. The first process in the mill is to **scour** the wool. This involves washing the wool in troughs of soapy, alkaline solution. The wool passes through several troughs, each being a weaker concentration than the one before it. This process removes all the dirt and grease from the wool. The next process, called **carbonizing**, involves treating the wool with acids and passing it through rollers. This removes materials such as straw and other plant materials. The cleaned wool is then passed through a **carding** process (see Fig. 6.2). The wool passes over and round rollers which are covered with sharp steel wires. This separates the fibres and makes them lie straight so that they are ready for **spinning** (see Fig. 6.3) into yarn and **weaving** (see Fig. 6.4) into fabric.

Fig. 6.4 Weaving machines

Properties of wool

Wool is a material that is very elastic. This means it can be stretched but will return to its original length. This elasticity helps to give strength to the material. Because it is able to trap air in its structure, it is a very warm material. Finally, it is capable of absorbing up to one third of its own weight in water. These properties are apparent in the uses of wool, some of which include clothing, bedding and carpeting.

Linen

This is a material that is made from flax, a crop which, in the UK, is particularly associated with Northern Ireland. Flax is an annual plant which, to obtain the best quality linen fibre, is harvested shortly before its seeds mature. The linen fibres extend the length of the stalk from the flowering head to the roots. Because of this the plant is generally pulled up by the roots so that useful fibre is not left as stubble. (The seed of the plant can be pressed to produce linseed oil, the remains can be used as a cattle food.)

The harvested plants are stacked and dried and are then passed through a process called **rippling**. This removes the seeds from the stalks. Following this process, the long fibres are extracted from the stalk by a process called **retting**. The stalks are allowed to decompose in water by the action of bacteria. The bacteria decompose material in the stalk other than the 'linen fibre' and, once a suitable stage of decomposition has been reached, these fibres can be separated mechanically. The separation of fibres is known as **scutching** and takes place on a machine that combs and beats the stalks. In this way impurities are removed with minimum damage to the long 'linen fibre'. The fibres are also made to lie fairly parallel to one another.

After the scutching process, the long fibres (called **flax line**) and the short fibres (called **flax tow**) are separated. The tow is used to make coarse material while the line is used to make high quality linen. Further processes, similar to the carding process with wool, make the fibres as straight as possible and work them into thin layers so that they can finally be spun into yarn and woven into fabric.

Properties of linen

Linen is very tough and durable as can be seen from the fact that Egyptian mummies are found wrapped in linen that is still quite strong. It is resistant to sunlight and heat and has an attractive lustre when woven. Linen is frequently used for such things as tea-cloths and table-cloths.

Fig. 6.5 *Egyptian cat mummy wrapped in linen bandages*

Timber

Though much of our timber is imported, since 1919 the Forestry Commission has been set the task of producing as much of our own timber as is possible.

Timber is divided into two major groups, **hardwoods** and **softwoods**. Generally, these names describe the type of wood very well—hardwoods are generally of a harder texture and are more difficult to work than the softwoods. There are some exceptions to this, however, for instance balsa is a hardwood.

These two different types of wood typically come from two distinctly different types of tree. The hardwoods usually come from deciduous trees—those trees that generally shed their leaves during the winter season. The softwoods usually come from coniferous trees—those trees that generally keep their leaves all year and have cones rather than flowers. The leaves are typically narrow or needle shaped.

Though the hardwoods include the densest, strongest and most durable timbers, some 75% of all timber used in the UK is softwood. This is the reason why up to 90% of the trees now planted by the Forestry Commission are softwoods. This policy, however, is criticized by many people and these criticisms are discussed in Chapter 7.

Timber may be used either in its solid, more or less unaltered form, or as a manufactured wood such as plywood, or as a paper product.

Properties of solid and manufactured wood

Whether or not softwoods or hardwoods are used for the purposes mentioned below depends upon the specific use in question. Nevertheless, some general properties of wood are as follows:

1　It is generally a good insulator and, when heated or cooled, does not expand or contract very greatly. Special joints are therefore not required even when changes in temperature are expected.

2　Because wood is fairly impermeable and has a high cellulose content, it is usually quite resistant to chemicals. Compared with metals, the resistance of wood to alkalis and weak acids is good.

Fig. 6.6 Sitka Spruce—the most numerous tree planted by the Forestry Commission

Fig. 6.7 *Machine stress grading of timber*

3   Wood has a high strength: weight ratio. This means that weight-for-weight, wood is stronger than many other materials.

Some general uses of different timbers are outlined below.

Structural uses—Douglas fir, Scots pine, European spruce

Joinery—ash, birch, sycamore, beech, oak, Scots pine, Douglas fir

Furniture—ash, birch, beech, oak, pine

Veneers—ash, birch, beech, oak, Douglas fir.

(A **veneer** is a very thin sheet of wood that is usually glued onto the surface of a 'manufactured board'.)

Manufactured board—in general, softwoods are very much preferred for this use though the type of softwood is usually not important.

Fig. 6.8   *The structural elements of the walls of this building are of prefabricated plywood panels; the building is timber-clad*

Manufactured boards include plywood, blockboard and hardboard. Plywood is made up of 'plies' and adhesives. The plies are peeled off a log that has been placed in hot water and then rotated against a sharp blade. The plies are bound together with the adhesive. This material is usually stronger and stiffer than solid timber. Blockboard is made of a solid core consisting of blocks of wood up to 2·5cm wide. The blocks are then covered with a veneer on each side. This material is useful for large, rigid panels. Hardboard is made from wood fibres and is often used in wall and ceiling linings and door faces.

The changes in moisture content of wood during use which would cause the wood to contract and perhaps distort are controlled in several ways.

1 **Impregnating** the timber with a solution of resin. This technique is restricted to small items such as knife handles.

2 **Surface coating** the timber with one of several preparations including aluminium-based primers (paints) and epoxy resin varnish.

3 **Seasoning**, which involves the controlled reduction of moisture content to a level suited to its final use. This process not only prevents uncontrolled shrinkage but also:

a) increases resistance to decay by fungi (less than 20% moisture prevents fungal decay)

b) increases its strength

c) improves heat insulation

d) makes it more suitable for impregnating, painting and glueing.

The two means of seasoning are **air seasoning** and **kiln seasoning**. Air seasoning works by protecting timber from rain, raising it off the floor and allowing for the free circulation of air. In the UK 17–23% moisture can be obtained by this method and wood seasoned in this way is suitable for rafters and joists. Kiln seasoning is necessary for all internal uses including joinery and furniture. The wood is heat-treated until its moisture content is reduced to as little as 8% (see Fig. 6.9).

Fig. 6.9 Drying timber in a kiln

4 **Preserving** the timber by treating it with a range of chemicals designed to give it protection from attack by fungi and insects. The preservatives that can be used include creosote (made from coal tar), copper naphthanate and zinc naphthanate. The methods of applying preservatives include:

a) **Brushing** over the surface—The liquid should flood the surface so that the timber absorbs as much as possible. Treatment needs repeating every 2–3 years.

Fig. 6.10 Cylinders for pressure impregnation of timber

b) **Dipping** and **steeping**—Dipping involves submersing the timber in preservative for a short period (up to 10 minutes) whereas steeping involves submersing the timber for several days. This allows deep penetration of permeable timbers and is suitable for timbers in contact with the ground. Fencing posts, for instance, are steeped in preservative at 80–90°C for maximum effect. The timber is kept in the preservative whilst it cools down as more preservative enters the wood during the cooling down period than whilst it is in the hot creosote.

c) **Pressure impregnation** (see Fig. 6.10)—This is generally considered essential for timbers in permanent contact with the ground such as telegraph poles. The timber may or may not be placed in a vacuum before the preservative is forced in.

Paper

Most paper is made from softwood trees, and of these, spruce is the main species. Though there are many types and qualities of paper, they are all made of cellulose fibres. (The first papers were made from the cellulose fibres present in cotton and linen.)

The bark is first removed from the trees and then the tree is treated in one of two ways.

1 The tree is forced against a grinding wheel and sprayed with water.

2 The wood is placed in a mixture of chemicals that will dissolve material other than the cellulose. The cellulose fibres float to the top for removal.

The material produced by the first process is called **mechanical** wood pulp and the material produced by the second technique is called **chemical** wood pulp. The best paper contains the highest proportion of chemical pulp.

The pulp is then mixed with water and poured onto a moving wire frame. The water drains away and the fibres that remain are transferred to a moving felt 'belt'. The web of fibres then passes round heated rollers so that the fibres are dried and pressed together to form the paper (see Fig. 6.11). China clay may be added to fill in the spaces between the fibres to give a smooth paper, and size may be added to make the paper water repellant.

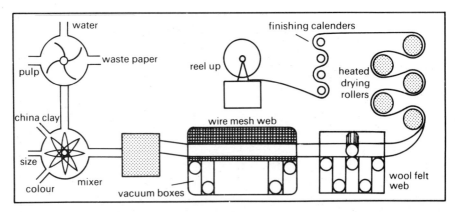

Fig. 6.11 *Paper manufacturing process*

The Environmental Effects of Producing Organic Renewable Resources

The environmental effects of producing wool and linen are minimal, though of course, local conflicts may arise between using land for these purposes and for other purposes. The environmental problems that result from forestry operations are discussed fully in Chapter 7 but include a reduction in the range of species of plant and animal in the environment. Many areas of forest also look unnatural because they have been planted with little thought to the natural land contours.

The conversion of these organic materials into the finished products may create environmental problems. The major problems are likely to be linked with the release of water used during the processes. This water may contain caustic or other toxic materials or may contain organic material that could eventually lead to a reduction in dissolved oxygen in rivers (see Chapter 4). The people involved in these processes naturally take great care to ensure that the release of these materials is kept to a minimum.

INORGANIC RAW MATERIALS

This is a very large group of materials including metals, building stone, salt, china clay, potassium and sulphur. In a book of this type it is only possible to look at a small sample of these materials. However, because they are all formed as part of the rock cycle (see Fig. 6.12) the next section is common to them all. Three parts of the rock cycle are of particular importance. These are volcanic activity, the construction and destruction of crustal plates and erosion and deposition.

Volcanic Activity

Whenever the Earth's crust is weak, there is the possibility that pressures present beneath the crust will break through it. When these pressures are released, hot gases and fluids (**magma**) that cause the pressure are often forced out through the crust and are visible as volcanoes. When these gases and fluids escape into the atmosphere (or come sufficiently close to it) they cool down and solidify. The solids that form from the solidified gases and magma are known as **igneous rocks** (see Fig. 6.13 and Fig. 6.14).

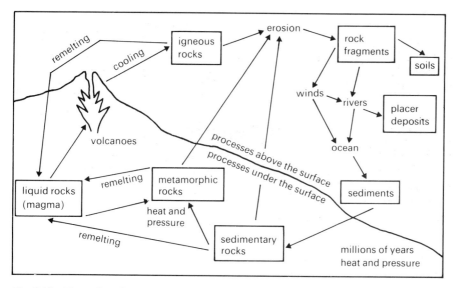

Fig. 6.12 *The rock cycle*

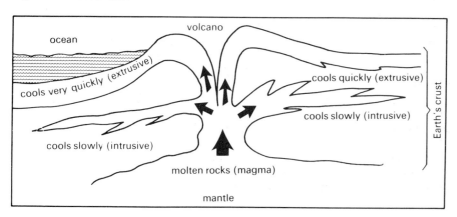

Fig. 6.13 *The formation of igneous rocks from volcanoes*

Fig. 6.14 *A volcanic plug—Wase Rock, Nigeria*

Fig. 6.15 *Granite is an instrusive igneous rock*

Two fairly distinct groups of igneous rocks can be formed. These are **intrusive** igneous rocks and **extrusive** igneous rocks. Intrusive rocks are formed when the gases and magma are only forced part of the way through the crust. When this happens the material cools slowly and gives the atoms that make up the material time to move together to make relatively large crystalline shapes. Granite is an example of this type of rock.

Extrusive rocks are formed when the gases and magma are forced through the Earth's crust into the atmosphere or the sea. This causes the material to cool very quickly so that there is little or no time for crystals to form before the material solidifies. Basalt is an example of an extrusive rock with relatively small crystals and obsidian is an extrusive rock that has cooled so quickly that no crystals appear to have formed (this type of rock is generally glassy in appearance).

Fig. 6.16 *The Giant's Causeway in Northern Ireland is composed of basalt*

The Construction and Destruction of Crustal Plates

It is now accepted that the Earth's crust is made up of a series of large pieces or **plates** (see Fig. 6.17). These plates are free to move across the Earth in different

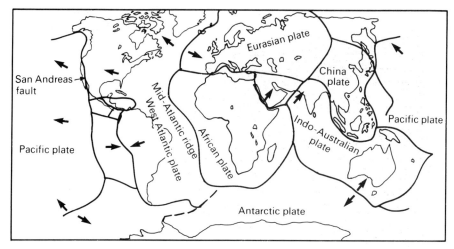

Fig. 6.17 *Continental and oceanic plates of the world*

directions. Because of this movement, we can see that two things must be happening.

Firstly, where two plates are moving in opposite directions from each other, material must come from below the Earth's crust to fill in the space that is formed. If this were not the case, there would be a large number of great big holes between each pair of plates that are moving apart! The material that comes into the gap is made up of the same substances as the magma that comes from volcanoes. When it cools down it forms new edges to each of the two plates. Because new edges to the plates are being made in these areas, they are called **constructive plate margins** (see Fig. 6.18) e.g. the Mid-Atlantic ridge. Volcanoes may occur close to the plate margins or actually be a part of the plate margin (as in Iceland).

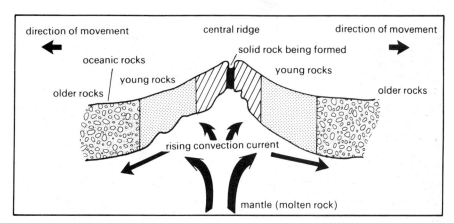

Fig. 6.18 *A constructive plate margin—material from the mantle fills the space left as the plates are forced apart by the rising convection current*

Secondly, where two plates are moving towards one another their edges collide. This tends to cause the edges to buckle both upwards and downwards so that the plate edges are destroyed. These areas are called **destructive plate margins** (see Fig. 6.19), e.g. the Andes and Himalayan mountain chains. Where this activity takes place, fractures occur in the crust which allow magma to be forced out into the atmosphere (as volcanoes). The magma then cools to form

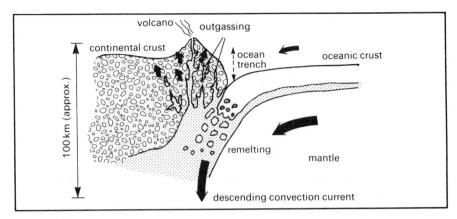

Fig. 6.19 *A destructive plate margin*

rocks. Both destructive and constructive plate margins can often be identified from surface features. Both processes give rise to volcanoes, earthquakes and mountain-building activities such as the buckling of the Earth's crust.

Fig. 6.20 *Volcanic ash on a town, Iceland*

Fig. 6.21 *Earthquake damage in Italy*

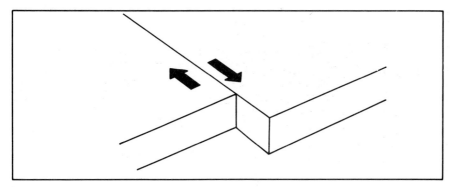

Fig. 6.22 *A sliding plate margin*

Some plates, such as those found along the San Andreas fault slide past one another and are neither destructive nor constructive (see Fig. 6.22). Earthquakes are commonly associated with these plates though volcanoes are not.

It must be understood that where plate margins are being made and destroyed, and where volcanoes are active there will be a great deal of heat and presssure. This heat and pressure is often sufficient to cause any sedimentary rocks (see below) in the area to change their form. This change is called **metamorphism** and the rocks that are formed are called **metamorphic rocks.** Examples of metamorphic rocks that have changed from sedimentary rocks are: marble from limestone, slate from shale, diamonds or graphite from coal.

Erosion and Deposition

Once rocks have been formed and are exposed to the weather they are likely to be worn away. Several processes may cause this to happen. Some of the major processes are discussed below.

1   When water enters cracks in rocks it may become frozen and turn to ice. As the water changes from liquid to solid it expands. As it does so, sufficient pressure is often present to fracture the rock. Pieces of rock weighing tens or hundreds of kilograms may be broken from mountains in this way. As these pieces fall, so they will be broken into smaller pieces and will be more easily worn away by other processes.

Fig. 6.23 *In this rock formation hard sandstone overlies softer sandstone. Can you see the effects of erosion?*

Fig. 6.24 *Freeze-thaw action formed these screes at Lake Wastwater in the Lake District*

2 When wind blows sufficiently strongly it may carry small particles of rock (grit and sand) in it. These particles are blown against other rocks and slowly wear them away. Sandstone, being soft, is particularly likely to be eroded in this way.

3 Rainwater is often slightly acidic (see Chapter 2) and is able to dissolve the rock material. Whenever the water evaporates it will leave behind the dissolved material as a solid.

4 In areas where temperatures change very quickly over a large range, the change in temperature may cause rocks to fracture. This happens when the different materials that make up the rock expand and contract at different rates.

5 Moving water such as rivers often carries material in suspension. This may be sufficient to wear away other rocks in the side and bottom of the river. Very fast moving water will even roll boulders along.

The material that has been worn away from rocks in the above ways may be carried many kilometres from the 'parent' rock, but will eventually be deposited. The deposited material may collect until it is tens or hundreds of metres thick. When this happens, the pressure of the material (together with natural 'glues' that are present) causes the particles to stick together to form rock. Rocks formed in this way are called **sedimentary rocks**. Examples are sandstone, mudstone and shale. Limestone is a sedimentary rock but is made from the shells and skeletal remains of sea creatures. When these creatures die their shells fall to the bottom of the sea. If a sufficient depth of them builds up, they may be crushed together to form rock.

During the process of rock formation, mineral ores may also be formed. Ores are bodies of rock which contain sufficient metal to make it worthwhile to extract it. These ores may be linked to each of the processes in the rock cycle.

Igneous Processes

One type of ore that is linked with igneous processes is present in **magmatic deposits**. In this case, metals that are present in solution in the magma may form solid crystals before the rest of the material present does so. When this happens, the metal material may sink down through the rest of the magma and may accumulate at its base. Another way for magmatic deposits to form is when the metals combine with sulphur. The sulphur compounds produced form globules that will not mix with the rest of the magma and so they separate out. Magnetite is an oxide of iron (Fe_3O_4) which is formed in the first of these ways and sulphides of copper are often formed by the second process.

A second type of ore linked with igneous processes is found in **hydrothermal deposits** (see Fig. 6.25). These deposits are the most common and most important to man. Examples include magnetite (Fe_3O_4), chalcopyrite ($CuFeS_2$) and galena (PbS). Hydrothermal ore deposits are thought to have been formed by hot solutions entering cracks or faults in the rocks and the materials dissolved in the solution crystallizing out.

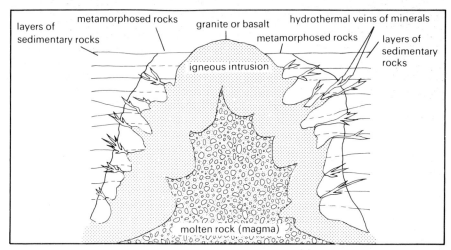

Fig. 6.25   *The formation of metasomatic and hydrothermal deposits*

Metamorphic Processes

Occasionally, when the temperatures and pressures in the magma are sufficient to cause metamorphic processes in rocks, **metasomatic deposits** may be formed. The hot liquids and gases present in the magma may react with some of the materials present in the original rock to form small, but rich, deposits of ore. Magnetite (Fe_3O_4) and haematite (Fe_2O_3) may be formed in this way as well as galena (PbS) and native copper.

Sedimentary Processes

These processes are important in the formation of iron, copper, lead, aluminium and other metal deposits. One way in which these processes are important is during the precipitation of material present in solution. Though the precise means of formation is unknown, it is thought that the materials were originally present in ancient seas. Something then happened to change conditions so that the material was precipitated out. Examples of this type of formation include haematite, magnetite, galena and chalcopyrite.

Another form of sedimentary deposit is the **placer deposit**. This may occur when water erodes and transports materials in suspension. The material is then deposited when the water speed is reduced (see Fig. 6.26). Gold is the metal most associated with this process, though some 50% of the world's tin (cassiterite, SnO_2) comes from placer deposits.

Residual deposits are also formed from sedimentary processes. In conditions of high rainfall and high temperature most minerals will dissolve in rainwater. Very often the least soluble materials will be left when all the other materials have been removed. The most important ore formed in this way is the

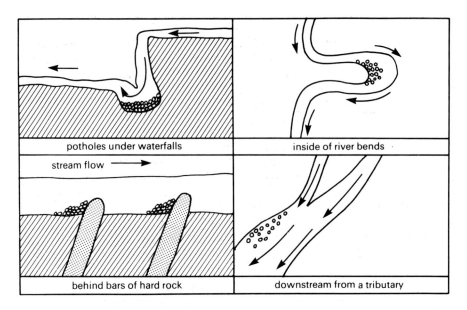

Fig. 6.26 *Sites of placer deposits. Minerals in suspension will tend to be deposited in places where the water speed is reduced*

aluminium ore called bauxite ($Al_2O_3.3H_2O$). The conditions that are most likely to lead to the formation of these deposits are found in the tropics. The soils that remain after everything but the aluminium (and often iron) has been removed are called **laterites** (see Fig. 6.27).

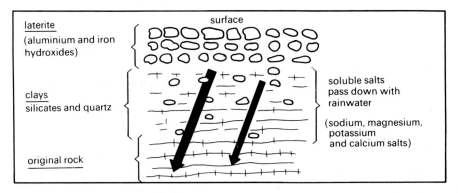

Fig. 6.27 *The formation of a laterite soil*

A final sedimentary process is that which leads to **secondary enrichment**. In this case, water moves down through the rocks and dissolves certain of the minerals. These may be precipitated lower in the rocks and become more concentrated. Chalcocite (Cu_2S) is an example of this process. Table 6.1 summarizes the modes of formation of the main ores of some major metals.

A number of materials such as salt and potassium are also of sedimentary origin. These materials are dissolved from rocks by flowing water and eventually enter the sea in solution. During the Earth's history many of these seas have evaporated. When conditions have been suitable, salt (sodium chloride, NaCl) and potassium (as potassium chloride, KCl; or potassium nitrate, KNO_3) have been deposited. These deposits are known as **evaporite deposits** (see Fig. 6.28).

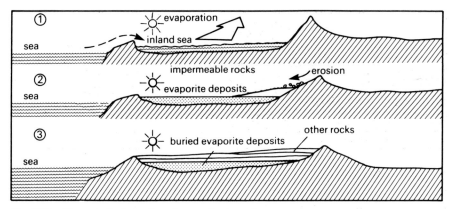

Fig. 6.28 *Stages in the formation of evaporite deposits*

Metal	Ore	Comments
iron	haematite (Fe_2O_3) magnetite (Fe_3O_4) siderite ($FeCo_3$) limonite ($Fe_2O_3H_2O$)	All major deposits are of *sedimentary* origin. However, hydrothermal, magmatic and metasomatic deposits are all possible
aluminium	bauxite ($Al_2O_3.3H_2O$)	These ores are formed as *residual* (or secondary) deposits in laterite soils
copper	chalcopyrite ($CuFeS_2$)	Most of the world's production is now from hydrothermal deposits, though there is still a lot produced from sedimentary deposits
	native copper (Cu)	Hydrothermal and metasomatic deposits
	chalcocite (Cu_2S)	Secondary deposits by descending water
tin	cassiterite (S_nO_2)	About half of the world's supply is from placer deposits. Magmatic deposits are the most important primary deposits
lead	galena (PbS)	Most lead is obtained from hydrothermal and metasomatic deposits though sedimentary deposits are becoming important

Table 6.1 *Modes of occurence of metal ores.*

Selecting Deposits for Exploitation

Once a deposit has been located, a decision has to be made as to whether or not it is worth extracting. The decision will be based upon a lot of factors. Some of the main ones are discussed below.

1 Size of deposit—It is important to decide whether there is likely to be enough material to make money. It is necessary to be able to sell enough material to make it worthwhile to extract.

2   Whether the deposit is deep or shallow—This will help to determine whether it will be possible to use open-cast techniques or deep mining. Building stone is most often extracted by open-pit techniques (or quarrying), but metal ores are frequently extracted in either way.

3   In the case of metal ores, the grade of ore present is obviously of very great importance. High grade ores are those that contain a high proportion of useful metal. Low grade ores contain a low proportion of useful metal. The grade of ore will help to determine how much metal will eventually be available. It will also determine the techniques and costs involved in the refining processes (these are the processes that are necessary to extract the useful material from the waste).

Open-cast techniques can be used with much lower grade ores than deep pit methods. It is also possible to extract nearly all of the ore present. However, it is likely that only about 85% of the useful material will be extracted from the ore. For deep mining, a higher grade ore is necessary to make it worthwhile constructing the mine. Only some 75% of the ore is likely to be extracted but up to 90% of the useful material will be obtained from it.

The final amount of useful material is likely to be higher in open-cast mines than in deep mines. However, the amount of waste produced by the open-pit mine is likely to be two or three times as great as that produced by deep mines. Many of the environmental problems caused by these two methods of mining are dealt with in Chapter 2. Other problems that are specific to different materials are discussed under each relevant section.

BUILDING STONES

The major stones in this category include granite, marble, slate, limestone, sand and gravel.

Stone tends to be relatively costly as a building material (with the exception of sand and gravel) because of the care that is needed during quarrying. The best stones are very durable, however, though damage can occur from atmospheric pollution, frost and from alternate wetting and drying.

The stone is obtained by blasting. Care has to be taken at this stage to prevent the rock from shattering. After blasting, the rock is broken into suitable sizes by hand. A number of holes are drilled into the rock and then a steel wedge is driven into each hole using a hammer. The wedges must be knocked evenly to prevent any uneven strain on the rock. This would cause the rock to split in the wrong places. After splitting, the rock may be machine-sawn before final finishing takes place. This finishing may consist of polishing or sand-blasting. The final finishing will also increase the final cost of the material.

Granites

Different granites vary greatly in colour, texture and mineral composition. They are very dense and hard, and this makes them expensive to quarry, cut and finish. Their extremely hard texture means that they are very resistant to abrasions and knocks, making the material very suitable for kerbstones (though it is now being replaced by concrete), jetties and steps. Although expensive to polish, it is possible to obtain a glass-like finish with granite. This makes it very suitable for external wall cladding where appearance is important. Granites are also used as coarse aggregates for concrete. The main sources of granite in the UK are in Scotland, Cornwall and the Lake District.

Marble

This rock, though resulting from the metamorphism of limestone, includes a range of other materials that are also associated with the original limestone. These other materials, including clay and iron oxide, create a range of colours in the rock.

Marble is similar to granite in that it is very dense, very hard, resists abrasions and can be highly polished. However, its uses are mainly internal because it loses its polish when it is exposed to the atmosphere. It is an expensive rock and so it is often used either as a cladding or in decorative work. As a cladding it is used as a thin layer of material about 2–2·5 cm thick fastened to another surface. In decorative work it is used for columns, balustrades, staircases, hearths and fireplaces. It is used a lot in churches for alters and pulpits and for counter tops in shops. It is also used as a sculpturing material. There is little high quality marble in the UK, most of it being imported from Norway, Sweden, Belgium, Italy and France.

Slate

Slate is also very expensive because of the skill involved in splitting the pieces of slate to the required thickness and because there tends to be a lot waste. The splitting is still done by skilled workers using a hammer and chisel. The best slate is one of the most durable of all building materials and can be found in colours ranging from grey to black through blue, green and brown. Though roofing slates are being replaced by tiles, slate is still used in flooring, wall-cladding and memorial work. Slate is still used as the base for billiard tables and in localized areas it is still imporant in the craft industry. Slate is obtained from North Wales, Cornwall and the Lake District but is also imported from France and Portugal.

Sandstone

The weathering qualities of this material are very variable and depend upon the composition. The very best sandstones are very durable but quickly tend to look dirty and unsightly. Though it can be used for paving and steps it is often restricted in use to the areas that quarry it. It is quite popular as a material for

Fig. 6.29 *Splitting slate (man on right) and dressing slate*

garden rockeries and may vary in colour from creamy white (e.g. Cotswold, Bathstone), through brown to red (e.g. Nottinghamshire and Staffordshire).

Limestone

This stone is generally less hard than sandstone and is easier to work. It is often sufficiently soft to hand-carve. Pure limestone is whitish but may vary through yellow and brown to almost black. Some limestone, such as that obtained from the Pennines, is very hard and can be used as concrete aggregate, road metal and wall-cladding. As a wall-cladding it has been used on St Paul's Cathedral.

Because it tends to be affected by atmospheric pollution it is more often used internally. A typical use is as an ornamental moulding (cornice) round the walls of a room just below the ceiling. Limestone is also a popular rock for garden rockeries.

Most of the limestone used in buildings comes from the south-west of England though for other uses it is obtained from a wide range of source areas. Some of these uses include its use in smelting iron, in paint manufacture, in glass-making and in making cement.

Portland cement is probably one of the most important manufactured products used in the building industry and is made from limestone and clay with a small amount of gypsum (calcium sulphate). The limestone often has to be crushed to a suitable size. It is then mixed with a suitable clay in the ratio 3 parts limestone to 1 part clay. Water is added to form a slurry and the material is carefully mixed. When it has been adequately mixed it is heated in a kiln. The final product is a 'clinker' which is cooled and ground to a powder. Gypsum is added to control the setting time of the cement (after it is mixed with water).

A particular difficulty arises from the blasting operation during the excavation of limestone. Because of its pale colour, the material that settles out of the air after blasting is very apparent and covers everything for tens of metres around the quarry. The effect is to make the surroundings very unsightly.

Sand and Gravel

This material is removed by open-pit techniques similar to those discussed in Chapter 2. The extraction of material from wet pits, however, may require the

Fig. 6.30   A dragline excavator extracting chalk from a wet pit

use of a suction dredger. This is most likely to be needed in deep pits. With loose, free-flowing material it is often possible simply to suck up the material using a machine rather like a vacuum cleaner. With harder material it might be necessary to include a cutter at the end of the suction pump. In wet pits that are shallower, a dragline excavator is often sufficient. Occasionally, in both dry and wet pits, explosives are used to loosen the material.

Once material has been extracted it is screened to separate the material into different sized products. Material that is too large may be discarded or crushed and screened again. Finally, the material is washed to remove silt or clay particles and if the material contains too much water it has to be dewatered. Very often it is possible simply to allow the material to drain naturally. Settling ponds often have to be used so that silt and clay particles are given time to settle from the wash-water before it is returned to the river.

A possible environmental consequence of sand and gravel treatment occurs if the wash-water escapes into water courses, though care is taken to reduce the possibility of this happening. The fine mineral particles that would escape in this instance would settle over the bottom of the rivers and destroy habitats. It will also reduce light penetration into rivers and make it a much more difficult environment for organisms to live in. The suspended material may also clog the gills of fish and other aquatic animals and so may kill them. Particular problems concerning wet gravel pits are discussed in Chapter 7.

Most of the sand and gravel that is extracted is used in the building industry for making concrete, mortar and plaster.

METALS

The major metals used by man are iron (and steel), aluminium, copper, tin and lead.

Iron and Steel

The importance of iron in modern industrialized societies is apparent when it is realized that several times more iron is produced than all the other metals combined. The main ores of this metal are haematite (Fe_2O_3), magnetite (Fe_3O_4), limonite ($Fe_2O_3.H_2O$) and siderite ($FeCo_3$). There are large deposits of siderite in the UK particularly in Lincolnshire and Northamptonshire, but unfortunately this is the lowest grade of iron ore. Because of this it is generally more economic for the UK to import the higher grade ores from other countries.

The preparation of iron from iron ore frequently requires preliminary treatment such as electromagnetic separation where the ore material is separated from the waste rock. The separated ore is then treated in a **blast furnace** (see Fig. 6.31). Iron ore, limestone and coke are fed into the top of the furnace together with **sinter**. Sinter is crushed ore mixed with coke (and sometimes water) that is heated until it fuses together to form a porous 'clinker'. The sinter makes the conversion of iron ore to iron more efficient in the blast furnace. It also helps to reduce dust that may be released from the the blast furnace, and removes some sulphur by oxidizing it to sulphur dioxide. The dust that is released often contains iron oxide which colours the 'smoke' orange/red. This is very unsightly if released from blast furnaces but can be reduced by the use of sinter.

The mixture of ore, sinter, limestone and coke is fired in the furnace and blasts of hot gases (800°C) are forced into the furnace through nozzles at the base. The heat produced (up to 1500°C) melts the ore and allows the impurities to react with the carbon and carbon monoxide from the coke.

$$2Fe_2O_3 + 3C \longrightarrow 4Fe + 3CO_2 \text{ (bottom of furnace)}$$
$$Fe_2O_3 + 3CO \longrightarrow 2Fe + 3CO_2 \text{ (top of furnace)}$$

The molten ore falls to the bottom of the furnace and the impurities react with the limestone to form a **slag** which floats on top of the iron. The slag and iron can be tapped off as required. The metal that is produced is **pig iron** which is 90%–95% pure and is very hard but very brittle. A large proportion of this iron is ued to produce **steel**. The properties of steel depend upon the amount of carbon present together with metals such as nickel, chromium, vanadium or molybdenum. Small amounts of these metals are added during the production of steel.

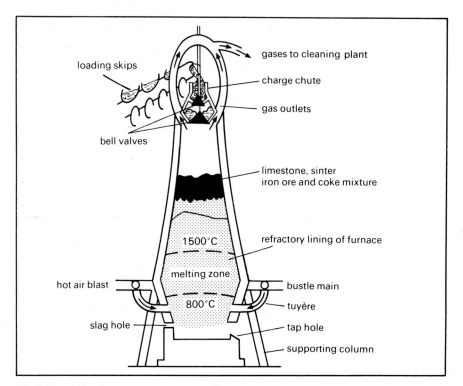

Fig. 6.31   A blast furnace

The three main steel making processes are the **basic oxygen, electric arc** and **open hearth** techniques. This last technique has declined since the early 1960s.

Basic oxygen furnace

In this technique, molten iron together with some scrap iron (up to 30%) is placed in the furnace (see Fig. 6.32). A **lance** is lowered into the furnace and very pure oxygen is forced down into the metal. The oxygen oxidizes impurities in the metal. Limestone is added and the oxidized impurities float in the limestone to form a slag on the surface of the metal. The metal is sampled at intervals and specific elements added until the required grade of steel is obtained. The steel is then tapped off and the slag is removed from the furnace. This process is rapidly becoming the main steel making process.

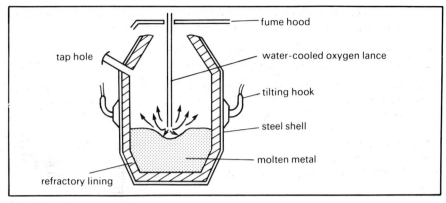

Fig. 6.32 *A basic oxygen furnace*

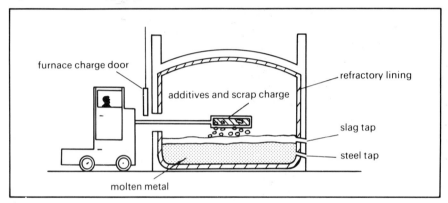

Fig. 6.33 *An open hearth furnace*

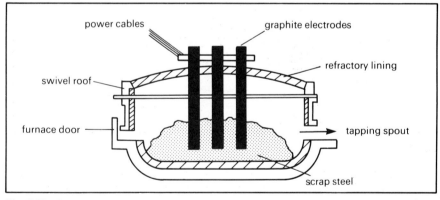

Fig. 6.34 *An electric arc furnace*

Open hearth furnace

Molten iron, scrap and limestone are again the starting points of this process. These materials are **charged** into the hearth of the furnace (see Fig. 6.33). Flames from a fuel such as oil or gas pass over the surface of the metal so that the impurities are oxidized. These combine with the limestone to form a slag which floats on the surface of the molten metal. The metal is sampled at intervals and elements are added to produce the type of steel required. This process is rather slow and is losing popularity.

Fig. 6.35 *Charging scrap metal into an electric arc furnace*

Electric arc furnace

This process uses only scrap iron and enables a very accurate control to be maintained over the final composition of the steel (see Fig. 6.34). Carbon electrodes are lowered into the furnace which has been charged with scrap (see Fig. 6.35). A very high current is passed through the electrodes and an electric arc is produced. This produces enough heat to melt the scrap. Lime and fluorspar are added and any impurities present combine with these as a slag. As with the other processes, samples are taken and elements added as required. The steel and slag are finally removed separately.

The environmental problems related to iron and steel production occur particularly during the reduction of the ore to iron and in the production of the coke that is used in the blast furnace. Because sulphur is present in the ore that is fed to the blast furnace, this becomes oxidized to sulphur dioxide. Much of this will escape to the atmosphere. The problems involving sulphur dioxide are discussed fully in Chapter 2. They include damage to the breathing mechanisms of animals, increase in the acidity of rivers and reduced growth in plants. The release of particulates from the blast furnace is also a problem. This is especially so with particles of iron oxide which often colour the atmosphere around the iron foundry a reddish-brown. This makes the area unattractive. Further problems involving particulate pollution are described in Chapter 2 and include effects on the global climate, reduction in plant growth and damage to breathing structures in animals.

Aluminium

The ore of aluminium is called **bauxite** and has the formula $Al_2O_3 \cdot 3H_2O$ (aluminium trihydrate). The ore is ground to a powder and made to dissolve in strong caustic soda (sodium hydroxide, $NaOH$) under suitable conditions of temperature and pressure. The impurities that are present in the ore (mainly iron oxide) are insoluble in sodium hydroxide and can be removed by allowing them to settle and then filtering them out. The sodium aluminate that is formed is cooled and agitated. Small quantities of pure, solid aluminium trihydrate are then added to the solution. This causes the aluminium trihydrate that is dissolved in the solution to precipitate out. The precipitate is separated by filtration. The pure aluminium trihydrate is then heated to 1300°C to remove the water and produce aluminium oxide.

Fig. 6.36 *Ring-pull cans are made of aluminium*

$$Al_2O_3 \cdot 3H_2O \longrightarrow Al_2O_3 + 3H_2O$$

This pure oxide is referred to as **alumina**. The oxygen is removed from this by **electrolysis**. Firstly, the oxide is dissolved in cryolite (Na_3AlF_6) at 1000°C to form the electrolyte. This is contained in a steel vessel with a carbon lining. The carbon lining acts as the cathode (negative electrode) and carbon anodes (positive electrodes) are suspended in the electrolyte. A current is passed through the electrolyte at about 5 volts and 100 000 amperes. Molten aluminium is produced at the cathode and sinks to the bottom of the cryolite where it can be tapped at intervals.

Aluminium is a metal which has a low density but is relatively strong. These properties, together with its resistance to corrosion, make it an ideal constructional material. It is a **ductile** metal (it can be stretched into a wire) that conducts electricity well. Because of these properties and its relatively lower cost, it is now used in place of copper in electricity transmission lines. It is also a good conductor of heat and is used in such articles as saucepans. Finally, because of its **malleability** (it can be beaten into sheets) it is used as a wrapping material in the form of foil or as ring-pull cans.

Because aluminium production requires very large quantities of electricity, aluminium smelters are often sited close to hydro-electric power stations where electricity is produced cheaply (1 tonne of aluminium requires about 18×10^3 kilowatt-hours or $64 \cdot 8 \times 10^9$ joules of electrical energy). Hydro-electric power stations are frequently sited in areas that are very attractive. Unfortunately aluminium smelters tend to look unsightly in these areas. Scotland, Canada and Scandinavia are amongst the areas in which aluminium smelters are situated.

Copper

Copper is very ductile and malleable. As such it is readily used in the form of wires, pipes and sheets. In particular, copper has a very high electrical conductivity and so is important in the electrical industry. Copper is also used as an **alloy** (Alloys are formed by allowing molten metals to mix together and solidify.) with either zinc to form brass, or with tin to form bronze. These alloys are used for decorative work, utensils, etc.

Though the metal has been mined in the UK, there are now no copper mines

Fig. 6.37 *The concentration of copper ore by froth flotation*

in this country and all our copper is imported. The main world producers of copper are the USA, Russia, Chile, Zambia and Canada.

Copper is occasionally mined as a pure metal, but is more usually found as the ores chalcocite (Cu_2S), malachite ($CuCO_3 \cdot Cu(OH)_2$) and chalcopyrite ($CuFeS_2$). The ore is first crushed, sieved and ground into fine particles in water. This fine material is separated by a process known as **froth flotation** (see Fig. 6.37). Chemicals are added to the mixture of ore and water in flotation cells and air is forced in. The air causes the chemicals to form a froth on the surface of the cells and the copper compounds float in this froth. The material that is concentrated in this way is roasted in air. This oxidizes the material and some of the sulphur is removed.

$$2CuFeS_2 + 3O_2 \longrightarrow 2CuS + 2FeO + 2SO_2$$

The material that remains is mixed with limestone and silica and melted in a **reverberatory furnace** (similar to the open hearth furnace in Fig. 6.33). Most of the impurities react with the silica and limestone and float to the surface as a slag. This is removed and the molten metal compounds are tapped off as required. This material is called a **matte**. The matte is melted in a **Bessemer convertor** at about 1250°C. Air is blown through to oxidize the impurities and produce a copper with 2–3% impurities. This material is **blister copper** and can be further refined in a reverberatory furnace with suitable fluxes and the addition of air.

$$CuS + O_2 \longrightarrow Cu + SO_2$$

Copper of an extremely high degree of purity can then be obtained by electrolysis (see Fig. 6.38 and Activity 11).

Tin

Tin is a soft, weak metal, though it is very resistant to corrosion. Its major use is in tin-plating, particularly in the manufacture of tin cans. It is a metal that easily forms an alloy with other metals. When tin is alloyed with copper or antimony it forms **pewter**. This is a metal that is popular for a range of ornaments. Of much greater importance, tin is alloyed with lead to form **solder**. This is a form of metal that is used to join wire and strips of metal together. In this way the tin is important in the distribution of electricity, water and gas, and is present in cars, televisions, radios, lights and very nearly every piece of electrically operated equipment.

The main tin ore is cassiterite (SnO_2) which occurs frequently in placer deposits (see Fig. 6.26). In this form it can be extracted by dredging. In other cases it is extracted by deep mining. After extraction the ore is powdered and washed. In this way the impurities are removed and the more dense tin is left behind.

To obtain tin from its oxide several processes are necessary. The washed and dried ore is first heated with lime in a reverberatory furnace at 1200°C. The mixture is stirred and the impurities react with the lime to form a slag. The slag floats on the tin and so the tin can be drained away. This tin is not very pure and needs further treatment. It is heated in a sloping hearth so that the tin melts. In this form it alloys with a number of other metals in the mixture (such as copper and iron) and runs off the hearth where it can be collected. The next stage is to heat the alloy until its melting point is reached. At this point air or steam is blown through the liquid. During this stage iron becomes oxidized and floats to the surface as a slag that can be removed. Following this, the liquid is heated further and sulphur is stirred in. This removes the copper as copper sulphide and leaves tin up to 99% pure.

Most of our tin has to be imported although some is mined in Cornwall. Major producers include Malaya and the West Indies.

Fig. 6.38 *Copper having 99.97% purity can be obtained by electrolysis. Impurities such as gold, silver and platinum are recovered during this process.*

Lead

This is a very dense metal with a low melting point. Though it is not very ductile it is readily rolled and can be formed into thin sheets (it is malleable). Approximately 25% of the lead used in the UK is used in the manufacture of batteries. Other uses include flashings on roofs to prevent water leakage and as a sheathing for underground electricity cables. At one time it was used to form water pipes but because lead is slightly water soluble there was a danger of lead poisoning and so lead is no longer used in this way. It is present in petrol as

Fig. 6.39 *Lead shielding allows scientists to work with highly radioactive materials*

tetra-ethyl lead to improve the performance of petrol engines, but this has recently given cause for concern (see Chapter 2). Because it is very dense, it is often used as radioactive shielding. As mentioned earlier, lead is alloyed with tin to form solder. The commonest ore of lead is galena (PbS) and is found in the USA, Australia, Spain and Mexico. Lead has been mined in Britain using deep mining techniques though it is now no longer profitable to do so.

The first process involved in obtaining lead is a froth flotation technique. The powdered ore is put into tanks of water which have been treated chemically and which are agitated. This produces froth in which the lead sulphide floats to the surface. The lead sulphide is removed and roasted in oxygen at about 800°C. In this way the lead sulphide is converted into lead oxide.

$$2PbS + 3O_2 \longrightarrow 2PbO + 2SO_2$$

The lead oxide is then fed into a blast furnace together with coke, calcium oxide and iron oxide. The coke reduces the lead oxide to lead.

$$2PbO + C \longrightarrow 2Pb + CO_2$$

The impurities that are present float in the slag formed by the oxides of iron and calcium. The lead that is produced is removed separately from the slag. The lead is further purified or refined to remove a number of impurities. Though the processes used depend upon the impurities, many of the impurities can be removed by heating the lead to 400°C and stirring it. Many impurities float to the surface and can be skimmed off.

The production of sulphur dioxide and particulates is a problem that is common to all of these techniques. The sulphur dioxide can be used in the manufacture of sulphuric acid and the particulates are removed from waste gases by electrostatic precipitation (see Chapter 2). Some of these substances do get released into the atmosphere, however, and their effects are discussed in Chapter 2.

A final environmental problem that can arise from the extraction and production of all these metals is related to the formation of spoil heaps. During the extraction of the useful metal, waste products are removed and generally dumped in piles around the site of the mining or refining operations. This waste will contain metals which have been concentrated to the point where they might become toxic. This is apparent from the fact that such waste heaps rarely support life. Water that passes through these heaps may dissolve the metals in toxic quantities and spread them through the environment. If this occurs, it may endanger human water supplies or may make parts of the environment unsuitable for plants and animals to inhabit. Some of these problems are summarized in Fig. 6.40.

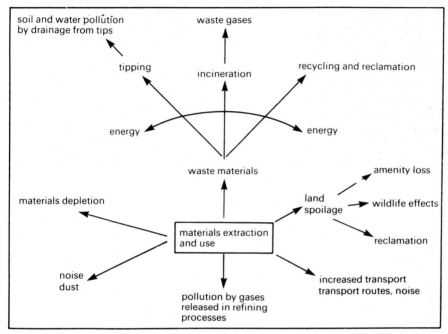

Fig. 6.40   *Environmental problems associated with the extraction of materials, their refining and use*

RECYCLING

Within this group of materials some concern is being expressed about the amount of some metals that are left in the ground. Table 6.2 gives an indication of how long our known reserves of the metals discussed in this chapter will last at the present rate of use. Some metals, such as mercury, gold and silver are expected to run out even before tin, lead or copper. Despite the controversial nature of values such as these, there is enough concern for people to become increasingly interested in recycling and reclamation schemes (see Chapter 1

Metal	Depletion date (years from now)
iron	250
aluminium	100
copper	25
lead	25
tin	20

Table 6.2   *How long the known reserves of the major metal ores will last.*

for a discussion of the problems involved in predicting depletion dates for different resources).

There are various forms of recycling, some of which have been common for many years. The most obvious of these is when milk bottles or mineral 'pop' bottles are returned to the supplier. Even more use could be made of this form of recycling because it is the easiest and often the cheapest. Another common form of recycling is when a substandard product is passed back to the start of a production line. This is especially common in paper making and metal works.

When most people think of recycling however, they usually think of **indirect recycling**. This is when something is recycled to produce a material that is used in a different way from the original material. Whether or not this form of recycling is practicable depends on a number of factors.

1   There has to be a steady and suitably large supply of material to be recycled. This generally means that a suitable collecting scheme has to be organized.

2   The technology must be available to recycle it. A typical problem here is when metals are required for recycling when they have originally been used as an alloy with another metal. Very often, the technology is not available to separate the metals.

3   The recycled material must not be more expensive than the same material produced from conventional raw materials.

4   There must be a suitable market for the final product.

The recycling of materials is not restricted to metals of course. The recycling of glass, paper and oil for instance are all possible and have been shown to be practicable under the right conditions. Because a great deal of material is thrown away from each home in the country, a lot of effort is being made to recycle normal 'dustbin' rubbish.

ACTIVITIES

Paper making

1   In this activity you are going to recycle some paper. First of all you will need to make a **mould** and a **deckle**. These are wooden frames made so that the internal dimensions of each frame is equal to the size of the paper you wish to make. To make the mould, stretch some fine gauze across the frame. Screen-printing nylon or finely perforated zinc or aluminium is suitable for the gauze.

a) Take 25g of newsprint (5 sheets of a full size newspaper or 10 sheets of a tabloid). Shred the paper into 2–3 cm^2 pieces and soak it in water overnight.

b) Take the newspaper (125g in weight) and divide it into 4 batches. Place one batch into a liquidizer. Add 650 cm^3 of water and turn on the liquidizer. Do not allow the liquidizer to run for more than 30 seconds. Liquidize in 30 seconds bursts until no particles of print are visible. Repeat the process, liquidizing one batch of your pulp with 650 cm^3 of water each time. Pour your pulp into a deep tray and add 5 litres of water. Stir until the water and pulp are well mixed.

c) Place the deckle on the mesh covered side of the mould. With the deckle on top, place it and the mould vertically into the end of the tray furthest from you. Tip the deckle and mould until they are horizontal in the pulp and water mixture. Remove the deckle and mould from the mixture and carefully shake them from side to side to distribute the pulp evenly on the mesh. Hold the deckle and mould over the tray while the water is draining away.

d) Place a piece of felt by your tray. Remove the deckle and tip the mould upside down over the felt. Carefully clear all the pulp from the mould. If you are not careful, the pulp will tear and ruin your results. Place another felt on top of the pulp and put this in a press. The pulp should be pressed for 2 hours. After this time, the sheet should be removed from the press, peeled from the felt and allowed to dry.

e) Compare your material with newspaper and writing paper. In what ways do they differ? Suggest what use could be made of the material you have made.

2 Select a mature tree for the following exercise. (A telegraph pole is a suitable substitute.)

a) Calculate the volume of wood in the tree (pole) using the following information.

$$\text{Volume of wood in tree} = \text{height} \times \pi r^2 \times \text{'form factor'}.$$

(The 'form factor' takes into account the fact that the tree tapers towards the top and is generalized at 0.5 although it varies from one species of tree to another.)

b) The weight of wood in 1 issue of the *Daily Digest* is 5.5 tonnes ($1.1 m^3$ of wood = 1 tonne), therefore how many trees are required?

c) If these trees are 3m apart, what area of land is required?

d) How much land is required if you assume that 50% of the timber used in the newspaper is recycled material?

Properties of different fibres

In these activities you could compare wool and linen with, say, cotton and one or two man-made fibres such as nylon or terylene.

3 Investigate the insulation properties of materials.

a) Obtain pieces of material you wish to compare.

b) Cut a piece of your heaviest material so that it will fit round a beaker and be as tall as your beaker.

c) Weigh the material.

d) Cut your other materials to the height of the beaker but sufficiently long so that their mass equals the mass of your first material.

e) Using a technique similar to that described for Activity 7, Chapter 2, compare the insulating properties of your materials.

f) What use could be made of this property of the materials.

4 If you can obtain strands of the materials of equal dimension, you could investigate the strength and elasticity of each material that you used in Activity 3. In what way would each of these properties be useful or cause a problem?

The structure of rocks

5 This experiment illustrates the structure of igneous rocks. During the experiment pungent fumes of sulphur dioxide are released. For this reason, the experiment should be done in a fume cupboard or a well-ventilated room.

a) Place a 2cm depth of powdered sulphur into a boiling tube. Have ready a filter funnel together with filter paper mounted in a stand over a beaker of cold water to catch any hot material that passes through the paper.

b) Heat the sulphur *carefully* until it just turns to a liquid. Do *not* heat the sulphur after it has liquified. If you do it will ignite and very pungent, toxic fumes will be released. If it does ignite, place a material that will not readily burn (e.g. a thick piece of wood) over the neck of the tube until the flame goes out.

c) Pour the hot liquid into the paper in the filter funnel and leave the paper until you see a thin skin appearing on the surface of the sulphur. At this time, *carefully* open up the paper (the sulphur will still be hot). If you have timed it correctly, you should see large needle-shaped (monoclinic) crystals of

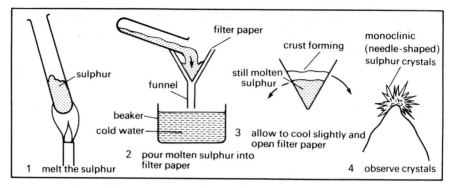

Fig. 6.41 *Investigating the formation of igneous rocks*

sulphur in the material. If the material is one solid lump repeat the experiment and open your paper earlier.

6   This experiment demonstrates the structure of extrusive igneous rocks. Heat a 2cm depth of sulphur in a boiling tube as described above. When the sulphur liquifies, pour it into a beaker of cold water. This will form a solid material with no crystals present (this material is called 'plastic' sulphur).

7   Use the results of experiments 5 and 6 and the information in the chapter to explain the differences in structure between intrusive and extrusive rocks.

Metals

Try extracting some metals from their ores. If you were to use real ore for these experiments you would have very little success in obtaining metals. It is suggested therefore that you use metal compounds. This will make your experiments similar to the industrial processes after the impurities have been removed by crushing and sieving or flotation (see text).

8   Obtain lead from lead sulphide (galena, PbS) by carrying out the following procedure.

a) Carefully mix 2g of lead sulphide and 2g of charcoal on a tin lid or some aluminium foil.

b) Heat the lid strongly from above for 5 minutes. Beads of lead should become visible as shiny balls. When the heat is removed the lead gains a grey oxide coat and can no longer be distinguished from the rest of the material.

9   Obtain copper from copper carbonate ($CuCO_3 Cu(OH)_2$) as follows.

a) Mix 2g of copper carbonate with 2g of charcoal on a square of aluminium foil.

b) Wrap the ore in the aluminium foil (to prevent it re-oxidizing) and heat it strongly from above and below for 5 minutes.

c) Quickly tip the contents of the foil into a beaker of cold water.

d) Decant the water and tip the residue onto a paper towel so that the copper can be isolated. The copper will look like small brown flakes of material.

10   Repeat experiment 9 but this time try to obtain iron from iron oxide (haematite, Fe_2O_3). After decanting the water, put the residue into a beaker and add sulphuric acid. If iron is present, hydrogen will be released and will be seen as bubbles.

$$Fe + H_2SO_4 \longrightarrow FeSO_4 + H_2 \qquad or \qquad 2Fe + 4HCl \longrightarrow 2FeCl_2 + 2H_2$$

11   Measure the energy required to obtain pure copper by electrolysis. The amount of energy required and the quantity of copper deposited will depend upon many factors, some of which are: the current flowing in the circuit, the

distance between the electrodes, the strength of copper sulphate, the size and number of electrodes. You might like to use the general procedure outlined below to investigate some of them.

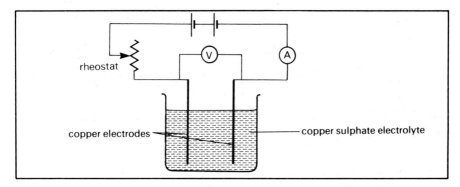

Fig. 6.42 *Obtaining copper by electrolysis*

a) Set up the experiment as shown in Fig. 6.42. Make sure that the electrodes do not touch and are held at the same distance apart throughout the experiment.

b) Adjust the rheostat so that a current of about 2 amperes passes through the circuit. Allow this current to flow for 10 minutes or until the ammeter or voltmeter shows an obvious increase or decrease in value (this would make your calculation more difficult).

c) From Chapter 1 you should recall that electrical energy (in joules) can be found from the relationship.

$$E=VIt$$

(where V=voltage, I=current, t=time in seconds). Calculate the amount of energy required to deposit 1 g of copper under the conditions present in your experiment.

d) In the industrial preparation of copper several electrodes are used. Some of these electrodes are made of impure copper and some are of pure copper. Pure copper is transferred from the impure electrode to the pure electrode.

From the results of your experiment, can you state whether the anode (positive electrode) or the cathode (negative electrode) is made of pure copper?

12   The weight of domestic refuse in the UK in 1978 was 20×10^6 tonnes.

a) Approximately 43% by weight of this material is paper and card. What weight of paper could therefore have been recycled?

b) Total imports of wood pulp in 1978 were 1.8×10^6 tonnes. How much of this material could have been replaced by recycling the paper in domestic refuse.

c) If 9% (by weight) of domestic refuse is iron and steel, what was the total weight of this material? In 1976 some 45×10^6 tonnes of iron and steel were produced in the UK. What percentage of this could have been provided by recycling domestic waste?

7 Land Use and Conservation

Most of man's activities affect the land either directly or indirectly, though until recently, little concern was ever expressed about these effects. The present concern about land has come about for two major reasons. Firstly, as our need for raw materials increases, so the extent to which we affect the land increases. Secondly, the number of people in the world is increasing and so the amount of space available to each one is decreasing. Because of this any adverse effect we have on the environment is becoming more noticeable.

LAND USE

The major activities of man that affect the environment include agriculture, forestry, industry, urban development, recreation, military activities and waste disposal. The extent to which each of these demands land in the UK can be seen from Fig. 7.2. Some of these land uses have a worse effect on the land than others. For example, hundreds or thousands of hectares of land used for extensive grazing of sheep will not disturb the environment to the same extent as an airport or open quarry or an industrial estate would do, even though these land uses may occupy much smaller areas of land. The ways in which many of these land-use catagories disturb the environment have been discussed in previous chapters, though a brief summary of each is given below as it affects the UK.

Agriculture

Though agriculture still uses the largest amount of land, concern is expressed because this value is decreasing each year. At present, this loss is averaging about 12000 hectares per year. The major reason for concern is the fear that farmers will not be able to continue producing an adequate supply of food. However, though agricultural land has been lost annually, agricultural

Fig. 7.1 How many forms of land use can you identify in this picture?

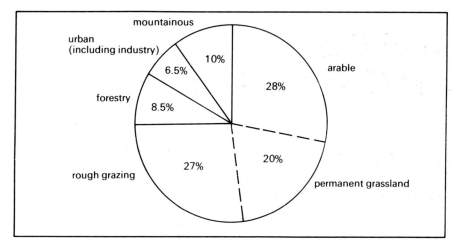

Fig. 7.2 *Land use in the UK*

production has increased by some 30% during the last twenty years. The means by which this increase has been achieved have themselves caused concern. This is because in many ways they have proved themselves harmful to the environment.

Fig. 7.3 *The size of farm machinery is increasing*

Firstly, a move towards larger machines that make harvesting more efficient has meant that many hedgerows have had to be removed. This removal means that not only is the patchwork pattern of fields, that has decorated the countryside of Britain for many years, disappearing but the habitat of a large number of plant and animal species is also vanishing.

Secondly, in order to cultivate as much land as possible, many areas of boggy marsh land have been drained. This again removes the habitat of many plants and animals.

Finally, the use of herbicides has reduced the number of 'weed' species and with them the food supply of a large number of animals including insects, birds and mammals. Pesticides have directly led to the deaths of many individual animals and have seriously reduced the numbers of some animal species to dangerously low levels. The application of fertilizers has led to the pollution of water courses. These effects are considered in more detail in Chapter 5.

Fig. 7.4 *Trees are often planted without thought to whether they 'blend in' to the landscape*

Woods and Forests

Some 8% of land in the UK is planted with woods and forests. Though some of these areas are privately owned, by far the greatest landowner in this category is the Forestry Commission. This is a government department that as long ago as 1919 was given the responsibility of encouraging the growing of timber in this country. The intention was that we should supply as much of our needs for timber as possible. Although the Commission now purchases land throughout the UK where plantings are economic, most land is acquired in upland areas, particularly Scotland, Wales and the Lake District.

The greatest criticism of the Commission has probably been the planting of imported coniferous trees rather than native broad-leaved trees. In 1970, 98% of new plantings were of coniferous trees. This trend is understandable, however, when it is appreciated that the Commission wishes to make as large a profit as possible. The market demands in the UK are for 90% conifers (soft wood) and 10% for hardwoods (deciduous, broad-leaved trees). Most of the areas planted by the Commission are unsuitable for deciduous trees.

Further criticism of the Forestry Commission is two-fold. Firstly, it is felt by many people that large areas of uniformly green trees are unsightly when planted without thought to the natural contours of the land. This is particularly so when they are necessarily arranged in rows and therefore present a fixed geometrical appearance to the observer (see Fig. 7.4). Secondly, it is pointed out that coniferous tree plantations reduce the amount of light reaching the ground. This means that few wild plants are found growing in the forests. As a result of this, the habitat is only suited to a very small range of animal species.

The Commission has attempted to modify its practices in an attempt to reduce these criticisms. It now plants areas of mixed conifers so that the areas are not uniformly green, and plants them in a more natural fashion so that they blend in more readily with the natural contours of the area.

Industry and Urban Development

Together, these land use categories claim about 10% of the land in the UK and this amount is increasing by some 25000 hectares every year. It is certainly arguable that these forms of land use most seriously disturb the natural environment. Even so, many species of plants and animals have adapted to conditions within large urban areas. The increase in urbanization is, in part, because of the increasing population, but also because of the movement of people from rural areas to urban areas. Since the industrial revolution, jobs have become more available in towns and less available in the countryside. Also, however, it is because people are now more concerned with the quality of

Fig. 7.5 *Urban and industrial land uses occupy some 25 000 hectares more land each year*

life they lead and so wish to have a piece of land of their own which separates them from their neighbour and in which they may relax. Houses are now, therefore, built further apart.

The increasing demand for industrial land has arisen again partly because an increased population requires more products. Another reason is because our increased standard of living means that each individual wants more, or bigger, or better products. This increasing demand for consumer goods has led to the development of industrial estates which often require areas of land up to 200 hectares. Two of the largest industrial developments since the war have been the petro-chemical industry and the electricity generating industry. Where petro-chemical industries are sited alongside oil refineries, up to 800 hectares of land may be required. For a large generating station with its associated fuel storage, cooling towers and ash disposal sites, a similar area of land may be needed.

Military

As the weapons of modern warfare have been developed, so the Services have needed to acquire large areas of land to test them. Land is also needed for the training of troops. In England and Wales the area of land in use by the Services is now approximately 340 000 hectares, though much of their land is used by farmers for the grazing of cattle and production of hay and silage. It is arguable that this form of land use offers refuge to wildlife, though of course few people would benefit from this.

Waste Disposal and Mineral Workings

As the 'consumer society' grows, so the amount of waste it produces increases. Much of the waste is disposed of into the air or into water and this has been dealt with elsewhere in this book. Solid wastes that are produced may occasionally be disposed of at unplanned sites and may cause unsightly piles of material to develop. Alternatively they may prove dangerous if toxic materials are dumped. These may eventually be dissolved in rainwater and pollute the soil locally or affect the environment over a wider area by being washed into rivers and streams.

Most of the waste produced by society, however, is treated in a responsible manner and is either burnt and the ash buried or, less frequently now, is buried directly. When these materials are buried properly areas of land are only temporarily disturbed—the topsoil is removed, the material is buried and the topsoil is returned. Also, material may be used to fill in disused excavations so that areas of land may be effectively reclaimed after they have been covered with topsoil and planted.

Fig. 7.6   *Waste disposal site from an old copper mine in Anglesey*

Mineral workings have also increased as people require more commodities that are dependent upon materials that have to be extracted from the ground. Major excavations in the UK include coal, sand and gravel, iron, clay, limestone and chalk, sandstone and china clay. Many areas of derelict land show man's use of the land for extracting these materials. It is estimated that nearly 45×10^3 hectares of land are occupied by unfilled quarries (this excludes quarries that are currently in use). Future predictions indicate that up to 4000 hectares of land will be required annually for open-cast mining and about one-third of this will be restored. The increasing area of derelict land in Britain is shown in Fig. 7.8.

The greatest permanent damage is probably caused by sand and gravel extraction. Unfortunately it is anticipated that the amount of quarried land used for this purpose will increase in proportion to all others. Many of these quarries utilize good agricultural land and up to one-third of the quarries are 'wet'. This means that excavations rapidly become flooded and such areas are difficult to restore. It is worth noting, however, that an increasing amount of this land is being developed for a range of recreational pursuits, particularly those that depend upon expanses of water such as boating and fishing.

All open-pit mining has the disadvantage of requiring overburden to be removed before work can start. (Overburden is the material lying on top of whatever is to be extracted.) The land is then removed from all other uses until

Fig. 7.7   *Mineral workings can adversely affect the environment*

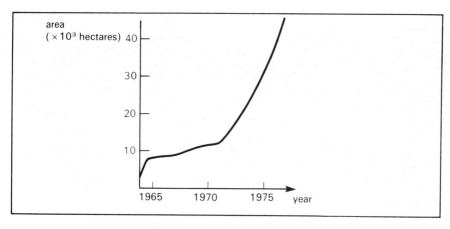

Fig. 7.8 *The increasing area of derelict land in the UK*

the material is fully extracted. This overburden may be used elsewhere for filling up holes or landscaping so an equivalent amount of land may be reclaimed. Strip mining or open-cast workings often allow for the overburden to be back-filled. As an area of mineral is extracted, so the overburden is used to fill the hole.

Water Catchment

It was noted in Chapter 4 that the land required for water storage must increase considerably if we are to maintain adequate supplies by the end of the century. Detailed problems were discussed in that chapter so it is sufficient to recall here that the two major problems are.
1   the flooding of areas of land that were previously used for some other purpose
2   the construction of possibly unsightly dams.
It should, however, be noted that water authorities are increasingly allowing their reservoirs to be used by the public for fishing and yachting. Great care is also taken to create dams that have pleasing designs and that are constructed of natural 'local' stone where appropriate.

Recreation and Land

Recreational activities have increased considerably during recent times. This has happened for several reasons. Firstly, there has been an increase in holiday time. Secondly, increasing standards of living leave people with more money to spend on recreation after they have purchased such essentials as food. Thirdly, there is a desire in people to live a more satisfying life. In particular this increase in recreation has been seen in those activities which demand the use of the countryside. These include such general activities as touring, camping, and caravanning, and more specialized activities such as rock climbing, horse riding and all forms of water sports.

This increasing demand for recreational land has tended to conflict with many of the land uses described earlier in this chapter. This is particularly so with forestry, water supply and agriculture. However, there is now a move by all parties concerned towards the idea that the land should be thought of as being capable of providing several different uses at the same time. This concept is known as **multiple land use**.

Fig. 7.9 *Climbers on Napes Needle in the Lake District* **Fig. 7.10** *Sailing on Trimpley Reservoir on the banks of the River Severn*

Recreation and forestry

People in the UK have in the past generally preferred the open country and the seaside to forests. Recently, however, there has been an increasing number of people using forests. For instance up, to 100000 people may visit the New Forest each day during the summer. To cater for this increase in visitors the Forestry Commission has created **open forests** where the public are allowed free access. They also provide **forest parks** (now covering some 174000 hectares) where a warden is appointed to manage the area. These parks are organized to allow for camp sites, picnic places and nature trails together with such possible activities as pony trekking and wildlife observation. Difficulties obviously arise during logging operations when the public are often instructed to stay clear. Also, increased numbers of visitors increases the possibility of fire. Nevertheless, the Commission is extending its policy of encouraging visitors to the forests.

Recreation and water supply

The primary aim of water authorities must obviously be to provide an adequate supply of clean, safe drinking water. Little work has been done on the effects of recreational activities on water purity, and in the past the authorities have often played safe. This has meant excluding the public from many of its water storage areas. More recently it has been shown that most activities are not as detrimental to water quality as was originally feared. Because of this the authorities are allowing a greater use of their bodies of water by the public. Some activities are not allowed, however, such as swimming, power boating and camping in the catchment area of the reservoir. It has been estimated that there are up to 84170 hectares of enclosed water in the UK and some 3000 kilometres of canals. Obviously there is a considerable area of water that could be developed for these activities.

Recreation and agriculture

Because farms are privately owned, farmers are not as subject to the pressure exerted to make areas of land available for recreation as are government agencies. Nevertheless, farms are increasingly organizing 'open days' where the public are allowed access to farms or are guided round. The problems involved in this form of recreation are very obvious, and enormous trust must be placed upon the public if the farmer is not to suffer large economic losses.

Recreation and the countryside

As well as creating conflicts with other land uses, recreation creates direct pressures on the countryside. These pressures might become apparent in several ways. Firstly, the landscape may be altered by developments such as caravan parks and car parks designed to cater for recreational pursuits. Secondly, erosion may occur because of the continued use of an area by walkers (see Fig. 7.11). The ecology of an area may be disturbed by changing conditions to suit certain species of plant or animal to the detriment of others. These effects may well be caused simply by too many people walking over **ecologically fragile** areas which are unable to tolerate the conditions.

Because of concern about certain land use activities and their effects, groups of people have been given responsibility for reducing the disturbance caused by these activities. Areas of land have also been selected in which the activities described above are severely restricted. The principles upon which these groups of people act, and upon which these areas of land have been selected, are generalized under the term 'conservation'.

Fig. 7.11   Footpath erosion caused by hill walkers

CONSERVATION

This can best be defined as the management of environments, including the plants, animals and land forms present, in a way that maintains or improves their quality. Also at the same time, wherever possible, access should be provided to the public for recreational purposes.

In the UK because we are a small, densely populated area (each of us having approximately 0·4 hectares of land), preservation as a means of conserving land is not generally possible. This is because of the many demands made on it. Also, much of the land in the UK is far from natural anyway. Many **ecosystems** (groups of plants and animals and the area in which they are found) require positive management to maintain them. An example of this would be the typical downland ecosystems which, if not grazed, would revert to a scrubland ecosystem.

The aims of conservation can be seen in four main areas: species conservation, habitat conservation, conservation of large areas of land and creative conservation.

Species Conservation

This form of conservation shows a concern for the protection of rare, interesting or beautiful species. It is the form of conservation with which people are generally most familiar.

Controversies occasionally arise over this form of conservation for a variety of reasons. Firstly, though there is rarely much doubt about which species may be classed as rare, many people argue that they have become rare because they have been unable to adapt to a changing environment. They suggest, therefore, that they should be allowed to become extinct in the same way as the dinosaurs or woolly mammoths did. Unfortunately these people conveniently forget that the changing environments with which these plants and animals are unable to cope are brought about by man at such a speed that few biological systems could possibly adapt. Many species throughout the world are in danger of becoming extinct. In fact it is estimated that one species of mammal alone becomes extinct every year while over 250 mammals and up to 1000 vertebrate species are regarded as being in danger of extinction. This number is dwarfed by the number of invertebrate species and plants at risk.

Secondly, the terms 'interesting' and 'beautiful' are always open to controversy because people's ideas of what things are interesting and what things are beautiful differ. Many people will always argue that certain species should not be conserved because they find them neither interesting nor beautiful!

Fig. 7.12 Early spider orchid—a species of plant in danger of extinction

Fig. 7.13 Common Sundew (Drosera rotundifolia) found in boggy areas

Fig. 7.14 *The conservation of otters now covers the whole of England and Wales*

BBC copyright photograph

Animals in the UK which have quite recently become subject to conservation protection include otters (see Fig. 7.14), bats and all birds of prey. Admirers of the osprey have taken extreme precautions (including a 24-hour guard on some of the nesting sites) to ensure its survival in Scotland where there are fewer than 20 breeding pairs.

Habitat Conservation

This form of conservation involves the maintenance of representative habitats of as many types as possible. These habitats may then be used to measure changes in similar habitats that are likely to be affected by man. Researchers can also learn more about how the natural world functions. This aspect of conservation is apparent in national and local nature reserves and in 'sites of special scientific interest' (see Fig. 7.15).

Fig. 7.15 *Scar Close—a national nature reserve in Yorkshire showing a 'limestone pavement' habitat*

Conservation of Large Areas of Land

This aspect of conservation concerns itself with the mangement of land. The aim is that the demand for recreation, water catchment, industry and forestry, etc. can be balanced against the ability and desirability of the land to support them. This aspect of conservation is particularly apparent in national parks and also in 'areas of outstanding natural beauty'.

Creative Conservation

This involves large-scale improvements to the environment, for instance by the reclamation of land from the sea, the reclamation of mineral extraction pits, and landscape planning in general.

These four areas of conservation are supported by five main arguments. These are ecological, aesthetic, recreational, economic and moral.

Ecological arguments in favour of conservation are based on the idea that the inter-relationships that exist in nature are extremely complex and interdependent. The arguments suggest that seriously reducing the number of a species, or removing it entirely, may have an adverse effect on many other parts of the environment that depend upon it. An indication that this argument is a reasonable one was seen when myxomatosis was introduced into the UK. This virus drastically reduced the number of rabbits in this country. At the same time, it was noted that many downland areas were losing there characteristic plants and associated animals. It was quickly realized that the rabbits were responsible for eating and thus controlling the numbers and heights of a range of plants, and thus allowing others to grow. Once the rabbits were removed the plants that were previously kept in check spread rapidly so that many other plant species were unable to compete. Animals or plants become extinct because of some adverse effect on the environment; an environment of which we are a part. This shows we are making our own environment less pleasing to live in.

Aesthetic arguments suggest that man needs to spend a part of his time pursuing interests that allow him to relax. This is becoming increasingly important as the pressures of life increase. Many people find this relaxation by spending time in the quiet surroundings offered by the countryside and surrounded by the sights, smells and sounds which we so much take for granted. Who can fail to be excited by finding the common sundew (*Drosera rotundifolia* (see Fig. 7.15) an insectivorous plant of peat bogs?

Economic arguments in favour of conservation are two-fold. Firstly, it is suggested that many species which we might thoughtlessly cause to become extinct may be of value to man as a food source. The most widely publicized example of this possibility is that of the whale. Many species of whale have been killed with the result that they are now in danger of extinction. It is still not certain that the species that are now conserved will increase their numbers again, and yet man is likely to reduce other species of whale to the same dangerous levels by hunting. It is further suggested that animals as yet unused as food may be used in the future.

Secondly, it is argued that species of plants and animals should be conserved in case we need to use them for purposes other than as a food source. As yet, we cannot know and probably never will know for sure, which organisms we may or may not need or want to use. The importance of this argument may be appreciated when it is realized that all our food crops were once 'wild' and that many of our drugs and medicines are obtained from wild organisms. As we kill off these organisms, so the material for further research into possible medicines and drugs will disappear.

Moral arguments are based upon the simple idea that it is wrong for man to cause an end to the existence of any species of plant or animal on this planet.

At the time of writing, a new Bill, the 'Wildlife and Countryside Bill' is fighting its way through Parliament. This Bill will hopefully extend the protection currently given to threatened species of plants and animals in the UK and will also help to conserve the remainder of our dwindling, though extremely important, specialized habitats. The present degree of legislation and the co-operation between conservationists and land users, though at first glance quite extensive and comprehensive, has not been sufficient to prevent a quite dramatic decrease in these habitats and organisms. There is at present, and has been in the recent past, a number of investigations into habitat loss. Most have been restricted to specific areas of the country, but throughout the picture is depressing. It is calculated that more natural and semi-natural woodland has been lost in the last 3 decades than in the last 400 years. In mid-Wales, agricultural improvements destroyed nearly 10% of the natural habitat from 1970–1976. Within the last 30 years, some 20% of mixed woodland, 61% of heathland and 10% of fens have been lost to agriculture and forestry in southern Scotland. Peat bogs, chalk grasslands, meadows, mosslands and deciduous woods are all being destroyed at an alarming rate throughout England. Even 'protected' areas are not safe; it is thought that some 4% of 'sites of special scientific interest' are lost annually to developments of one sort or another.

The present Bill is contentious in that many conservationists feel that it will still not afford the necessary protection. If this proves to be the case, and given that another Bill is extremely unlikely this decade, then at the present rate we could lose 10–20% of our natural habitats in the same period. The outlook for our countryside is very bleak indeed.

In 1980 a document was produced jointly by the World Wildlife Fund, the International Union for the Conservation of Nature and the United Nations Environment Programme. This document was entitled *World Conservation Strategy* and set out a 'plan of action for all nations of the world to co-operate in a move to conserve all that is good in the environment and to minimize all that causes harm'. The document informs that the environment is suffering more now from the activities of man than it has ever done in the past, and that it is essential that we act now. It also points out that there has never before been a global conservation plan despite the fact that environmental pollution or degradation in one nation invariably affects many others. Though there is not the space here to detail the strategy, it is relevant to note that the plans that are proposed are designed to meet three aims. These are:

1   to understand and maintain the world's natural ecological processes (an introduction to these processes is given in Chapter 3)
2   to maintain as wide a range of plants and animals in the world as possible to maintain 'genetic diversity'
3   to manage the world's ecosystems on the basis of a 'sustainable yield basis' (see Chapter 6).

CONSERVATION IN THE UK

Countryside Commission

This Commission was originally the National Parks Commission and was given its new title in 1968. It is a government-financed body and has several functions. As well as being able to decide upon any future national parks and 'areas of outstanding natural beauty' (AONB), it provides grants and advice to local authorities when they wish to set up country parks. It has also set up the 'long distance footpaths' that exists in England and Wales (e.g. Pennine Way, Offa's Dyke Path, Cleveland Way).

National parks

Ten national parks have been set up in England and Wales (see Table 7.1). These parks are large areas of land which have been selected because of their outstanding natural beauty. Though the land within each national park is not owned by the Countryside Commission, the Commission is able to restrict the types of developments that take place there. The purpose of these parks is to prevent the areas of land from being spoiled so that people should be able to enjoy the natural countryside. This aim, however, has to take into account the fact that people live and work within the national park boundaries.

National Park	Area (km²)	Area (square miles)	Area (hectares)
Pembroke Coast	583	225	58 300
Exmoor	694	265	69 400
Dartmoor	945	365	94 500
Northumberland	1031	398	103 100
Brecon Beacons	1357	524	135 700
Peak District	1404	542	140 400
N. Yorks Moors	1432	553	143 200
Yorkshire Dales	1761	680	176 100
Snowdonia	2170	838	217 000
Lake District	2243	866	224 300
Total Area	13 620	5 256	1 362 000

Table 7.1 *National parks cover 5·65% of the surface area of the UK.*
Source—Countryside Commission

'Areas of outstanding natural beauty'

These areas are much smaller than national parks though in many ways they serve a similar purpose. They have been set up to allow people to enjoy the countryside. Though the Countryside Commission makes the decision as to which areas are to become 'areas of outstanding natural beauty', no organization actually manages them. Developments within these areas are controlled very carefully by local authorities.

Long distance footpaths

These have been set up by the Commission to allow people to walk for long distances through areas offering a range of scenery, wildlife and history. Eight such footpaths have been designated and cover over 2500km in distance, the longest single path being the Pennine Way which covers some 400km.

Nature Conservancy Council

This body was set up in 1949 'to provide scientific advice on the conservation and control of the natural flora and fauna of Great Britain' and 'to establish, maintain and manage nature reserves'. In 1965 it became a part of the Natural Environment Research Council (NERC). It has responsibility for national nature reserves and sites of special scientific interest.

Fig. 7.16 *In upland regions national nature reserve signs are often built into a cairn*

National nature reserves

These are areas of land that have been specially chosen by the Nature Conservancy Council because they display particularly important types of plants and animals, or have particularly important physical or geological properties. All these reserves are managed by the Conservancy Council but the Council does not necessarily own them. Over half of the one hundred and thirty or so reserves have been set up under agreement with an existing landowner.

Sites of special scientific interest (SSSI)

These are areas of land that the Nature Conservancy Council consider to contain rare species of plants or animals or show features of special geological interest. In this way they are similar to national nature reserves. The Nature Conservancy Council has no control over these areas but has to be informed of any developments that are being planned within the areas. Generally speaking, it is able to advise on their management so that their special character is preserved.

National Trust

The Trust was formed in 1895 by a group of private individuals whose intention was to protect land and buildings from destruction and to allow the public to enjoy them. The Trust now owns some 150000 hectares of land and several hundred buildings. Free access to the public is allowed on most of this

Fig. 7.17 *Dyrham Park, Avon. A National Trust property*

land. Though the Government assists the Trust through relief from taxation, the main sources of income are from donations and members' subscriptions. Anyone can become a Trust member by paying a small annual subscription fee.

Forestry Commission

Though the Commission was formed in 1919 to develop and manage timber in Britain, it has more recently become involved in conservation and in public recreation. A number of forest nature reserves have been set up in conjunction with the Nature Conservany Council and these have the same purpose and status as national nature reserves. 'Sites of special scientific interest' also exist within the Commission's forests. The Commission has also opened large areas of their land to the public. In many of these areas they have arranged for picnic areas and nature trails to be provided for public enjoyment. In 1974 the Commission said that its aim is to 'improve forests as wildlife habitats and to integrate balanced conservation and wood production in a pattern of good land-use and sound management'.

Local Authorities

These authorities have the power to control all developments within their own area and so necessarily have an important role in conservation. Local authorities are responsible for the management of country parks, local nature reserves and (with the exception of the Lake District and Peak District) national parks.

Country parks

Local authorities are able to obtain a 75% grant from the Countryside Commission to help in developing country parks. These areas of land or water are developed especially for recreational purposes. They are generally situated quite close to urban areas so that they are easy for people in cities and towns to get to.

Local nature reserves

Many of these reserves are established by local authorities and may be owned by them or maintained as reserves by agreement with the existing landowner. Several hundred local nature reserves have also been established by trusts and other bodies.

Green belts

These are areas around large urban areas where planning control is strict. The purpose of green belts has changed a lot since they were introduced. Initially, the idea was to limit the size of a town by having a 'green belt' round it. However, the developments simply tended to leap over it. What tends to happen now is that the green belts exist as wedges of land within urban areas. Though farming may take place on this land it is now more usual for it to be used for golf courses, playing fields and hospitals that have large expanses of green land.

ACTIVITIES

1   Fig. 7.18 shows an imaginary town in the West Country. It is a tourist attraction in summer. Oil and gas have been discovered in workable quantities in the sea south of the town. The following developments are proposed over the next 10 years.

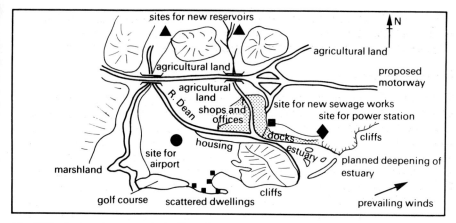

Fig. 7.18 *An imaginary town in the West Country*

a) expand industry and docks;
b) deepen estuary;
c) build airport, power station, motorway, reservoirs;
d) extend housing, shops, amenities, sewage works;
e) build gas terminal;
f) build oil refinery;
g) build docking facilities for tankers or offshore docking facility with pipeline to refinery.

Naturally all this is going to need land, will upset many local people and change this region completely, *if* the plans are accepted. It has been decided that the only way to thrash out all the problems is to hold a public inquiry where all parties can have their say. There are *six* basic points of view each proposed by a different representative at the inquiry:

a) Town and Country Planning Officer;
b) villager's action group;
c) spokesman for oil company with drilling rights;
d) industry and employment spokesman for town;
e) anti-airport and motorway lobby supported by the Conservation Group (also against town expansion and destruction of this peaceful little town);
f) local farmers' lobby.

This activity may be played by yourself or by a group of pupils (up to a full class of 30).

Class organization—The class will be divided into groups of up to 6 individuals. Each person in the group should choose (or be allocated) one of the roles. Each person should adopt a role and should construct arguments to fit the role. Each group of six individuals will debate the issues involved, each individual being given the opportunity to speak. The class should represent the 'public' and should be free to ask questions of the 'experts'. Either the Town and Country Planning Officer can be selected to make a final decision on the various proposals or a teacher can act as the Minister concerned.

Individual organization—As an environmental scientist, you should be able to see many sides to an argument. You should choose two or more opposing roles from those suggested and construct an argument that could be used by each in turn.

Role 1—Town and Country Planning Officer—Your job is to stay neutral and listen to all the arguments put forward by the various speakers. You must therefore invent some detailed questions that you can ask every speaker in turn. You must be able to pick holes in the arguments of people whose arguments you basically agree with.

*Role 2—Local villagers' lobby—*You are against the plans and proposals and are speaking on behalf of all the local villagers. Your arguments might be—tourism in summer is enough of a headache; we want this area preserved; there are rare plants and animals living in the area. You must expand this basic theme not only with arguments but also with questions you can put to other speakers.

*Role 3—Spokesman for oil company—*You are strongly in support of all the proposals and can quote evidence from your geologists and engineers. An accident of nature means the oil is here. We need to use it (say why). Deanmouth is the nearest port so it must come here. Every precaution will be taken to prevent pollution. Expand your argument to include pipelines, cost, oil depth, quantity, etc.

*Role 4—Local industry and employment spokesman—*The basic argument is that people in the town are sick of winter unemployment and only holiday work—they want full-time work. It is all right for these rich villagers who have retired here from London in their little cottages to talk about rare plants and ecology. But we locals want work and this oil is a golden opportunity for us to get work and money to feed and clothe our families. It will make this a rich and prosperous area.

*Role 5—Conservation Group—*The Conservation Group lobby are against the whole scheme but are generally realistic—giving sensible arguments against the scheme. But also rather eccentric with 'odd' ideas about solar energy and the need to phase out the use of fossil fuels completely.

*Role 6—Local farmers' lobby—*Where will we stand in all this, we won't be able to get farm workers, they will all be at sea getting fantastic wages or in the docks building rigs. How much land will be bought from us under compulsory purchase orders? Build arguments around all this.

2　　There are 10 national parks in the UK. They are: Lake District, Snowdonia, Peak District, North York Moors, Yorkshire Dales, Northumberland, Brecon Beacons, Pembrokeshire Coast, Dartmoor and Exmoor.

These National Parks are outlined in Fig. 7.19. Place each name on the map alongside the correct area.

There are 7 Long Distance Footpaths (though in fact the South West Peninsula Coast Path comprises several paths). These are: Pennine Way, Cleveland Way, Offa's Dyke Path, Pembrokeshire Coast Path, South West Peninsula Coast Path, North Downs Way and South Downs Way.

These paths are marked in Fig. 7.19. Label each of these paths.

Fig. 7.19 *National parks and long-distance footpaths in England and Wales*

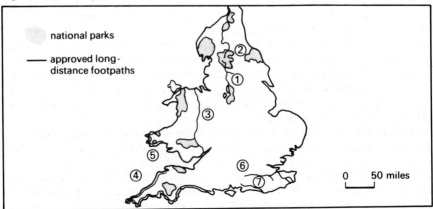

Populations 8

A **natural population**, as distinct from a **human population**, is considered to be the number of organisms of a species which freely interbreed. Often, the limits of the population are fairly well-defined by geographical barriers. For instance, the number of mice on an island may be regarded as a population. Mice on a neighbouring island would be thought of as a different population because the two groups would be unable to interbreed. The boundaries between populations may not be as obvious as in this example. The rats present in Britain would not normally be regarded as a population because the area involved would not allow free interbreeding between individuals. It would, however, be acceptable to speak of the population of rats present in a town or even perhaps a city. Geographical barriers will be more important to some animals than to others, of course. Many birds for instance will be less influenced by these types of barrier than other animals.

Human populations are rather different (in terms of definition) from natural populations. Firstly, though we are all of the same species *(Homo sapiens),* we do not freely interbreed for one of two major reasons. The first of these is geographical. Even with the advent of such forms of transport as Concorde, people in different countries do not frequently meet and breed. The second reason is cultural. Even when individuals of our species live in the same country or town, it is still the exception rather than the rule for people from different cultures to interbreed. The term 'population' in human terms is therefore used rather more loosely than in terms of natural populations. It is generally used to describe all the people living in a certain area. This may be a town, a country or the world.

Factors Affecting Population Size

The size of both natural and human populations tends to be controlled by similar factors. These factors are food, water, space, the build-up of waste materials, disease, migration and predation. In addition to this list, however, the size of human populations is partly determined by religious, economic and social factors. These factors are discussed later in this chapter.

The factors listed above (with the exception of migration) work by increasing or decreasing birth rates (**natality**) or death rates (**mortality**). Migration means the movement of individuals from one area to another. Migrations may be *into* an area (**immigration**) or *out* of an area (**emigration**). To calculate the change in size of a population because of migration, subtract the number of emigrations from the number of immigrations.

Birth rates are a measure of how many births there are in every hundred or every thousand individuals in a population in a given time. The time period used is usually one year. A value for birth rate is obtained by finding the total number of births in the population and dividing by the total number of individuals in the population. The value obtained by doing this is then multiplied by either 1000 or 100. For instance, if a population of 500 individuals gives birth to 25 individuals in a year, then the birth rate would be

$$\frac{25}{500} \times \frac{1000}{1} = 50 \text{ per thousand per year} \qquad \text{or}$$

$$\frac{25}{500} \times \frac{100}{1} = 5 \text{ per hundred (5\%) per year}$$

Death rates express a similar value—the number of deaths there are in every hundred or thousand individuals in a population in a given time. Again, a period of one year is normally taken. If, in the population of 500 individuals given above, there are 10 deaths, then the death rate would be

$$\frac{10}{500} \times \frac{1000}{1} = 20 \text{ per thousand} \qquad \text{or}$$

$$\frac{10}{500} \times \frac{100}{1} = 2 \text{ per hundred (2\%)}.$$

Population Growth Rates and Growth Curves

The change in size of a population is found by calculating the difference between birth rate and death rate and is known as **population growth rate**. (This assumes no change resulting from migration.) In the example given above, the population is changing at a rate of 50−20=30 per thousand per year. As a percentage it would be 5−2=3% per year. Because this is a positive number (there are more births than deaths) it indicates that the population is increasing in size. If the growth rate is a negative number (there are more deaths than births), then the population is decreasing in size. This is often referred to as a **negative growth** and the rate of growth is known as a **negative growth rate.**

In theory, if a normal population of individuals made up of males and females are given ample food, water and space, it would be expected to increase in size until it reaches a balance with its environment. This will generally be when there is just sufficient food, water and space, etc. to maintain a given number of individuals. If this type of population growth is drawn as a graph, then the graph will appear as a **sigmoid curve**. An example of this is shown in Fig. 8.1.

The population represented in Fig. 8.1 can be seen to have three distinct stages A–B, B–C, C–D. The stage A–B represents a population with an accelerating growth rate. Stage B–C represents the period during which the growth rate is slowing down. The population will reach a point where it will neither increase nor decrease. It will have reached a balance with the environment (Stage C–D).

Fig. 8.1 *A population growth curve*

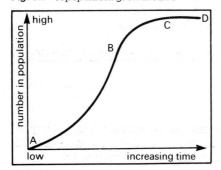

Fig. 8.2 *Curve showing 'population collapse'*

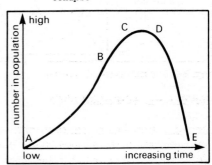

The stage of growth represented by the curve A–B shows **exponential growth**. In this case, the number of individuals will successively increase by a certain factor during a given period of time. For example, a population of 500 individuals might be increasing exponentially such that its numbers double every ten years. At time zero, the number is 500, in ten years—1000, in twenty years—2000, thirty years—4000 and so on. Obviously this form of increase results in a very rapid increase in numbers.

Often, populations will not remain as constant as Fig. 8.1 shows at stage C–D. If the population has consumed all of its food for instance, and there was no new input of food, then the population would collapse as shown in Fig. 8.2. More often however, the population at point D will tend to fluctuate around a certain optimum number as shown in Fig. 8.3.

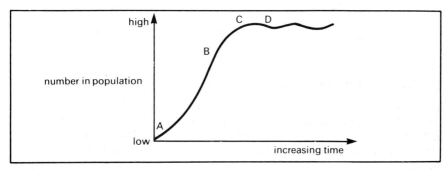

Fig. 8.3 *A fluctuating population*

In the natural world, of course, the factors that determine population size will tend to fluctuate, and so natural populations will deviate from the expected curves given above. Also, different populations will tend to influence one another, either as competitors for such things as food, water and space, or by displaying predator-prey relationships. A simple example of this last type of relationship is given in Fig. 8.4.

A final important statistic of populations is **population density**. This value is a measure of the number of individuals in a unit area. For instance if 500 individuals populated an area measuring $10\,km^2$ then the density of population would be.

$$\frac{500}{10} = 50\,km^{-2}$$

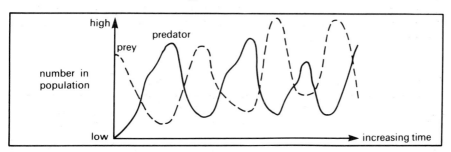

Fig. 8.4 *Predator-prey relationship*

NATURAL POPULATIONS

Because population numbers and densities are so important in ecological studies, various techniques have been designed to enable these studies to be done scientifically. Some of the basic techniques are described below.

Investigating Plant Populations

Generally speaking, plant populations are rather easier to study than animal populations because they remain still while you count them!

Quadrats

The basic tool used in describing plant populations is the **quadrat**. This is a square frame, the size of which varies depending upon the area being studied. Frequently, if the area being studied is small, say the side of a wall, or a tree trunk then the quadrat may measure 10 cm × 10 cm. If larger areas are studied, then the quadrat may measure 50 cm × 50 cm.

It is essential in any scientific work that wherever possible, the measurements taken are *objective*. This means that they do not depend on an individual's interpretation. One of the most satisfactory means of doing this when the area of study is fairly uniform is to use a **random quadrat** technique. (The term 'random' means that all parts of the area being studied have an equal chance of being selected each time the quadrat is placed down.) Using this method, the area is reduced in shape to a square or rectangle and the sides measured. Then, starting from one corner of the area, two random numbers are obtained from 'random number' tables. These numbers are then measured out along the *x* and *y* coordinates of the area. The quadrat is placed down at the point where the coordinates meet and the plants present are recorded. (Random numbers could be obtained by placing numbers in a container and removing two without looking.)

Suppose the area given measures 8 m × 8 m. Choosing corner A in Fig. 8.5 two random numbers are taken—say 2 and 6. These numbers are then measured out, 2 m along the *x* axis and 6 m along the *y* axis. The coordinates meet at point B and so the quadrat is placed at that point. This procedure is repeated a number of times, depending upon the size of the area. The greater the number of repeats the more accurate will be the results. It is important to start at corner A and measure along the axes in the same order each time.

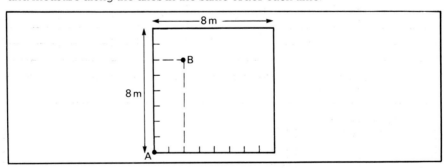

Fig. 8.5 *Placing a quadrat using random numbers*

The purpose of taking random numbers is to remove any personal selection (bias) in the area covered by the quadrat. Given personal preference, we may choose to select those places in the study area in which the 'interesting' plants are growing. Alternatively, we may wish to avoid the nettles! In this way, the results would not be accurate. They would not give a representative picture of the whole area.

The actual recording of the plants could occur in several ways. The two most satisfactory means are either by counting the individual plants or by estimating their percentage cover. Counting is usually best when it is practicable, but on many occasions it is not possible. For instance, if the area contains grass it is often difficult to tell one plant from another. Also, of course, there may simply be too many plants to count.

The final results can be totalled and, where percentage cover is being used, an average value calculated (see Fig. 8.6 and Fig. 8.7). The results of these investigations can also be presented as a bar chart (see Fig. 8.8).

plant species	quadrat number											
	1	2	3	4	5	6	7	8	9	10	11	totals
A	4	7	11	16	12	6	0	0	5	8	7	76
B	3											
C	1											
D	0											
E	8											
F	2											
G	2											
H	4											
totals	24											

Fig. 8.6 Frequency grid showing the total number of plants present in a given area

plant species	quadrat number											
	1	2	3	4	5	6	7	8	9	10	total	average
A	10%	5%	4%	11%	21%	68%	31%	14%	8%	3%	175%	17.5%
B												
C												
D												
E												
F												
G												
H												
I												
J												

Fig. 8.7 A frequency grid showing percentage cover. This system is useful when it is not possible to count individual plants

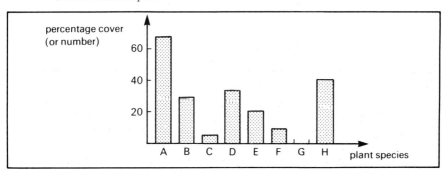

Fig. 8.8 A bar chart showing the result of a quadrat investigation

In certain circumstances, for instance when many small plants are present, a **point frame quadrat** can be used. This consists of a horizontal bar with ten 'points' or steel needles fixed through it. The points covered by the quadrat are chosen by using random numbers as above, and a record made each time the needles (either the point or the shank) touch a plant. Finally, the results of all the quadrats are totalled. Knowing the number of points in the frame and the number of quadrats taken, then the frequency of each plant can be calculated. For example, if 10 points are in the frame and the frame is used 40 times then there have been 400 sampling points. A plant that has been recorded 80 times will have a frequency of

$$\frac{80}{400} \times \frac{100}{1} = 20\%.$$

This indicates that there are 20 examples of the particular plant present in every 100 plants in the area.

Though both techniques have their faults, they are generally satisfactory for most types of work. So that other people considering the results of your surveys can appreciate the accuracy of your results, it is always essential to provide a description of the technique you use, the measurements of the area chosen, the size of quadrat used and the number of samples taken.

Line transects

On occasions when the plants in the area being studied are not distributed evenly, then a line transect is probably most satisfactory. In this instance, a line is placed on the ground to stretch across the area being studied. Starting at one end of the line, quadrats can be placed on the ground alongside the line at regular intervals. The intervals chosen will depend upon the size of the area and the frequency with which the plant types change. The plants present in each quadrat can either be counted or an estimate of their percentage cover can be made. The results of this type of survey are often best presented in a graphical form where the horizontal axis represents the line along the ground and suitable intervals along it are chosen to represent those plants found in each quadrat. The vertical axis of course represents the percentage cover or number. An example of such a graph is given in Fig. 8.9. If samples of soil are also taken from each quadrat and analysed, then a hypothesis could be drawn up to suggest reasons for the change in vegetation across the area that has been described.

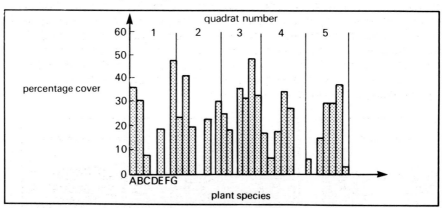

Fig. 8.9 *Graphs can be useful when trying to identify patterns of growth*

Finally, though it is preferable to use an objective measurement of vegetation whenever possible, it is occasionally necessary to use a more subjective approach. In this instance, the investigator should walk over the area under investigation and list all of the plants that are present. Having done this it is necessary to walk over the area again. This time, however, the investigator should attempt to place one or more of the named plants in an order of abundance. This order will correspond to a place on the **DAFOR** scale. The initials in this word represent a particular description of abundance and they are: Dominant, Abundant, Frequent, Occasional and Rare. After repeatedly walking across the area being investigated, it should be possible to place each plant somewhere on the DAFOR scale. Because this technique is subjective, there are some problems that the investigator should be aware of.

1   It is easy to overestimate the abundance of conspicuous plants.

2   It is easy to underestimate the abundance of inconspicuous plants. For instance, suppose a pasture contains buttercups and clover. Also suppose that the buttercups are flowering but the clover is not. In this case, the buttercups will appear to be more abundant (because they are more obvious) though the reverse may be true.

3   Each individual investigator may vary in his idea of just what abundant or (say) frequent means.

4   A decision must be made as to whether the dominant plant is the one present in the greatest number or is the one that most influences the other plants. Occasionally this is obvious, for instance in an oak wood, oak trees may be most abundant and so would also have the greatest effect on the other plants. What would be the situation though where two large oak trees stand in a field of 1 hectare?

Investigating Animal Populations

The techniques for investigating animal populations are more varied than those used for plants because the techniques used depend very largely on the animals being studied. Some examples are given below.

1   **Sweep nets**—Using a 'butterfly net' on a handle, an area is crossed at slow walking speed and the net is swept from side to side in front of you. This technique is suitable for sampling animals present in areas of long grass. The numbers of each species are recorded. The speed with which you walk and the area you sweep should be the same for different areas being compared.

2   **Pit-fall traps**—This involves digging a hole and placing a container such as a jam jar in it. The hole is filled in so that the jar fits it exactly, both in circumference and depth. The container must then be covered to prevent rain entering, remembering to leave a space for the animals to fall in (see Fig. 8.10). This technique is suitable for catching relatively mobile animals that live in leaf litter, etc. Such animals include beetles, wood lice, centipedes and spiders. Pit-fall traps must be visited frequently and any captured animals removed or they may die of lack of food or eat one another.

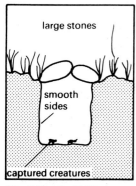
Fig. 8.10   *A pitfall trap*

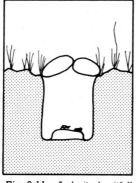
Fig. 8.11   *A baited pitfall trap*

Fig. 8.12   *A bait trap*

3   **Baited pit-fall traps** (see Fig. 8.11)—These are a refined version of the pit-fall trap. They are set up in the same way but contain a bait to attract the animals you hope to catch.

4   **Other baited traps** (see Fig. 8.12)—Hollowed out potato or carrot can be used to capture a similar range of organisms as the pit-fall traps.

5   **Longworth mammal traps** (see Fig. 8.13)—These are commercially made traps designed to capture small mammals without harming them. The investigator must be very careful to visit the traps regularly to remove the animals captured or they will die from lack of food. The trap is a metal box with a telescopic section so that its size can be adjusted to accommodate large or small rodents (shrews, mice, voles, etc.). When the animal enters the trap, it trips a rod which shuts the lid to the trap and so traps the animal inside.

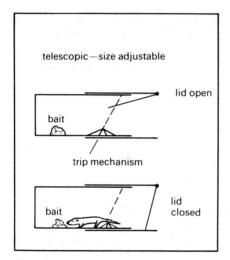

Fig. 8.13   *The Longworth small mammal trap*

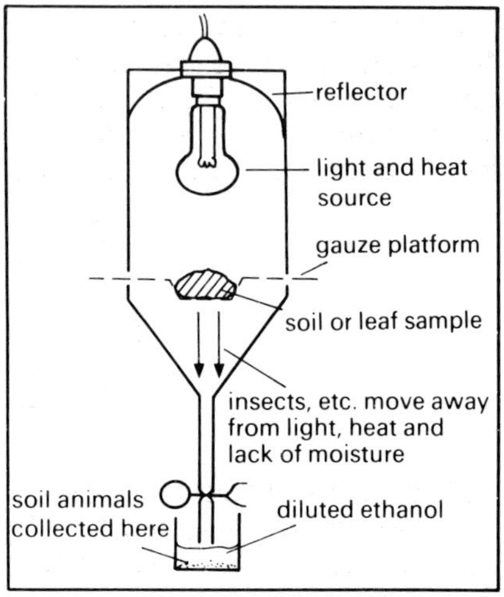

Fig. 8.14   *The Tullgren funnel*

6   **Tullgren funnel** (see Fig. 8.14)—This is a piece of apparatus that has been designed to extract small, mobile organisms from soil. Basically, it is made up of a funnel, a lamp and a gauze platform as shown in Fig. 8.14. As the lamp is turned on, so the soil organisms move down through the soil. They do this to move away from the light and also to move out of the upper layers of soil that begin to dry out. The soil must not be allowed to dry out too quickly as the organisms will dry out and die in the soil. This is managed by placing the lamp at a distance from the soil to obtain a temperature gradient of about 15°C between the top and bottom of the soil. A specimen tube should be placed under the funnel to collect the organisms as they fall through.

Many more techniques are possible, and variations of those given above may be used. Whatever method is used, it must be described in detail along with the figures obtained so that the reader may judge the validity of the results.

Finally, it is worth mentioning a technique used to estimate the total number of animals in an area based upon the animals caught. The technique requires that the animals can be marked in such a way that they can be recognized again. The mark, however, must not place the animals at a disadvantage in their environment (e.g. make them more obvious to predators) or enable you to capture them more easily. On reasonably large animals such as woodlice or beetles, a spot of dark green or brown paint might be adequate. The technique is called the 'capture, mark and release, recapture' technique.

Firstly, the animals are caught, marked and released again into their environment. After a suitable period of time has passed to allow the animals to disperse in the environment, the area is sampled again. It is necessary to use exactly the same technique as was originally used. All animals caught must be taken and no effort must be made to select the marked animals. The means of calculating the total number of animals in the area is shown below using a simple example.

Suppose that 50 animals were originally caught, marked and released. On resampling the area, the animals caught contain 10 of the original sample (i.e. they are 'marked' animals). The number of animals recaught is thus

$$\frac{10}{50} \times \frac{100}{1} = 20\%.$$

of the number released. From this it is assumed that you are able to capture 20% of all the animals in the area in which you are interested. The original 50 animals therefore represent 20% of the total number in the environment. As estimate of the total number present can therefore be calculated from the equation below, where x is the number in the population.

$$\frac{50}{x} = \frac{20}{100}$$
$$20x = 50 \times 100$$
$$x = \frac{50 \times 100}{20} = 250$$

The total number of that type of animal in the area is thus 250.

This section on sampling populations will be helpful if you attempt any practical work on food chains and pyramids of number, etc. as discussed in Chapter 3.

The description of particular communities of organisms, in particular environments, is of great importance. By doing this, it is possible to estimate the effect that man's activities might be having on the environment. (An obvious example of this application is given in Chapter 2.) By sampling the communities of animals present in a river and comparing them with the biotic index, an idea of the level of pollution can be obtained. By comparing the population of different organisms in a natural deciduous woodland with those in a forestry plantation, the effects of planting coniferous trees may become apparent (see Chapter 7 for a further discussion of this).

In concluding this section, it is essential to remind readers that whenever sampling occurs in the environment, the minimum of disturbance should occur. If samples are removed, they should be as few in number as possible and, where possible, should be returned. These precautions not only prevent damage to the environment, which must be of the greatest importance to us all; if you remove organisms from the population then your results will be meaningless because your activities will have changed the area so that anybody repeating your work will obtain different results.

Colonization and Succession

Communities of plants and animals are rarely stable but tend to undergo change. The changes that occur tend to follow particular trends and are called **successions**. These successions usually lead to an increase in the number of species of plants and animals in an area. (This increase in the number of different species is referred to as being an increase in **diversity**.)

The increased complexity and diversity of communities tend to make them more stable until a point is reached where changes only occur very slowly over relatively long periods of time. At this stage the community is said to have reached a **climax.** It will support the greatest number of plants and animals under the climatic and geological conditions that prevail. Each community of plants and animals that occupies an area during its progression to a climax is known as a **sere**.

HUMAN POPULATIONS

Many of the factors which cause changes in the size of plant and animal populations also cause changes in human populations. This is the case despite the fact that man is able to control many of the causes of these changes.

The factors in common with natural populations are food, water, climate, disease and predators.

As we live in a country that is regarded as 'developed' we tend to forget that in the 'developing' or 'underdeveloped' countries, food and water shortages frequently limit population size. We are, however, made aware of this fact on those all-too-frequent occasions when famine in the developing world makes news in our country. The photographs of unfortunate individuals having to queue for what could possibly be their last meal very often moves us to offer aid to these nations. Despite this aid, however, death by starvation often has catastrophic effects on Third World populations. In years of poor food harvests, up to 60% of deaths in the world are a result of a lack of food. In Biafra in 1968 some 1 million people died of starvation. In some areas, the number of deaths reached one thousand each day. The hunting and gathering peoples of the world such as the Australian Aborigines and the African Bedouin are also restricted in number by the availability of food and water.

Occurences such as typhoons, floods and droughts claim large numbers of lives in many parts of the world. Also, the climate limits the amount of food and water that can be made available to sustain life.

During the history of man's development, diseases have often appeared and decimated the population. The population of England, for instance, was reduced by nearly half in the thirty years from 1348 as a result of Bubonic plague (Black Death). Even with man's considerable medical knowledge, diseases such as malaria and cholera still claim tens of thousands of lives every year. This is particularly true in the developing countries where public health measures such as sewage treatment and clean water supply are very simple or non-existent. It is estimated that some 25×10^6 people die every year from a lack of clean water for drinking or for sanitation. Medical aid is also not very widely available in these countries.

Though man is rarely preyed upon by other animals, self predation in the form of wars still operates to limit our population size.

Factors influencing human populations that do not affect natural populations are social, religious and economic factors. These factors may, at different times and in different circumstances cause increases or decreases in birth rates and thus increase or decrease population size. One example of each of these factors is given below, though there are many more examples.

In the UK, though the situation is undergoing change, there is a great deal of social pressure on people to get married. In particular, women tend to be regarded with pity if they are not married by the time they are thirty or thirty-five. Once people are married, social pressure then determines that they have children. Other couples, both friends and family, frequently enquire if children are planned or, 'When are you starting a family?'. Even television adverts tend to show a family situation (including two or three children) when advertising everything from toothpaste and toilet rolls to motor cars. All of these pressures tend to suggest to people that it is the norm to have children and it is in man's nature to conform to the norm.

Though there is a move towards a more tolerant view of birth control techniques, the Roman Catholic Church for instance looks unfavourably on the most effective contraceptive devices. The reduced ability of Roman Catholics to prevent pregnancies inevitably leads to an increased birth rate.

Economic factors may be used to make it easier for people to raise a family or to make it more difficult. In the UK Child Benefit is payable to every mother with a child up to the time when the child leaves school. This allowance helps to ease the necessary financial burden of raising children.

In China however, if couples have more than two children the father has to pay extra taxes and might forego promotion at work. These measures obviously make it financially more difficult to raise a family.

WORLD POPULATION

As can be seen from Fig. 8.15, the world's population has increased at all times during man's history. Fig. 8.15 also shows that the *rate* of change has been increasing. At the present time, the population is increasing exponentially. This means that the population is increasing by a certain fixed quantity during a certain period of time. At present the world's population is increasing at a rate such that it will double every thirty-five years or so. If this present rate of growth continues, the population could reach 6500×10^6 (six thousand five hundred million) by the year A.D. 2000. This rapid increase, however, is not occuring evenly throughout the world. At the present moment, the underdeveloped countries of the world contain the greatest proportion of the population and this proportion is increasing. The greatest cause of this increase is the reduction in death rates in these countries due to such things as improved sanitation and medical aid.

Eventually, perhaps, the underdeveloped countries will reduce their birth rates so that the overall growth rate will not be so rapid. This type of situation occurred in the UK during the nineteenth and early twentieth centuries. If you consider Table 8.1 you can see that in the early part of the nineteenth century,

Fig. 8.15 *World population growth over the past 2000 years*

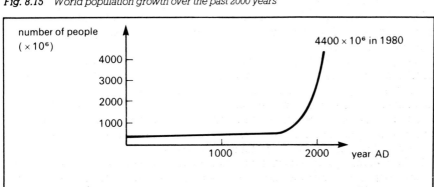

Year	Natality (per thousand)	Mortality (per thousand)	Growth rate (per cent)	Population (millions)
1700	34	32·8	0·12	9·4
1750	35	30·4	0·5	
1800	35	22·5	1·0	15·9
1840	35	23·	1·3	
1860	35	22·5	1·1	38·2
1880	33·6	19·7	0·4	
1900	30·6	17·3	0·5	
1920	23·1	12·7	0·55	50·2
1940	14·6	13·7	0·80	52·7
1950	16·3	12·1	0·96	
1960	17·5	11·8	0·55	55·2
1966	17·8		0·4	56·2
1968	17·3	11·6		
1971	16	12		57·7

Table 8.1 *UK population statistics since 1700.*

both mortality and natality were relatively high. Mortality, however, began to fall (for much the same reasons as in present day underdeveloped countries). As this happened, so the population growth rate rose until natality began to fall during the latter part of the nineteenth and into the twentieth centuries. It has since been suggested that natality fell because people realized that the children who were born had a better chance of surviving until they reached old age. It was no longer necessary to have a lot of children to make sure that some of them survived.

The change from high mortality and high natality to low mortality and low natality is referred to as the **demographic transition**. This change took place gradually in the UK and possibly it will occur in the underdeveloped countries. The problem, however, is one of time. A reduction in mortality in many underdeveloped countries (of about 1%) has taken only one or two decades. While we wait for a possible reduction in natality to compensate for this (something that took the best part of one hundred years in the UK), the population could reach such levels that other natural checks such as epidemics and mass starvation may begin to operate.

In conclusion, it is probably true to say that most of the environmental problems that have been discussed in the other chapters in this book are mainly the result of an increasing population (together with a desire for an improved standard of living). As populations increase, so more energy, materials and land are used and there is a greater demand on such resources as water and food. The use of all these resources is producing waste products at such a rate that the environment is becoming unable to cope with them. The environment is unable to make the waste harmless (degrade it) within acceptable time limits.

ACTIVITIES

Questions

1　In 1965, 600 field mice were found in a field of 5 hectares. In 1975, in the same field, the population of field mice was 870.
a) Calculate the density of the population in 1965 and 1975.
b) What was the rate of change of density during this period?
c) Suggest 3 possible reasons why the change in density would be likely to fluctuate during this time.

d) If the rate of change had been negative what would this tell you about the population of field mice?

2 Draw a bar chart of the data below relating to a population of voles and owls in a wood.

Year	Voles	Owls
1970	30×10^3	15
1971	24×10^3	18
1972	30×10^3	14
1973	46×10^3	18
1974	80×10^3	28
1975	5×10^3	58
1976	18×10^3	17
1977	38×10^3	18
1978	20×10^3	28

Table 8.2 *Population statistics of voles and owls in a wood.*

a) Describe the changes in the vole population from 1971–1974.
b) What explanation does the graph offer to explain what happed to the voles in 1975?
c) Suggest two other possible explanations for the change in vole population in 1975.
d) Why are there more voles than owls?
e) What would be the likely long-term effect of the owls in this wood being killed off?

3 A species of amoeba is introduced into a culture media which is kept constant in terms of volume and nutrient. Fig. 8.16 shows the change in population number.

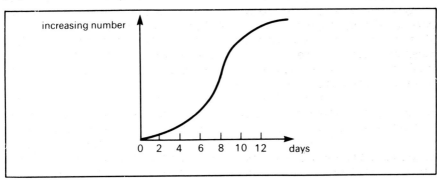

Fig. 8.16 *Changes in a population of amoebas*

a) What features of the environment are likely to operate to restrict the population growth?
b) What conclusion can you draw about relative mortality and natality on day 2, 6, 10?

4 A population of aphids was kept in the laboratory and allowed to 'settle' or equilibrate. At this point (A) numbers were relatively constant and births were equal to deaths. This is shown in Fig. 8.17. At point (B), however, a separate chamber containing a population of ladybirds was joined to the aphid chamber by a tube. Ladybirds were allowed into the aphid chamber during the daytime but were all removed in the evening.

a) What effect did the ladybirds have on the population of aphids?

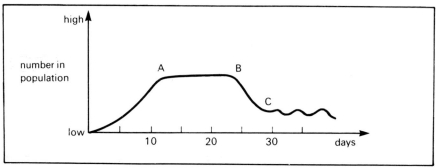

Fig. 8.17 *Population graph for aphid experiment*

b) At point (C) the population appears to have steadied out at a lower level than previously. Can you explain why?

c) Beyond point (C) the graph waves up and down. What does this tell you about the population?

d) What relationship exists between aphids and ladybirds?

5 Suppose 10 bacteria cells are innoculated into a nutrient medium and that the cells divide into two every 20 minutes.

The change in numbers for the first 3 hours are shown in Table 8.3.

a) Graph this data.

b) Consider the graph you have produced. Do you consider it likely that the population increase will continue unchecked?

c) If not, suggest 3 factors that might operate to prevent its increase.

d) Sketch a graph to show the population as it stabilizes.

e) Suppose the nutrient medium occupies $100\,cm^2$, what is the density of population at 20 min, 1 hour, 2 hours, 3 hours?

Time (minutes)	Number
0	10
20	20
40	40
60	80
80	160
100	320
120	640
140	1 280
160	2 160
180	5 120

Table 8.3 *Increase in number of bacteria cells over a three hour period.*

6 State 5 instances with which you are familiar where man purposely controls population numbers. In each instance suggest *why* man controls the population and what you think would be the consequences if he didn't do so. Finally indicate the *means* by which the control is exercised.

7 Use the techniques described in this chapter to investigate the following:

a) the populations of plants in a field;

b) the populations of invertebrate animals in a hedgerow;

c) a comparison of the range of species of plants or invertebrate animals in a deciduous wood and a coniferous plantation;

d) the effect of footpaths over a field.

Index